BLOWN

THE INCREDIBLE STORY OF JOHN GOLDSMITH, GAMBLER, RACEHORSE TRAINER AND WARTIME SECRET AGENT

Death is like any untamed animal.
He fears a scornful eye.

IAN FLEMING

Quoted in *Goldeneye* by Matthew Parker, Hutchinson, 2014

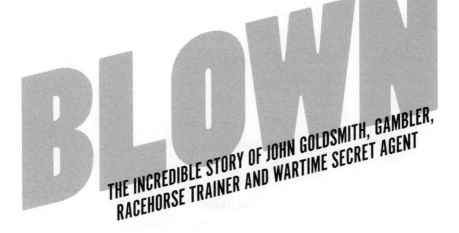

BLOWN

THE INCREDIBLE STORY OF JOHN GOLDSMITH, GAMBLER, RACEHORSE TRAINER AND WARTIME SECRET AGENT

Jamie Reid

RACING POST

First published in Great Britain in 2015 by
Racing Post Books
27 Kingfisher Court, Hambridge Road, Newbury, Berkshire, RG14 5SJ

10 9 8 7 6 5 4 3 2 1

A catalogue record for this book is available from the British Library.

ISBN 978-1-910498-06-4

Cover designed by Jay Vincent

Typeset by J Schwartz & Co

Printed and bound in the UK by CPI Group (UK) Ltd, Croydon, CR0 4YY

www.racingpost.com/shop

CONTENTS

DEDICATION

My privileged post-war generation have never had to fight for their survival. I should like to dedicate this book to all those who did. Amongst them my uncle Ian Reid who, in July 1944, was shot down and killed in a Lancaster Bomber over Cambrai, northern France. He was 21 years old.

CAST OF CHARACTERS

John Goldsmith – *English racehorse trainer and gambler, born in Paris in 1909*

Annette Helen Bell Clover, also known as Tiny – *John's second wife*

Edna Booth – *John's third wife*

Harold Yorke Goldsmith, better known as Jack – *John's father, a horse dealer in Paris*

Florence – *John's mother*

Gaie Johnson Houghton, b. 1941, and Gisele Steel, b. 1949 – *John and Annette's daughters*

SOE

Colonel Maurice Buckmaster – *head of F Section*

Vera Atkins – *Buckmaster's right-hand woman*

Brigadier Colin Gubbins – *a tough Highlander and student of irregular warfare*

Selwyn Jepson – *talent spotter*

Major Roger de Wesselow – *Commandant of Wanborough Manor Preliminary Training School, June 1941 to February 1943*

CAST OF CHARACTERS

Lieutenant Colonel James Young – *Commandant of Arisaig Paramilitary Training School, May 1942 to January 1943*

Captain Eric Sykes, better known as Bill – *formerly of the Royal Shanghai Police; SOE expert on demolitions and silent killing*

Henri Déricourt – *former Air France pilot; F Section air movements officer, 1942 to 1943*

Gilbert Norman, James Amps, John Young, Rowland Dowlen, Arthur Staggs – *John Goldsmith's fellow recruits in SOE Training Party 27P*

Peter Churchill, George Starr, Francis Suttill, Brian Rafferty, Sidney Jones, Fergus Chalmers-Wright, Jack Agazarian, Francine Agazarian, Andrée Borrel, Yolande Beekman, Diana Rowden, Noor Inayat Khan – *F Section agents*

France

General Charles de Gaulle – *self-appointed leader of the Free French in exile; haughty and obstreperous*

General Henri Giraud – *senior and highly respected French General; seen by the British as a possible alternative to de Gaulle*

General René Chambe – *Giraud's principal staff officer*

André Girard – *artist and poster designer; head of the Carte resistance network on the Côte d'Azur*

Henri Frager – *a Nice architect and Girard's second-in-command*

André Marsac – *Girard's courier and reckless associate*

André Bartoli – *insurance salesman and Carte member*

Paulo Leonetti – *a hairdresser and former Mayor of Antibes; Carte member*

Dr Costes-Broussard – *Giraudist Secret Army organiser in the south*

Commandant Pierre Lejeune – *Giraudist officer*

Commandant Pierre Du Passage – *Giraudist officer*

Guillaume Lecointre – *Parisian banker's son and Resistance member*

Edouard Grosval – *a wounded ex-soldier and Resistance member*

Madame Tantzy – *a Romanian actress*

Monsieur Henri – *Madame Tantzy's lover*

SS Sturmbannführer Hans Josef Kieffer – *head of counter-espionage at the Sicherheitsdienst or SD headquarters at the avenue Foch in Paris*

Dr Josef Goetz – *head of the SD wireless direction finding teams*

Henri Lafont (a former gangster and pimp) and Pierre Bonny (an ex-police inspector) – *heads of the French Gestapo*

Madame Cecily Beaufort – *an old Parisian acquaintance of John Goldsmith's from the 1920s*

Georges Wall – *Madame Beaufort's younger brother*

Camille Rayon – *Maquis chieftain and Gaullist staff officer in the Vaucluse and Provence*

Lieutenant Colonel Philippe Beyne – *head of the Gaullist FFI, or Forces Françaises de l'Intérieur, in the Vaucluse and Provence*

General Friedrich Wiese – *Wehrmacht commander of the German 19th Army in Avignon*

'Noel' – *a German spy*

Horse racing

Robert Mathet-Dumaine – *a wealthy Parisian racehorse owner and old friend of John Goldsmith's; SOE sympathiser*

Antoine Munat – *a French racehorse trainer in the 1920s and 1930s*

Paul 'Popol' Blanc – *French lightweight jockey*

Bobby Bates – *French jump jockey, born in Marseille*

Javier Cruz-Valer – *French racehorse owner and black marketeer*

Percy Thompson – *a high-stakes Mayfair bookmaker and gambler*

Max Parker – *a high-stakes East End bookie*

Hughie Rowan, also known as 'The Old 'Un' – *Australian card player and con man*

PROLOGUE

It was shortly after 3 a.m. on the night of 23 June 1943 and Paris was sweltering in a mid-summer heatwave. John Goldsmith was sweating in a locked third-floor room in the Hôtel Continentale on the corner of the rue de Rivoli and the rue de Castiglione. The Gestapo had warned him that his interrogation would continue at ten o'clock the following morning and the Englishman had no illusions about what to expect.

Goldsmith had been brought to the hotel from his previous accommodation at number 82 avenue Foch, his captors bundling him at gunpoint into the back of a black Citroën Traction Avant and driving him up the allée de Longchamp, around the Arc de Triomphe and on down the Champs-Elysées. The blacked-out streets were eerie and deserted. There was an acute petrol shortage in the capital and the few French cars were mostly reserved for doctors or members of the government and friends of the occupying forces. Everyone else walked, took the Métro or rode around on bicycles, but the curfew restricted all movement from 11 p.m. until 5 a.m. the next day.

In the first few years of the Occupation, Paris had been the Germans' favourite playground. But by the summer of 1943 there were almost daily acts of resistance – a grenade attack here, an assassination attempt there – further taxing an army already stretched to the limit on the Eastern Front. Senior Nazis and their collaborator cronies still dined at Maxim's and the Tour d'Argent but ordinary soldiers no longer went out alone or on foot after dark.

The Continentale and its five-star neighbours had been turned into billets for high-ranking members of the German General Staff. Carl Heinrich von Stülpnagel, the Military Governor of France, was asleep in his suite at the Meurice a few doors down, while the Luftwaffe had moved into the Ritz around the corner on place Vendôme. As John Goldsmith was brought in through the Continentale's revolving door, passing the sandbags and the sentries, a number of Wehrmacht officers were still sitting around smoking and drinking coffee and brandy. Goldsmith could smell their distinctive cologne along with their cigars and their polished leather boots. It was the scent of the Occupation.

When the officers saw the new arrival, accompanied by the burly men in suits, they smiled and exchanged knowing looks. To satisfy the German obsession with paperwork, the prisoner was required to sign the hotel register. He used his own name: 'Captain John Goldsmith. RAC.' Told to add an address, he wrote 'Warminster, near Salisbury'. The desk clerk stared at the entry in amazement but the Gestapo escorts grinned and nodded triumphantly. One of the uniformed officers strolled over to the desk and read the entry out loud in perfect English. He patted Goldsmith on the back. Salisbury. He knew it well. He had enjoyed some very good fishing near there before the war. The captive didn't feel inclined to swap memories.

There was more mocking laughter from the onlookers as Goldsmith was led away to the stairs, the lifts being out of service to save electricity. The procession made their way up the carpeted staircase and along the corridors, German military orderlies sitting dozing in chairs on each landing. The third-floor room was incongruously comfortable with a double bed, with clean linen sheets, a red counterpane and brass and glass Art Deco lamps on the bedside tables. There were heavy floor-to-ceiling curtains, a large armoire, a dressing table and two chairs in the window which was covered by a blackout curtain. There was also a private bathroom.

A redheaded Gestapo operative told Goldsmith that he would be brought coffee and shaving tackle at 8 a.m. But a few hours later they would be back to collect him. 'And then?' the redhead sneered. 'Well maybe the Englishman would like a bath?' They went out and locked the door, taking the key with them. They had removed Goldsmith's jacket and belt in the avenue Foch along with his wallet, money, identity card and other vital documents. He was left standing in the trousers of his black marketeer's suit, shoes with no laces and a collarless open-necked shirt.

Head pounding and sweat pouring off his body, Goldsmith lay down on the bed and tried to collect his thoughts. He had been betrayed, that much was clear, but by whom? Was it just him? Or had a whole Special Operations Executive network been blown, putting countless names and operations at risk? He mustn't talk. He must give them nothing they didn't already know. But when his interrogation resumed and he was subjected to the various tortures that the Germans and their French auxiliaries had devised and refined, how long would he be able to hold out? His handlers had repeatedly drilled into him that the first 48 hours were crucial. Time enough for fellow agents and their contacts to discover that the circuit had been rolled up and run for cover. He had been arrested at 8 p.m. the previous evening so by 10 he would already have bought himself 14 hours. He somehow had to withstand another 34. He had thrown away his cyanide capsule weeks before. But he mustn't talk. He must die if necessary.

The 33-year-old's mind turned briefly to God. But John Gilbert Goldsmith, racehorse trainer, gambler and one-time playboy, had never seriously believed in the Almighty. 'What will be will be' was his motto, and let tomorrow take care of itself. It was surely too late in the day to place his faith in divine intervention. Yet as Goldsmith lay there listening to his heartbeat hammering against his ribcage, his maverick and bloody-minded side rebelled against the idea of being a Gestapo punch bag for the next two days and nights. His commanding officer, Colonel Maurice Buckmaster, and his Baker Street colleagues had seen in the racing man what they described, admiringly, as 'unusual qualities of bluff and daring'. The same qualities that had enabled him to talk his way out of the SD, or Sicherheitsdienst, headquarters at avenue Foch and into a German officers' mess. But the deception couldn't last much longer. Had he used up his share of luck? Or did he yet have the nerve and the ingenuity to escape?

He started prowling around the room, feeling like 'a bag fox' that has been caught and locked up in a stable the night before a hunt.[1] Outside the door was an orderly wearing an infantry belt and a bayonet. If Goldsmith tried to force the lock the orderly would hear the noise at once. He switched off the lights and eased back the blackout curtain on the window, but the catch wouldn't budge. Turning the lights back on, he stood on the bed and examined the ceiling, then rolled up the rug and studied the floor. But he could find nothing to help him. He went into the bathroom. Washbasin, bath, shower, bidet. There were even clean towels on the rail.

---

1   *Accidental Agent*, p.101. The next day the fox was taken in a bag to a covert, then released to be chased by the hounds.

Goldsmith ran the tap and splashed some water on his face. And that's when he noticed that there was a small window open up above the lavatory, and it looked just big enough for a body to squeeze through. He placed one of the bedroom chairs on the lavatory seat and climbed up gingerly. Fearful that at any moment his stool might collapse, alerting the guard outside the door, he put his head out. He was about 60 feet up. The room faced on to an inner courtyard and the glass roof of a conservatory and palm court with a fountain and some tables and chairs. But below him was a narrow ledge about 18 inches wide. Goldsmith could see that it ran along the wall beneath the next bedroom and, after being interrupted by a drainpipe, continued along the wall at right angles to his own where he could just make out an open bedroom window.

Trying to make his way along that ledge, even for a short distance, might be well nigh impossible. Especially for a man who had suffered from vertigo all his life. But then the alternatives weren't that promising either. Goldsmith drew his head back in and climbed back down off the chair. If he was going to make a move he would have to wait until it was nearly daylight and the curfew had ended. Otherwise, even if he did manage to get out of the hotel, he might be picked up immediately by a German patrol.

Breathing heavily, he lay back on the bed and started counting. Fifteen minutes. Thirty. Forty-five. When he reckoned about an hour had passed he tiptoed back into the bathroom and climbed up into a kneeling position on the chair. The first light of another fine summer's day was just beginning to break in the Parisian sky. As quietly as he could manage, Goldsmith started to wriggle out of the open window. It was a slow process but, despite the bruises, he was fit and slim and not too big to squeeze through. He had to get his head and shoulders out first and then, by supporting himself with one hand on top of the open window and one on the sill, he managed to ease out first one leg and then the other before gently lowering his feet on to the ledge. The chair wobbled and threatened to fall noisily to the floor but there was nothing he could do about it. He had his face to the wall and his back to the abyss.

It was, as they say on the racecourse, neck or nothing.

1

AN ENGLISHMAN ABROAD

The journey that brought John Goldsmith from his beloved 'trim little stable yard in Oxfordshire' to that Parisian ledge had begun with a meeting in London almost 18 months before. But his progression from the world of the Turf to the role of wartime secret agent might never have happened had it not been for his early life and upbringing in France.

Harold Yorke Goldsmith, better known as Jack, was a member of the expatriate British sporting community living in Paris in the early 20th century. Families like the Carters, the Heads and the Cunningtons had come over to work in racing stables in Chantilly and Lamorlaye, married French women and become fluent French speakers, and in many cases naturalised French citizens. Jack Goldsmith and his English wife Florence had a stable yard down a leafy *voie privée* in Neuilly in the affluent 16th arrondissement. A friend and neighbour was the boxing promoter Jim Pratt who brought the first black world heavyweight champion, Jack Johnson, to Paris in 1913 and gambled on racing, boxing and cycling.

Pratt broke in yearlings and owned a couple of stallions which he rented out to commercial breeders. Jack Goldsmith sold moderate all-purpose horses which he bought out of the local abattoir at Vaugirard but then dressed up as hunters, hacks, steeplechasers or military steeds depending on what his customers were looking for. Dissembling and guile played a key part in these transactions, as his son would soon learn.

John Gilbert Goldsmith was born in Paris on 15 August 1909 and his childhood home was the house and stables at number 119 rue de la Faisanderie, just around the corner from the boulevard Flandrin and avenue Henri Martin. It was a select, residential neighbourhood. Signs outside the bigger houses discouraged hawkers and warned 'Attention Chien', and each morning there was a polite queue for the brioches and fresh bread in the boulangerie on the corner of rue Dufrénoy. A few doors down from 119 was the Polish Embassy, and just beyond that was a police station where the infant John liked to watch the gendarmes come and go in their traditional blue kepis and capes.

The stable was pulled down in the 1930s and replaced by a typical Parisian apartment building with a beady-eyed concierge keeping watch from her ground-floor rooms near the foyer and the cage lift. Nowadays the area is dominated by smart young professionals and the sounds of the traffic moving to and from the western suburbs into the city, but a century ago horses were more commonplace than cars.

The English boy went to the École Primeur on rue Singer near the Porte de Passy, walking there and back each day with his mother and enjoying the bustling street life. By Christmas 1914 some quartiers were filled with wounded soldiers and homeless families from Flanders and the Marne. But in Passy older gentlemen continued to smoke and drink and read the racing papers on the terrace of the Café le Chalet and the market next door still sold John's favourite saucissons as well as live rabbits and chickens.

Goldsmith was a quick learner who was soon speaking French like a local, and at the age of 11 he moved on to the Lycée Janson de Sailly on rue de la Pompe. The 19th-century school building had brown double doors, stone floors and wide staircases. Discipline was strict in the high-ceilinged classrooms and teaching traditional and by rote. Young Goldsmith cordially loathed both school and school teachers but he saw it out until he'd completed his baccalaureate in 1927 by which time he'd added a good knowledge of Parisian street slang to his formal vocabulary.

John was by now an accomplished rider, having first sat on a horse as soon as he could walk, and in his teens he was often required to assist his father in his commercial dealings. One of his first jobs was to groom newly arrived stock with a small bottle of petrol and a wisp of twisted hay. An hour and a half of dogged labour would transform a refugee from the slaughterhouse into a seemingly glistening thoroughbred who, Jack Goldsmith would say, wouldn't have looked out of place in the Grand Prix de Paris at Longchamp.

When a customer came calling, Jack would say he had 'just the right animal for them' and that he would 'put the boy up to put him through his paces'. His son would duly take the reins like a budding jockey and trot the horse up and down, doing his best to conceal any nervous or unwilling traits it might possess and concurring 100 per cent with his father's glowing description of its abilities. Remarkably it was a sales trick that never seemed to fail though, as John confessed later, 'to look a man straight in the eye and tell him a lie' requires years of practice. But it's a skill acquired, necessarily, by many a racing, gambling and horse-dealing man, and John Goldsmith would one day be grateful for the dexterity with which he learned to control his face and play a part.

John rode in a few Chevaliers or amateur-riders races and played polo with a smart crowd. His first job after leaving school was as manager of the Polo Club de Roubaix whose members met regularly at St Cloud and in the Bois de Boulogne. They partied hard in the evenings and at weekends and it was fun to be a sporting young man about town in the Paris of the late 1920s. The bilingual Englishman was tall, slim and good-looking with piercing blue eyes and hair swept back from his forehead. He loved French café society and French cigarettes, wine and oysters, and he loved French girls and they adored him.

In 1929 John became assistant to Antoine Munat at his stable at Maisons-Laffitte. The Frenchman trained steeplechasers and hurdlers to run in the metropolitan meetings at Auteuil and Enghien-les-Bains and sometimes he had runners on the flat at Longchamp too. The Parisian racecourses were glamorous, leisurely, tree-shaded places. The horses were sleek and well fed and the owners included a Marquis here and a Comte there along with assorted industrialists and self-made men accompanied by a fleet of expensive-to-run women. Munat's yard wasn't afraid to put the money down when things were going well and Goldsmith had further training in dissembling and keeping his counsel in public so as not to affect the odds.

John loved the early mornings on the forest gallops with the dew and the sun getting up and he loved the evenings too with what Ernest Hemingway, in his 1923 short story *My Old Man*, called the 'Maisons Gang' at the Café de Paris in town or the Café de la Paix near the Opera. If Munat had a big winner he might take a table at one of the famous restaurants that were frequented by the flat racing fraternity, like Lapérouse or Gallopin, and then afterwards they might go on to see Josephine Baker at the Casino de Paris, or

Chevalier and Mistinguett. They often didn't get to bed until 3 a.m. even though the working day began again only a few hours later with a cup of black coffee and a cigarette.

It was an expatriate English gambler who raced horses in both Britain and France who encouraged John to come 'home' in 1933. A stable yard, The Paddocks at Sparsholt near Wantage in Oxfordshire, was available to rent and several owners offered their support. The chance to make a name for himself in the UK and to be his own man rather than an assistant seemed too good to pass up.

John announced himself with a hat trick at Wolverhampton races in November 1933. But most of the horses he trained in that decade, and there were never more than about a dozen of them, were what are known in the trade as 'platers' – modest types capable of winning on their day but at a fairly low level. But while there may have been no champions among them Goldsmith soon established a reputation for the skill with which he placed them and their readiness to run when the money was down. If a horse was a bit better than plating class you needed to disguise its ability in the run-up to the race and then not have it win by too far, otherwise it would have too much weight to carry next time out – and the élan with which John mastered these details didn't go unnoticed by the big racecourse gamblers.

John's best horse before the war was a steeplechaser called Black Hawk who should have won the 1939 Grand National. The level of betting on the race in that era was phenomenal with high-stakes bookmakers like the Mayfair-based Percy Thompson and the East End brothers Max and Snouty Parker staking and winning millions of pounds in modern money. Ten days before the '39 National, Black Hawk won a three-mile steeplechase at Wolverhampton 'a shade cleverly', as the *Sporting Life* correspondent Meyrick Good put it.

Afterwards the gelding's owner, Mrs Christine Jones, revealed that she had backed her horse for Aintree at 50–1, placing a bet for herself and the Goldsmith stable. By the day of the race, Friday, 24 March, Black Hawk's odds had contracted to 40–1 but the hot favourite was Kilstar, owned by the compulsive gambler Dorothy Paget and the subject of a 50-strong police guard at the racecourse stables for fear that he might be got at.

The race offered a much-needed release from the nationwide tension and fear of another European war that had been building since the Munich crisis the previous autumn. For every page of newsprint about the Liverpool runners and riders (and there were sheets of it) there was comparable coverage given to the latest moves of the fascist dictators and their henchmen. German troops had just marched into Prague as Czech leaders, abandoned by Britain and France, gave in to Hitler's ultimatum, while in Spain Franco's forces were about to enter Madrid, and in Poland, Mussolini's son-in-law Count Ciano was demanding protection from 'Jewish terrorists' as he travelled to Cracow in a special train. The German propaganda minister, Josef Goebbels, insisted that war was 'not inevitable' as he joined the Führer at his 50th birthday concert in Berlin (where one of the guests was the Conservative peer and Nazi sympathiser Lord Brocket), while Field Marshal Hermann Göring, whose ample girth and preposterous taste in uniforms fascinated the British press, embarked on a five-week holiday in San Remo with his wife and family. But the British Easter holiday and talk of more modest excursions to the likes of Paignton, Scarborough and Bognor Regis was overshadowed by the grim news that special gas masks for babies would be ready in a month as a parliamentary report warned that in week one of a war bombs would kill 100,000 British citizens and wound up to 200,000 more.

The nation was desperate for some light relief, and the National, run in bright sunshine, drew an estimated crowd of 200,000 that included the King's brother, Prince George, and Lady Diana Cooper, who was sporting a fur coat and one of the new season's fashionably short hemlines. The first prize of £7,284 went to the Irish challenger Workman, a 12–1 chance who was ridden by Tim Hyde, but it should have been Black Hawk in the winner's enclosure. Goldsmith's runner, with the experienced Jack Molony in the saddle, was in fourth place as he jumped Becher's Brook second time round and he took up the running going to Valentine's a few fences later. With less than a mile to run the race looked to be his but, at the fourth last, Workman jumped into the back of him, giving Molony a 'big shove' as he did so. The jockey, who said he 'hadn't moved at the time', came down and Mrs Jones's and the stable's wager hit the deck with him. The bookmakers were almost as disconsolate as Molony and Goldsmith and were said to have paid out over a million pounds nationwide (£50 million today) as a result of Workman's victory.

Jack Molony, for whom Aintree had been a perennial hard luck story, took the train back down to London to drown his sorrows, ending the night in the Turkish baths on Jermyn Street. At least John Goldsmith had the new love of his life to console him on the long drive back from Liverpool to Wantage. From his early teens in Paris John had always been surrounded by attractive female company. As well as a ready sense of humour he had a way about him, and when he lit up a Gitanes (which he purchased from a tobacconist's in Soho a bit like Ian Fleming ordering his Morland Specials) he looked a lot more exotic than most conventional British racehorse trainers of the time. By 1939 he had already been married once, briefly, and divorced. Then he met Annette Helen Bell Clover, another passionate racing and riding enthusiast whose parents owned Foxhills, a 19th-century house surrounded by 70 acres of woodland and paddocks near Northwich in Cheshire.

The 21-year-old Annette was a beautiful willowy blonde who was known, despite her height, or perhaps because of it, as 'Tiny'. Vivacious and optimistic with more than a passing similarity to the actress Madeleine Carroll, her extrovert personality was the perfect foil to the moodiness and depression that could sometimes assail a trainer worried about the health and well-being of his horses. She was also relatively well off and had first met John when she sent him one of her horses to train. She started riding out with him on the gallops and before long she was working as his unpaid secretary too, typing the entries on her lap in a chair in his sitting room as he poured them both generous measures of gin and grapefruit juice and discussed running plans through a haze of French cigarette smoke.

The day before war broke out, Saturday, 2 September 1939, John had been due to have some runners at Folkestone but the meeting was abandoned due to the state of emergency and the horses returned to the yard. For the time being all sporting entertainments were suspended, but after a month had passed with no bombs, air raids or poison gas attacks, a semblance of normality returned. British and French politicians assured their citizens that their armies were secure behind the 'impregnable' Maginot Line and that, in the face of such defences, Hitler would be mad to attack.

At the end of October racing resumed at Newmarket (and Newbury and Thirsk) and Marcel Boussac, the textile tycoon and biggest racehorse owner in France, sent his top two-year-old Djebel over to win the Middle Park Stakes. When the seasons changed there was a limited programme of jump racing too with icy weather seemingly more of a worry than the Germans. On 5 March 1940 John Goldsmith ran his dual winner Nocib, owned by 'Miss Clover', in the

Eastergate Selling Hurdle at Fontwell Park and the little French-bred gelding finished second. War or no war, a day at the races was still an extremely popular day's sport. The *Times* racing correspondent noted that he had 'never seen more visitors at the Sussex track than was the case yesterday', adding that 'it would be churlish not to call attention to the excellent catering arrangements made by Messrs Elliott whose luncheons were as good as, if not better than, in times of peace'.

In April 1940 John Goldsmith and Miss Clover were married at Marylebone Registry Office, but within a month the 1930s racing and sporting Elysium that had persisted throughout the phoney war was shattered. By late May the Germans had invaded Norway, driving out the British Expeditionary Force, overrun Holland and Belgium and launched their blitzkrieg assault on France. Neville Chamberlain's comment the previous year that Hitler had 'missed the bus' looked risible and on 20 May he resigned and was succeeded as Prime Minister by Winston Churchill.

Extraordinarily, horse racing continued at Lewes on 3 June even as special trains piled high with remnants of the British Army evacuated at Dunkirk were passing up the line only a few miles away. Numerous racing men were caught up in the disaster. The Duke of Norfolk and the amateur rider and breeder John Hislop got away unharmed but the journalist Roger Mortimer was captured and the gallant Corinthian jockey Lieutenant Kim Muir was killed.

John Goldsmith, who felt loyal to both Britain and France, longed to get involved, and in September he attempted to join the RAF. But the recruiting officer in Reading laughed at him and said that at 31 he was too old to be a fighter pilot. He should go back home and wait and if, or when, he was needed to perform some subsidiary role he'd be contacted. John tried the army but got an identical response. (He was experiencing the same frustration felt by Nick Jenkins, the hero of Anthony Powell's *Dance to the Music of Time* novels, who discovers that if you are over 30 in 1941 it isn't easy to get a commission in the British Army and that you just have to put up with what you are offered.)

In December 1940 Goldsmith closed his yard and sent his horses home to their owners. His last runner was Nocib, who was unplaced at Cheltenham on the 15th. The following month he started work in a civilian position at the RAF depot at Milton in Gloucestershire. It seemed that most of his fellow clerks and drivers were ex-fairground workers who regarded the RAF stock, especially the petrol and tyres, as their entrée into the black market.

A few months later Goldsmith was accepted as a trooper in the Royal Armoured Corps and, after five desultory months in Cheshire and a further three weeks' training at their barracks in Warminster, he started driving tanks over Salisbury Plain. Well used to manoeuvring heavy horse boxes he took to the new vehicles with aplomb. Indeed such was the ease with which he steered the Valentine Infantry Tank – which saw extensive action in North Africa – that his commanding officer offered him the job of tank instructor with the rank of an, unpaid, Acting Lance Corporal.

It was meant to be a compliment, but to John Goldsmith, and more importantly to his wife, it seemed like a dead end, and Tiny wasn't prepared to leave it there. She told her well-connected sister, who was about to get married herself, all about her lovely fit, strong, handsome husband who was a fluent French speaker. The sister described John in turn to her London solicitor who was recovering from injuries sustained on a parachute course. The lawyer had injudiciously admitted, under questioning by his attractive client, that he had been involved in talent spotting for a new undercover enterprise that was just gathering pace.

The lawyer made enquiries and spoke in turn to the sister's fiancé, Captain Lionel Cecil, who was an officer in a pukka cavalry regiment. At the end of 1941 Cecil wrote to John telling him that he would be hearing about a job that might be available to him. A dangerous but important job that he could be ideal for. A couple of months later Goldsmith was summoned into the presence of his Warminster CO and told that a letter had come telling him to report to a mysterious address in London the following day. He was given the details along with a 48-hour pass and a travel warrant.

As he left the Colonel's office, still in his trooper's khaki Tank Corps uniform, John wondered what the summons might entail. Dangerous yet rewarding Lionel Cecil had said, hinting that France might in some way be involved. Like John Buchan's hero Richard Hannay when he gets his summons to the Foreign Office at the beginning of *Greenmantle*, was this a call to high adventure at last?

2

FIFTY-FIFTY

The room was completely empty except for a table and two chairs. John was directed to sit in one. His interlocutor took the other. The spartan setting seemed appropriate in this third, stripped-down winter of the war. Goldsmith hadn't been in London for more than a year and the face of the capital had changed dramatically. Making his way on foot from Paddington Station he had passed streets littered with rubble and buildings pockmarked with bomb damage. Windows were blown out, there were no railings in the parks, once-smart private gardens had been turned into allotments and the pavements were crowded with Allied servicemen and women from more than 20 different countries.

The address he was looking for turned out to be in a large mansion block near Baker Street. A Corporal took his name and told him to have a seat, and then, about fifteen minutes later, he was shown up into a room on the third floor. The man sitting across from him, who was wearing a captain's insignia, was tall and thin with a face like a weasel. He didn't introduce himself then, but the weasel's name was Selwyn Jepson and, appropriately for a man engaged in clandestine warfare, he was the author of mysteries and detective stories with titles like *Rogues and Diamonds* and *I Met Murder*. He told John that the conversation to follow would take place entirely in French, which was Jepson's second language as he'd taken a graduate degree at the Sorbonne after his studies at Cambridge.

They began with some bland and straightforward questions about Goldsmith's birth and background in Paris. Then Jepson moved on to French life and politics. What did Goldsmith think of Marshal Pétain, the elderly silver-haired soldier who had signed the armistice in June 1940 and become head of the puppet Vichy government? John replied that he'd had a pretty low opinion of senior French army officers both before and after the German invasion. Jepson wanted to know what his impressions were of the strength of resistance to Vichy and the Germans, and how strong did he think the Communist Party was in France? These were mostly uncharted areas for a racehorse trainer so the weasel turned to French culture. What were John's favourite French films and actors and actresses? What did he think of Picasso and modern art, and what about jazz? What French newspapers did he read, what cigarettes did he smoke, and what were his favourite drinks and meals? And how was his knowledge of French geography? What were the main industries of Metz and Toulouse, and if he was asked to take a train from Marseille to Paris which station would he arrive at in the capital? John had to admit that not having been to France since the Grand Steeplechase de Paris in 1938 his knowledge of some of these topics was not as good as it should be.

Jepson changed the subject to John's racing career. He asked about Black Hawk's Grand National and the planning and attention to detail that he imagined must be necessary to prepare a horse for a big race. And what about the risks involved when the stable's money was at stake? How did John cope with that pressure? Not quite sure where this was going, John agreed that bravery and steady nerves were important elements of any life involving training, riding and backing horses.

Goldsmith had assumed that he was being vetted for a job as a translator, possibly with the Free French forces in London. But then Jepson, speaking English now, told him that he would be called back for another interview in three weeks' time. Until then he must say absolutely nothing to anyone about their conversation or where it had taken place.

'Not even to my commanding officer?' asked John.

'Especially not to your commanding officer,' Jepson replied.

'Can you give me any further idea of what's involved?' asked John.

The weasel shifted in his chair. 'You have been recommended as potentially suitable for special employment,' he said. 'If you are selected you will be dropped into Occupied France, probably by parachute, to carry out subversive work against the Germans. We'll do everything we can to prepare and support you but if you're caught, you're on your own.'

Goldsmith was staggered.

'What about my wife?' he asked quietly.

'Should you agree to volunteer your next of kin will be kept informed by us by letter, once a month, of your well-being. We estimate your chances of coming back alive as around fifty-fifty. That should appeal to a betting man.'

It most certainly did appeal. Selwyn Jepson would say after the war that his task at this point was to decide whether he could risk a man's or woman's life but that they had to decide for themselves whether they were willing to risk it. John Goldsmith had no such doubts.

Three weeks later he was summoned to the RAC Colonel's office for the last time.

'You've been posted, Goldsmith,' said the Colonel. 'What's it all about?'

'I'm not entirely sure, sir,' John replied, truthfully. Two days earlier he had received a letter telling him he would be leaving the Royal Armoured Corps regiment and giving him a new address to report to in London. Number 68 Orchard Court. He had just been waiting to hear the date of his departure.

The Colonel, annoyed to be losing a useful instructor, bade him a not entirely fond farewell, warning that he would regret spurning the opportunity to see out the war in the relative safety of a barracks on Salisbury Plain. Fifteen months later John might have agreed with him, but that April morning he could hardly wait to be gone.

He spent that night in a small hotel in Paddington, and the next morning he set out to find Orchard Court, which turned out to be a block of flats reached through an archway off Baker Street opposite Portman Square. Goldsmith approached the doorman who wore a dark suit and tie and was told to take the lift to the second floor. The building was completely silent and there was no sign of anyone else around. John walked down the corridor and knocked at number 68. After a few minutes Jepson appeared and ushered him into a smart, modern flat, all 1920s and 1930s chrome and Art Deco. They passed several closed doors one of which, Goldsmith later discovered, led to an exotic bathroom with a black tiled bath and an onyx bidet. Newcomers and returning agents were sometimes made to wait there while another meeting was concluded so that as few people as possible would see them and discover their identity.

The conversation took place in the dining room and, as before, there was no one else present. There was no preamble or offer of coffee or tea either. Jepson told him that he had been selected to undergo special training which would begin in a week's time. The whole course would involve sabotage, subversion, security and political warfare. Oh, and parachute jumping. If he came through it all satisfactorily he would be considered for action in the field. If not, he might be found some other wartime role or – and this made John's heart sink – he might be returned to his unit. It all depended on him.

There was also the question of rank, said Jepson. Temporarily John was to be awarded a commission as a Second Lieutenant and he could go off straight away and buy the pips. Other than that he was being given a week's leave in London, accommodation provided in a South Kensington hotel – and he could ask his wife to join him. At the end of it he should report back to Orchard Court.

Within half an hour it was all over and John was back out on the street with his future transformed. So how exactly did he feel? Excited, yes, and curious too, but surely there was also some trepidation, though not enough to put him off. The interview had taken place only a few days after his daughter's first birthday. The baby girl's name was Gaie and she had her mother's blonde hair and impish good looks. But would her father ever live to see her grow up? It was the kind of question that he knew he had to push to the back of his mind. He had despaired of army life at Warminster and longed for a proper role. Now he was going to get one, and better not to think too much about what it might lead to or where it would end.

By April 1942 the war was global, stretching from North Africa to Russia, the Pacific and beyond. More than 60,000 British and Commonwealth servicemen had been captured at Singapore and in Darwin, Australia, the population were steeling themselves for Japanese air raids. In France Pierre Laval's minister of the interior in the Vichy regime had been assassinated and the French Gestapo were out hunting his killers. In the North Atlantic there had been

114 attacks on Allied shipping in 54 days. There was talk of new fuel and coal rationing, eggs were to be restricted to five a month, and all the time the bombing of British towns and cities continued.

On 25 April the Luftwaffe launched the so-called 'Baedeker Raid' on Bath. It was the first time a cultural centre had been targeted and, initially, it was assumed the planes were heading for Bristol, further west. Over 400 people were killed, some of them machine-gunned as they ran for shelter, and more than 1,000 historic buildings damaged or destroyed by the combination of incendiaries and high explosive dropped on three successive nights. An antique sedan chair was one of the casualties too, leading the pro-German propagandist Lord Haw Haw to inform listeners to his nightly radio transmissions from Berlin that Bath had been targeted as it was 'a meeting place of the English upper classes', hence the 'smashing Luftwaffe raids'.[2]

But experiences of wartime Britain weren't only about suffering and hardship stoically endured. It wasn't just mugs of tea and huddling round the wireless set listening to Churchill's speeches. There was also a sense of excitement and liberation from conventional restraint that the day-to-day nature of life and constant presence of death intensified. There were still sporting entertainments to enjoy too. Vice Admiral Sir Gerald Dickens, appalled that horse and greyhound racing was taking place while sailors were dying, had recommended that 'slackers in all classes ought to be shot'. Sir Stafford Cripps, the socialist Leader of the House of Commons, took a more relaxed view. He ruled that 'dog and horse racing and boxing will only be prevented in so far as they impede the intention to achieve

2   Lord Haw Haw was the nickname given to William Joyce whose broadcasts, 'Germany Calling', were conducted in an affected upper-class accent. Despite being an American citizen brought up in Ireland, Joyce was hanged for treason in January 1946.

victory'. This was music to the ears of the Jockey Club. Desperate to preserve the domestic breeding industry and undeterred by the risk of air raids in public spaces, they had been given approval for another limited programme of flat racing on Newmarket's July course, the Rowley Mile having been taken over by the RAF.

John Goldsmith kept in touch with the racing news whenever he could, and during his April leave he had time to go racing with Tiny at Salisbury. John had rarely been in better spirits. After leaving his meeting with Jepson at Orchard Court he had bounded into a men's tailoring shop in Piccadilly Arcade. As well as all the acres of tweed and the flat caps and covert coats, the shop stocked service ties and badges and had a long association with the military. But when John asked the elderly assistant if he could sew his pips on to his battle dress jacket, the salesman wore a pained expression as if he had just been asked to parachute naked into St James's Park. He regretted that it would be impossible. Staff shortages. As John looked around the otherwise empty shop he couldn't see much evidence of urgent assignments that needed tackling. He suspected that if he had been a prospective Brigadier or Colonel rather than a mere Lieutenant, help might have been forthcoming. Refusing to allow his enthusiasm to be dampened, he carried on up Piccadilly to the Hyde Park Hotel which he knew well from convivial pre-war evenings with his racing cronies. He hurried down the stairs to the Gents cloakroom where the porter greeted him like an old friend, and while John stood guard at the cubbyhole, the porter – who had formerly been a gentleman's gentleman – sewed on the pips.

John paid him five shillings for a job well done and then dashed back upstairs to the front desk where he asked the receptionist if she could put a call through to his wife, Mrs Goldsmith, in Sparsholt. He lit a cigarette and whistled excitedly under his breath as he looked forward to telling Tiny he had been made an officer. But when he was handed the phone she seemed to know about it already. John was flummoxed. How on earth could she have heard? 'Don't be silly, darling,' she said sensibly. 'The hotel receptionist said Lieutenant Goldsmith was calling so it was obvious that you had got the job and been given a commission.'

The week's leave passed happily, amorously, and all too soon. Gaie had been left with Mrs Clover up at Foxhills so one night the couple dressed up and went out in the blackout to the Berkeley Hotel. Even the grandest restaurants were restricted to charging no more than five shillings per person for a three-course meal. But luxury items like oysters and caviare weren't included and in places like the Berkeley and the Savoy the food wasn't rationed either, so if you could afford it and cover the bar bill and tips, you could still eat very well. The hotel was full of that distinctive wartime mix of officers and their wives and sweethearts, slackers, swindlers, black marketeers, distressed aristocrats and continental royalty on the run. The Lieutenant and his wife danced to the former Savoy Orphean Al Collins and his band who played 'With All My Heart' and 'Moon Over Miami', and the next morning Tiny felt sick and was inclined to blame it on too much gin and too many of John's French cigarettes. A week later she was back up in Cheshire with her mother and her baby girl, but by then her husband had already embarked on his journey into the secret world.

3

SET EUROPE ABLAZE

The hundreds of men and women who obeyed a summons to 68 Orchard Court were never told the specific name of the organisation they were going to work for. Some of them came to refer to it as 'the outfit', although Maurice Buckmaster preferred 'the firm', but they were deliberately kept in ignorance of its proper title and structure.

The Special Operations Executive had been founded in July 1940 less than a month after the fall of France. Its first chairman was Hugh Dalton, the Minister for Economic Warfare, who wrote of the need to set up a new body to 'co-ordinate, inspire, assist and control the citizens of oppressed countries' who must be direct participants in its efforts. The quixotic, cloak-and-dagger nature of the venture appealed to the vivid imagination of the new Prime Minister and Churchill gave it his blessing using one of the most famous catchphrases of his career. 'Set Europe ablaze', he said to Dalton.

The price paid for that rallying cry would be a high one both in terms of agents' lives and losses among civilian populations. There are some who point to the loss of life and question SOE's methods and achievements. Encouraging resistance in places like Yugoslavia and the Balkans way well have contributed to the region's problems to this day. But those arguments are easy and painless with the benefit of hindsight. As Professor M. R. D. Foot observed in his official history *SOE in France*, the new service was trying to wage war by new and unorthodox means and it had to battle numerous inter-service rivalries in order to do so. More conventional espionage types were suspicious of what they regarded as 'military bohemianism of the most raffish sort'.[3] The Foreign Office initially felt there was something ungentlemanly about covert warfare and drew the line at damaging private property, and the exiled General de Gaulle and his Free French colleagues in London were deeply suspicious of SOE's efforts even as the British were supplying them with wireless sets, ammunition and guns. The jobs that SOE's agents were asked to do were rarely as straightforward or clean-cut as in the pages of Sapper, Buchan and Dornford Yates[4] and some of their missions – to Holland, for example[5] – ended in disaster. But had it not been for Churchill's boyish enthusiasm, the organisation might have been stillborn and the many inspirational examples of courage and resistance that its humanity gave shape to would not exist.

SOE divided itself into different country sections and the job of F Section was to try to work with French Resistance members of all types from de Gaulle's Free French to ardent Communists, far

---

3   *The Military Philosophers, Dance to the Music of Time* volume 9, by Anthony Powell.

4   Sapper, the pen name for H.C. McNeile, and Dornford Yates, aka Cecil William Mercer, wrote popular thrillers about gentleman heroes tackling foreign villains between the wars. Sapper's most famous creation was Bulldog Drummond. John Buchan, a much better writer, was the author of the classic spy novels *The Thirty-Nine Steps* and *Greenmantle*.

5   The entire SOE network in Holland was penetrated by the Germans and more than 50 agents were sent to their deaths. They were either the victims of incompetence by the service chiefs in London or sacrificed as part of a 'double double agent' sting run by the Secret Intelligence Service (SIS).

right Catholic royalists, trade union leaders and sundry others who detested the Vichy regime but refused to co-operate with one another. De Gaulle's prime objective was to set up a single resistance movement and Secret Army inside France. But, to begin with, the British weren't entirely convinced that the General, who had never been elected and had effectively appointed himself, was the best man to lead it.

In 1941 SOE had set up a special RF (République Française) Section to try to improve their relationship with de Gaulle's counter-espionage service.[6] The Free French headquarters were at 4 Carlton Gardens but they also had offices in Duke Street, in a house that had been the pre-war headquarters of Bertram Mills Circus and SOE joked that the circus had never really moved out. Duke Street was not far from Orchard Court and Maurice Buckmaster occasionally met his Free French counterpart, Colonel André Dewavrin, in the mews that backed on to both their buildings. Discussions invariably focused on de Gaulle's latest grievance or fit of pique, but what Buckmaster didn't say was that SOE were trying to find out if there were other military figures inside France who would be easier and less disagreeable to deal with.

On the morning of Monday, 27 April 1942, Buckmaster was at Orchard Court to welcome John Goldsmith and nine other prospective agents. Veterans would remember the Major, as he still was then, sitting on a desk, swinging his legs and smoking a cigarette. Outwardly relaxed and amenable and often accompanied by his dog, Buckmaster was working intense 18-hour days, dividing his time between briefings at Orchard Court and the main SOE offices around the corner on Baker Street.[7] That morning he was joined by

---

6   Free French counter-espionage was run by the BCRA, or Bureau Central de Renseignements et d'Action.

7   F Section HQ was in Norgeby House at 83 Baker Street.

Selwyn Jepson and a tall Frenchman, André Simon, who was the son and successor to the wine expert of the same name. Simon, who was in RAF uniform, had already been on two undercover operations and he was going to be the new group's conducting officer. The mysterious Vera Atkins, who as Goldsmith would discover was Buckmaster's indispensable right arm, was there too. The recruits hardly noticed her at first but she would play an increasingly important part in their lives as their missions approached. There were also a number of FANY (Female Auxiliary Nursing Yeomanry) officers present. These were bright and often extremely attractive young women from 'good families' whose tasks included everything from chauffeuring Buckmaster and his staff around London and the Home Counties to working as telephonists, administrators and cipher clerks.

The SOE leadership were mostly from traditional backgrounds. Buckmaster himself had been to Eton and had gone to France to work as a journalist on the daily newspaper *Le Matin* before joining Schroders merchant bank. His last job before the war was as the Ford Motor Company's representative at Asniéres near Paris. He spoke fluent French. He had joined the Intelligence Corps in 1939, fought at Dunkirk in 1940 and moved to Baker Street a year later, becoming the head of F Section in October 1941. By comparison most SOE agents had little if any previous military experience and came from all backgrounds and classes. The firm weren't particularly interested in conventional masculine stereotypes. They preferred individuality and flair on the one hand and homespun anonymity on the other.

John Goldsmith's intake was a typically diverse group. The most conspicuously military figure was Gilbert Norman, who was a Major in the Durham Light Infantry and had been brought back to London from Egypt. The 27-year-old had been born in Paris like John and educated at a lycée in Versailles. Short and broad-shouldered, he had a thin black moustache which he fingered constantly.

A very different type was the jockey James Amps, a stocky red-faced little man who had grown up in Rueil-Malmaison outside Paris. With minimal formal education, he had been apprenticed at the age of 13 to the Chantilly trainer Frank Carter and had been working at his stable when the war broke out.

Rowland Dowlen was a naturalised Italian who had been adopted by an Englishman at the age of five. Dowlen had spent ten years working in the Paris branch of the Royal Bank of Canada before returning to the UK. In his spare time he was a scoutmaster in Poplar in the East End of London.

John Cuthbert Young, dark-haired and handsome, had been a fire insurance surveyor in Newcastle and had married a French woman. He loved the French countryside with a passion but Goldsmith felt his accent sounded worryingly English. In marked contrast Arthur Staggs, the cockney son of a Thames sailing barge skipper whose family had moved to northern France in the 1920s, spoke faultless working-class French.

None of the volunteers had any prior training in espionage. Unlike the more conventional agencies, the new service was looking for a range of orthodox and unorthodox characters and there was no one definitive SOE type. Future F Section recruits would include bank managers, teachers, barristers, boxers, a couple of acrobats, a racing driver, a head waiter, a chef at a golf club, a hairdresser, a gay musical comedy actor and a *Vogue* fashion artist.

There was little time for Goldsmith and his fellow students to introduce themselves that April morning. After a few encouraging words from Buckmaster they were escorted downstairs, out of the back entrance to Orchard Court and out through the black wrought-iron gates that led to Seymour Mews. Waiting for them was a 15-hundredweight army truck. A Sergeant got into the driving seat, the conducting officer sat beside him, and the recruits piled into the back. The lorry sped away along Fitzhardinge Street and around Portman Square and before long they were crossing the river and passing through Richmond and Twickenham and heading out into the suburbs. The men, who had no idea where they were going, chatted together after a fashion. But as the morning wore on and their journey continued through wooded countryside and down increasingly minor roads John remembered a silence descending on the lorry, each man preoccupied with his own thoughts.

The group's immediate destination was Wanborough Manor in Surrey. The redbrick 17th-century house with tall chimneys, mullioned windows and fir trees in the grounds was situated in a small village near Guildford. Nowadays the surrounding countryside of woods and fields seems forever to be within earshot of the traffic roaring along the Hog's Back, but in 1942, although only 30 miles from London, the village was peaceful and remote.

The Manor, and its neighbouring farm, dates back to the Norman Conquest and in the 19th century was lived in by Sir Algernon West, private secretary to the Liberal Prime Minister, Gladstone, and a director of the South Eastern Railway Company. By the 1930s the house had become the property of a Guildford timber merchant who installed an open-air swimming pool in the back garden. But in the autumn of 1940 the timber merchant's family moved out and Wanborough was requisitioned by the military. Its new designation was Special Training School Number 5, one of a number of SOE preliminary training schools set up in similar big houses in the south of England.

The ambience at Wanborough Manor, and at West Park in Finchampstead and Brickendonbury Hall near Hertford (where a certain Mr Philby and Mr Burgess were tutors), was like a cross between a boarding school and one of those rather gloomy but comfortable country residences that crop up in Agatha Christie novels.[8] The Commandant was Major Roger de Wesselow, an urbane former Guards officer who saw his role as a combination of headmaster, host, mentor and guide. Peter Churchill, who went to France by submarine in January 1942, was one of Wanborough's first students and in his book *Of Their Own Choice* he described his arrival at the Manor and de Wesselow's welcoming address.

'Gentlemen,' began the Major, 'you will be given three weeks' intensive instruction in this school for subversive activity. There will be lectures and practical exercises in map reading, demolitions, weapons training, Morse code, fieldcraft and close combat. French will be spoken at all meals. You will be worked very hard and I think I should warn you in all fairness that your reactions and progress during the course will be carefully noted. There is no limit to the number of candidates acceptable for the tough and lonely life of this organisation for which you have volunteered, but the requirements of physical endurance, patience, technical knowledge and security are high.

'I cannot sufficiently stress the importance of security. Nobody outside this school knows what goes on here and nobody must know. All letters written from here or received are carefully censored. The telephone must not be used. When the course is over, those of you who have passed – and I hope you all do – will be sent up to Scotland for the second course of advanced training. There will be no leave between the

8   The Cambridge spies Kim Philby and Guy Burgess were both employed briefly as SOE instructors in political warfare and sabotage techniques.

courses; only after the parachute course which comes third. In conclusion you will find the food here to be good and plentiful, the bar well stocked and the beds excellent. That's about all. Any questions?'

Nobody said a word.

The Major went on to assure them that he and his staff would always be at their disposal 'for any problem you might have. And now, as you would no doubt like to get acquainted with one another before lunch, I will leave you. A ring on that bell will produce the Corporal who handles the drinks. That's all.'

John Goldsmith and his companions got the same speech, and at the end of it the bell was duly rung, the Corporal swiftly appeared, and preliminary training began with a stiff gin.

Many former students have testified to de Wesselow's charm, an aura that, happily for John Goldsmith, had been honed in the convivial milieu of pre-war racing journalism. Born in 1890, the Major had served with the Coldstream Guards in World War One and been injured in a mustard gas attack. After the war he built a career as a publisher and businessman. His company, Welbecson Press, had offices in Mayfair and published *The Racehorse*, which was considered essential weekly reading for all Turf enthusiasts.

The then Lieutenant de Wesselow remained on the reserve list and in June 1939, three months before war broke out, he was called up. Promoted to the rank of Captain, his task for the next 18 months was guarding government installations including the Prime Minister's country retreat Chequers. But in 1941 he was contacted by Colin Gubbins, an old friend from the trenches and a tough, dynamic soldier who had recently joined the Baker Street Irregulars. Brigadier Gubbins was something of a self-taught expert on guerrilla warfare having studied how the IRA operated under Michael Collins while serving with the British Army in Kildare during the Irish War of Independence. SOE had charged him with setting up training schools and facilities and establishing a good working relationship with the Admiralty, the Air Ministry and the Joint Planning Staff. He was in the process of appointing a new Commandant at Wanborough Manor and he felt that de Wesselow's experience of active service on the one hand and unconventional peacetime life on the other was just what SOE were looking for. The Major, as he now became, had been to Neuchatel University as a young man and spoke French, and Gubbins regarded him as a good judge of character.

De Wesselow and his wife Rosamund arrived at Wanborough on 10 June 1941 and made an instant impression on everyone they met, especially the French students. As the Orchard Court matriarch Vera Atkins testified years later, the Major had the ability to get on well with people from all walks of life without ever quite losing the timbre of a Guards officer.

Peter Churchill was rather dismissive of de Wesselow's linguistic skills but the students soon became aware of the steel beneath the surface of their commanding officer. The Major and his staff of hand-picked Sergeants and Lance Corporals were continually assessing the inner man as well as his outward proficiency at the allotted tasks. The school day was a long one, beginning with a wake-up call at 6 a.m. and then, to the sound of the dawn chorus, an hour's strenuous PT on the lawn in front of the house. After a quick shower they were served a hearty breakfast before settling down to a succession of classes, some inside the Manor or in a disused outbuilding, some outside in the kitchen garden or in secret places behind the rhodo-dendron bushes and the compost.

There were moments when it all felt like a child's game of pirates or hide and seek but then, as they sat down on the lawn in front of the copper beeches, a Sergeant Major would unveil every known

variety of revolver and light and automatic weapon then in existence. They learned to fire a Thompson sub-machine gun, ripping
volleys into an old tree, a Sten gun (which, John was warned, was
notoriously unreliable), a Browning, a Colt 45, a Schmeisser, two
different types of Luger, a French light machine gun and a 28-calibre
Belgian pistol. The Warrant Officer instructors took each of the guns
apart and put them back together again and then the students were
told to follow suit.

They were given simple lessons in wireless coding and operating
and taught how to put a detonator into a primer and how to put
the primer into a gun-cotton explosive or 'six inch brick'. The last
class before lunch was French platoon and arms drill, conducted by
a French officer and designed to ensure that any agent whose cover
story involved service in the French army could prove it if required.

In the afternoons they would attend lectures on the precise
amount of plastic explosive required to destroy a train or bridge.
They would then go back outside for a practical introduction to the
almond-scented paste. Moulding it like plasticine, they learned the
difference between time fuses, instantaneous fuses, the pull switch
and the press switch. They also discovered that if you handled the
plastic long enough in a confined space it gave you a headache.

Sometimes they would go on a cross-country run, Major de
Wesselow joining in. When one recruit, the gay musical comedy
actor Dennis Rake, declared that at the age of 39 he was too old to
go running, de Wesselow accompanied him on a long walk instead.[9]

Unarmed combat lessons began with all-in wrestling with the
PT instructor who casually threw the students around the lawn as if

9   Rake was initially suspected of being a drug addict due to his reliance on sleeping
     pills but he managed to kick the habit while he was at Wanborough Manor. He went
     to France twice, displaying great courage, and was subsequently awarded the MC.

he was tossing away an empty cigarette packet. Afterwards they all went for a swim in the timber merchant's pool.

There was afternoon tea at 5 p.m. and drinks before dinner at 7.30.

John Goldsmith enjoyed every minute of it. As a racehorse trainer he was used to early morning starts and plenty of fresh air and exercise and the physical challenge didn't bother him. As a bon viveur he also appreciated the creature comforts which were a world away from the RAC barracks at Warminster. De Wesselow was right: the food was excellent and the breakfasts, lunches and dinners, prepared by a Yugoslav chef who had been recruited from the Major's favourite restaurant in Soho, included fresh milk, eggs, butter and poultry from the home farm as well as other rationed items not freely available to the general populace. There was none of the tedious minutiae of army life with its by-the-book procedures and social distinctions rigidly adhered to. After dinner the Sergeants and NCOs would join the students in the bar, though not just to be sociable. They also wanted to test their reaction to alcohol. Sometimes one of the Sergeant Majors would have just bought everyone another round when one of his colleagues would announce a night compass march beginning in 15 minutes. One night a couple of students who'd drunk too much beer got lost and took a short cut across the Southern Railway line outside Guildford. One of them stepped on a live rail and it was only thanks to his stout army boot that he wasn't electrocuted.

As the days wore on the tempo increased. There was target practice each morning along with an assault course, and they were taken to a nearby quarry to throw grenades and learn how to handle more powerful explosives. They had to cross the road along the Hog's Back without being seen by their instructors, they had to learn how to approach a guarded house noiselessly and surprise the sentry, and then finally they were each placed in charge of an exercise and given marks depending on how quickly and efficiently they carried it out and how well they managed their fellow students.

At the end of it all de Wesselow compiled his reports in conjunction with his instructors. Of Gilbert Norman, the man with the black moustache, Lance Corporal Revay wrote, 'one of the best of the party. Very good work, above average throughout.' De Wesselow, while acknowledging Norman's physical prowess, was more cautious. 'Inexhaustible and a very fair athlete,' he said, 'but fond of his own voice and talks too much . . . popular with the others and probably regarded by people of his own age as good company.' De Wesselow also noted that Norman walked in 'a rather slouching Latin manner'.

As for the jockey Jimmy Amps, the Lance Corporal had reservations. 'I consider this man quite satisfactory,' he wrote. 'He has a sense of humour and gets on well with everyone. But his uncultured mind does not appreciate the finer points of security. He also talks quite a lot about his private affairs and his family abroad.' That was a characteristic that John Goldsmith had noticed too. Amps had left his French wife and mother-in-law behind in occupied Paris and was understandably worried about their safety. De Wesselow agreed with Lance Corporal Revay that Amps 'lacks personality' but felt he was 'full of guts and bonhomie and is just the man to pass in a crowd and get away with it. Not a brain worker but find the right job and he would do his best. An imperturbable beast.'

John Young, Arthur Staggs and Rowland Dowlen were each considered 'promising' by the instructors, and they were all impressed with John Goldsmith's self-reliant and security-conscious way of going about things. He could assess a task practically and sensibly and accomplish it with cunning if required – a throwback to those days in the Neuilly stable yard with his father and a reflection of the guile that was an integral part of a racing and betting man's life. Lance Corporal Revay wrote, 'Is very steady in all his ways. Takes time to learn something new but thinks before speaking and is one of the most security minded of the party and very keen in all his work.' 'Not an intellectual,' remarked de Wesselow approvingly. 'But has all the qualities for leadership.'

John was recommended for the second-stage paramilitary training along with Norman, Amps, Staggs, Dowlen and Young. En route for Scotland the group had to pass, one by one, through Orchard Court. When it was time to leave for Euston Station, John noticed that of the original ten only six of them were left.

4

ARISAIG

The gloomy bars and lounges and dimly lit corridors of Glasgow's Central Hotel were packed with servicemen and women. Some were grabbing an hour or two's sleep on whatever sofa, chair or floor they could find. Others were in the middle of romantic reunions or tearful farewells. The hotel led directly on to the concourse of Glasgow Central Station and dozens of sailors, kitbags in hand, were waiting to go out along the Clyde to join their Royal Navy or Merchant vessel. Ahead of them lay a rendezvous with the Home Fleet in Scapa Flow and then battle stations in the North Atlantic or another perilous Arctic convoy to Murmansk.

The six SOE students in Party 27P had travelled up from London overnight. It was one of those typical wartime train journeys, blacked out, overcrowded and slow. John Goldsmith had brought the racing papers with him so that he could catch up on the news of the 1942 substitute 2,000 and 1,000 Guineas run at Newmarket on 12 and 13 May. The two classics had resulted in a famous double for the King whose two runners, Big Game and Sun Chariot, each of them ridden by Gordon Richards, won easily. The royal horses were now to be aimed at the substitute Oaks and Derby the following month as

racing continued to maintain a severely restricted (and not univer-
sally popular) fixture list.

At least the racing headlines were cheerful, unlike the war news.
The Americans had managed to halt the Japanese naval advance at
the Battle of the Coral Sea but the Philippines had surrendered, Allied
shipping losses had intensified and the Germans had launched new
offensives in North Africa and on the Eastern Front.

In the coming months the F Section recruits were going to learn
a lot more about German military dispositions and the Nazi Party
security apparatus that underpinned them, but first they had to be
toughened up. When their train arrived at Glasgow Central there
was time for a quick cup of tea and a roll and a wash and brush-up
in the hotel's subterranean men's cloakroom. Then they had a brisk
early morning walk to Queen Street Station to board a shorter and
less crowded train, pulled by an ageing locomotive, that was going to
convey them 150 miles up into the north-west Highlands.

The journey took them past the warships in the Clyde estuary,
along the shores of Loch Lomond where bluebells were in flower on
the banks and braes, and on across the treeless wilderness of Rannoch
Moor, passing Ian Fleming's family shooting lodge, Black Mount, on
Loch Tulla. Further north there was snow on the mountaintops as
the single-track line hugged the foot of Ben Nevis and then ran into
and reversed out of Fort William. For the last 40 miles they headed
west towards the sea, entering one of the wildest and most beautiful
landscapes in the British Isles.

The rugged mountains and shores of Lochaber and Moidart were
part of a 440-square-mile 'protected area' that had been set up in
1940 and which eventually covered all the land west of Loch Linnhe
from Morvern in the south, north to Fort William and then by the
line of the Caledonian Canal to Inverness. Anyone living within the

area had to obtain a special permit to enable them to leave it and return, and anyone from outside wishing to enter had to apply to the Military Permit Office for the relevant documents – and they'd better have a damn good reason for enquiring.

This vast tract of land, once a hotbed of Jacobite resistance to the Hanoverian monarchy, had been chosen by SOE as the ideal setting in which to conduct the paramilitary training of scores of potential agents. Not just from Britain either but from France, Poland, Czechoslovakia, Holland, Norway and all the occupied countries. The rough, sparsely populated terrain could scarcely be bettered for clandestine purposes. It had a direct rail link from the south as far as the fishing port at Mallaig. It was guarded by Cameron Highlander NCO detachments and motorcycle patrols at the landward points of access and by water on all the other sides, and west of Inverailort there were at least a dozen large houses that could be requisitioned. The owners were, in most cases, aristocratic families from the south who maintained their Scottish properties for the shooting, fishing and deer stalking and had what the army called 'acceptable accommodation' elsewhere.

It amused the wartime government that two of the requisitioned houses, Inverie Lodge and Glaschoille, were part of the Knoydart Estate which belonged to Lord Brocket, the aforementioned Nazi-loving chairman of the Anglo-German Fellowship Society and birthday guest of the Führer in 1939. His Lordship, an absentee landlord detested by his tenants, had bought his slice of the Highlands in 1935. But Arisaig House, the headquarters of Special Training School 21 and the largest house in the area, was part of an 18,000-acre estate that had belonged to the same family since the mid-19th century.

The greystone Victorian mansion, with Arts and Crafts interiors, is hidden among pine trees down a drive within sight and sound of the roiling Borrodale Burn. Across the field at the bottom of the garden is the shore of Loch nan Uamh where Bonnie Prince Charlie landed in 1745, and where he left from a year later at the end of his disastrous insurrection. Nowadays an extremely comfortable hotel, Arisaig House offered a dozen bedrooms into which two or three beds could easily be fitted, a spacious hall, a dining room, a drawing room, a library, a billiard room and bar, drying rooms – indispensable given all the wet-weather exercise – a beautiful terrace for drinks before dinner and a croquet lawn which became an outdoor classroom for unarmed combat. Seventy years later SOE's footprints are not hard to find, from the bullet holes in the wall of what was then a basement firing range to the bothie where the ammunition was stored and Bonnie Prince Charlie's Cave where bombs and explosives were tested every day.

Arisaig House was where John Goldsmith, Gilbert Norman, Jimmy Amps and the others in Party 27P were bound for. They left the train at Beasdale, a request halt in the woods four miles east of Arisaig village where the railway crossed the A830 by a gated level crossing. It was the ideal spot for troops to be set down with no one else to see them except the solitary station porter who also manned the level crossing.

The Commandant at Arisaig in May 1942 was Lieutenant Colonel James Young, a former Warrant Officer in the Brigade of Guards who had been a tea planter in Ceylon before the war. The students under his command had to cram what ought to have been weeks of vital training into one intense and exhausting month, and to help him knock them into shape 'Jimmy' had a staff of ten officers, ten sergeants and 40 other rank-and-file troops including a nursing orderly, three batmen, cooks for the officers' and sergeants' messes, six drivers and a motorcycle orderly.

Recruits could look forward to spending 44 hours on demolitions, 38 on map reading, 32 on weapons training, 22 on ropes and assault courses, 15 on fieldcraft, 12 on silent killing, 12 on daylight 'schemes' (and a further nine preparing them) and 19 on missions after dark. All the while the instructors were trying to train them to withstand fatigue and find it in themselves to pull out that last extra bit of energy which might make the difference between life and death. As Maurice Buckmaster wrote in his 1952 book *Special Employ*, they 'walked, they ran, they swam, they bicycled – and how useful a bicycle was going to prove in Occupied France – they learned to avoid skylines, to move silently through undergrowth, to use the natural back of rough country and to get unobserved from one point to another'. A month of mountain air, Buckmaster concluded, sent the party back south 'with ravenous appetites and a feeling of physical well-being'.

To some lonely Belgian and Polish recruits, confronted with a month of mist and rain, their bodies continually wet, water rushing down the slabs and spurs of rock and their feet sinking into the squelching mud of a peat bog, Scotland seemed a miserable and benighted place. But Party 27P were lucky in that their month in the Highlands coincided with a spell of almost Mediterranean weather and John Goldsmith loved the long hikes across the mountains with their jagged peaks and innumerable small lochs, home to deer and wild birds and belts of hazel, ash, birch and mountain oak.

Having never been a great swimmer or sailor, John was less enthusiastic about the waterborne exercises. But then he discovered that the *Orca*, a yacht that had been requisitioned by SOE and moored in Loch Morar, belonged to a wealthy racehorse owner he had known before the war. The owner had sailed the yacht up from Lymington in Hampshire bringing along his manservant who acted as a combination butler, valet and first mate. One afternoon

Goldsmith was invited aboard the saloon to catch up on the racing news while downing generous measures of gin poured by the butler.

Jimmy Young and his kilted officers sometimes went out after 9 p.m. to drink in the back room of the Station Hotel in Morar or to a dance in Mallaig. But the recruits were not permitted out at night. They had convivial evenings in their houses and once again the meals were excellent, with local venison, scallops, lobster and salmon, but the days were so exhausting that most students were happy to be in bed by 10 p.m. The intensity at Arisaig was on an altogether different level to the preliminary training schools and there was no sitting around beneath the copper beeches. By the autumn many of the students would be 'in the field' in Vichy or Occupied France and they were already being prepared for the possibility of an escape by foot across the Pyrenees. The ability to walk 20 or 30 miles a day up- and downhill with a Spanish smuggler as guide could be crucial to their survival.

Agents also needed to be able to live off the land, and to assist them the instructors called up not only the best gamekeepers and ghillies in Lochaber but the most notorious poachers too. These hard, wily, weather-beaten characters, amused to be on the same side as the keepers for once, taught the students how to fish, stalk, shoot birds and trap rabbits and hares, and how to skin and gut their food. Competition between recruits was encouraged, a bit like the wagers in John Buchan's novel *John McNab*, and much to the horror of the ghillies, unconventional methods were allowed. One Londoner allegedly threw a small slab of plastic explosive into a salmon pool. The accompanying explosion sent a 24lb fish flying into the air. The stunned salmon was wrestled to the shore, where it expired, and it was later cooked and served up for dinner to an approving Jimmy Young in the mess at Arisaig House.

The poachers and gamekeepers were good company, especially once drink was proffered. But of all the instructors at Special Training School 21 none made a bigger impression on the students than Captain Eric Sykes, known to everyone as 'Bill'. A bespectacled, grey-haired Lancastrian with 'a clergyman's demeanour', Bill Sykes was the SOE expert on demolition, shooting and silent killing. In the 1920s and 1930s he had been an officer in the Royal Shanghai Police gaining a fearsome reputation for his ability to handle the Chinese gambling syndicates and waterfront gangs.

Sykes and his equally formidable sidekick William Fairburn had been recruited by SOE in 1940. The 'Heavenly Twins', as they were nicknamed, patented their own commando knife which was used by agents of all the Allied countries. Light, but with a heavy grip, the blade was about seven inches long and was made to order at the Wilkinson Sword works in Sheffield.

In March 1942 Fairburn was poached by the Americans to work at the fledgling OSS (Office of Strategic Services) school in Canada which was the forerunner of the CIA. From that point on it was exclusively Bill's role to teach SOE pupils how most effectively to send their enemies to heaven or hell by whatever means at their disposal. He started out by telling them to forget about rules. This was war, not sport. They were facing an opponent of unprecedented ruthlessness and their watchword had to be to attack first and kill.

It was said of Bill Sykes that he had been 'the fastest gun in the east', and that he had been able to draw a gun from a shoulder holster, cock it, fire and hit the target in a third of a second. He taught John Goldsmith and his companions the finer points of shooting a .22 and .45 calibre handgun, including how to fire without using the sights. He taught them how to kill with a knife and a garrotte. He explained the musculature of the human body and its most vulnerable points and how always to fight with your hands open and use your fingers, thumbs and nails. Using an old West Highland Railway locomotive running back and forth between Arisaig and Morar he taught them how to jump from a moving train, rolling down the embankment like a hobo or a bandit. He taught them how to blow up bridges and track. He taught them how to destroy and demolish, how to attack and kill Germans, how to hit and run and, hopefully, to survive.

Everyone revered Bill, none more so than the Czechs. Brave, exuberant and passionate young men, their country had already been invaded by the Nazis, their homes destroyed and their families murdered. Indifferent to their own chances of surviving the war they just wanted to hit back, and Bill Sykes helped them. Sometimes they were a little over-enthusiastic in training. On one occasion they destroyed half the pier at Swordland Bay after using too much plastic explosive, a bit like Butch Cassidy dynamiting the Union Pacific. On another they enlivened a children's party at Meoble Lodge with a fireworks display featuring detonator fuse wrapped around trees and tracer bullets ricocheting from rock to rock. Jan Kubis and Josef Gabcik, the two Czechs who killed Reichsprotektor and Nazi mass murderer Reinhard Heydrich in Prague in May 1942, had both been trained at Arisaig. The final radio message they sent back to England after they had been parachuted into Czechoslovakia ended 'Give Bill Sykes our best wishes. Tell him we won't miss.'

Many of Bill's pupils died in action or captivity, Gabcik and Kubis included. John Goldsmith, boarding the train back south on the morning of Sunday, 21 June, was determined not to be one of them. All of Party 27P had enjoyed themselves in Scotland. The athletic Gilbert Norman had been determined to walk faster and further than anyone else. Jimmy Amps had struck up a friendship with Arthur Staggs and had stopped worrying about his wife long enough to demonstrate impressive marksmanship with a handgun, and both of them, along with Rowland Dowlen, John Young and John Goldsmith, had loved being out on the hills.

John had excelled under Bill Sykes' tutelage, particularly at silent killing, reflecting that the only thing missing at Arisaig was a real live German to practise on. He and the others would now go on to do the parachute course at Ringway, Manchester, and then to the SOE finishing school at Beaulieu in the New Forest. After that he would go to war. He would carry out the mission he was given, hit and run, and come back alive. That's what he assured Tiny as he wrapped his arms around her in another SOE Kensington hotel room at the beginning of his leave a week later.

5

JEAN DELANNOY

As darkness fell on the evening of Wednesday, 23 September 1942, a small Mediterranean fishing smack, or felucca, slipped out of Gibraltar and headed north-north-east into the open sea. The boat, known as the *Seadog*, was skippered by a bearded Pole, Jan Buchowski, and he had a one-man Polish crew.

There were five passengers on board. Three of them – John Goldsmith, Sidney Jones and Fergus Chalmers-Wright – were virgin SOE agents on their first venture into 'the field'. Chalmers-Wright, who was born in Brussels, had worked at the British Embassy in Bucharest before the war while Sidney Jones had been the Elizabeth Arden representative in Paris. The other two travellers were a chubby Frenchman on some unspecified mission for de Gaulle and a Pole hoping to link up with an escaped armoured warfare specialist in Marseille. Buchowski's orders were to land the quintet on a quiet stretch of beach at La Napoule near Cannes. The 20-ton felucca was 47 feet long with a top speed of 8 knots. It was going to be a slow and extremely uncomfortable voyage but, weather permitting, Buchowski expected to get there in seven days.

As the felucca left port John Goldsmith was on deck, sitting on the hatch cover smoking a cigarette. It was a warm night and the sky was clear and he could see the lights of Tangier away to the south. This wasn't the journey he'd been preparing for. He'd expected to drop into France through a hole in an aeroplane at 600 feet. The parachute course at Ringway had gone satisfactorily and, after a week's training in the gymnasium, Goldsmith, Norman, Young, Staggs, Dowlen and Amps – who had never been up in a plane before – had completed three practice jumps without mishap. The only jolt to their confidence came when they saw the body of a regular paratrooper whose chute had failed to open lying on the ground about 50 yards away from where they'd landed. But when John got to the finishing school at Beaulieu he learned that there was more than one way for an agent to get to France. A parachute drop might have been the safest (in the sense of attracting the least attention) but other means included landing by Lysander single-engine aircraft and travelling by submarine or felucca. The Lysander flight was the more comfortable option but Goldsmith was going to the south of France and the Riviera Run was always made by boat.

The mission that Baker Street had originally had in mind for him was much further north. They wanted someone with Arisaig training to target the railway lines between Amiens and Boulogne and the CIE Mécanique d'Albert works which maintained locomotives and track for the SNCF du Nord. But the intelligence officers at Beaulieu decided that as Goldsmith hadn't been in France since 1938 it would be a good idea for him to spend a month re-acclimatising himself in the south first. The Riviera coast was in the Vichy Zone and, as the Germans were not yet present there in the same numbers as up in Paris or the Pas de Calais, it would be an easier place for John to grasp the tenor of French wartime life.

43

But it wasn't going to be a holiday. SOE had a task for Goldsmith in the south too. They wanted to know more about a Resistance network known as Carte which was named after the code name of its founder, André Girard, a painter and patriot from Antibes. Word had got back that Girard, by all accounts a charming and persuasive character who had designed publicity posters in Paris before the war, had excellent contacts among the French Army of the Armistice that had surrendered in June 1940. It was said that proud, patriotic elements of the defeated force were prepared to rise up and that a Secret Army some 300,000 strong might eventually return to arms. Nicholas Boddington, the SOE F Section second-in-command, had met Girard on the Riviera in July and returned to London with glowing reports. But not everyone was convinced and it was hoped that John Goldsmith might be able to find out how credible Girard's plans for sabotage and guerrilla warfare really were and establish what SOE could do to assist him.

Then there was the question of General Henri Giraud, whose surname was confusingly similar to Girard's. But unlike the mercurial Resistance leader Giraud was a respected and very senior French officer who had just escaped from a German prison. The General – who had also escaped from the Germans in World War One – had been held in Königstein Castle, a Colditz-style eyrie atop a rock face near Dresden. In April 1942 he'd executed a daring getaway, shinning down the cliff on a homemade rope. After making his way to Switzerland he was now believed to be in hiding in the Vichy Zone, and Allied commanders wanted to organise his exfiltration to Algiers. They saw him as an alternative figurehead to the increasingly obstreperous de Gaulle and hoped to persuade him to take command of the French forces in North Africa currently under Vichy control. But in the treacherous climate of French Resistance politics they felt it was also important to make contact with Giraud's staff officers living in France as their assistance might be instrumental in getting the Secret Army on the move.

If John Goldsmith was going to communicate with these French generals as well as Carte he needed an identity that would enable him to travel around freely by train. The Intelligence Bureau at Beaulieu decided that his French cover should be that of a black marketeer and 'dealer' who would do business with both the occupiers and the occupied. SOE didn't normally favour a guise that was too conspicuous but 'spiv' seemed the ideal role for a racing man. Goldsmith chose the name Jean Delannoy which was also the name of a French actor and director of the period. To add authenticity John was to use his own history for the first 23 years of the fictitious Delannoy's life. But the SOE forgers who made his passport put his date of birth back a few years as there was a risk that, if picked up, young men of military age could be shipped east as forced labour.[10]

A Corsican by the name of Toto Otoviani, who lived in Nice, was to be John's point of contact for black market items like cigarettes and stockings, and to help him get into character before leaving England he was taken to a Savile Row tailor who had been provided with cloth and patterns in vogue in France. The tailor made John a splendidly sharp suit that would've been the envy of any self-respecting wide boy and he was equipped with shirts, ties and socks to match. Much to Goldsmith's amusement, and his wife's embarrassment, he

---

10 On 4 September 1942 Pierre Laval's Vichy government had introduced the Service Travail Obligatoire which 'encouraged' young, able-bodied Frenchmen to work in Germany in return for the release of French prisoners of war. The so-called *relève* was basically just a mechanism to allow the Germans to compensate for their loss of manpower as more and more German males were called up and sent to the Russian Front. By February 1943 the bitterly resented STO would become compulsory throughout France, unintentionally acting as a recruiting tool for the Resistance.

was told to wear his new costume whenever he went out so that it would be suitably worn in before he left for France.

The wardrobe fittings offered a light-hearted break from the serious background briefings that comprised a large part of John's time at Beaulieu. By the summer of 1942 the official ration in France had fallen from 2,400 calories a day to 1,200 and, in the words of the author Gilles Perrault who lived in Paris during the Occupation, 'food haunted the imagination from morning until night'. Spivs and racketeers were very popular with French peasant farmers who were selling a third of their butter, eggs and pork, a quarter of their potatoes and half their chickens to the black market, thus ensuring that the expensive restaurants patronised by German officers and their friends could continue to offer a good service. But the thousands of ordinary French men and women without money were suffering daily depredations.

France was being plundered of its wealth, its food and its raw materials, and the political warfare tutors at Beaulieu continually impressed upon their students that, before the Nazis could be defeated, the population had to see the Vichy authorities as every bit as odious and responsible for their suffering as the Germans. Agents were taught about the Vichy government's fawning veneration of Marshal Pétain, of whom it was said 'he can neither be wrong nor can he wrong us'. The staunchly Catholic Pétain had told the people that France had been corrupted by its pre-war 'love of pleasure and degenerate books' but that by going back to the traditional verities of marriage, family, church and squire, the nation would rise up once again. SOE seized on these platitudes and urged their pupils to shatter them as resoundingly as they might blow up a bridge or train.

At Beaulieu they also briefed Goldsmith on the German counter-espionage services and secret police. By the time they'd finished, the easy-going, pleasure-loving trainer and gambler who'd admitted to little prior interest in politics was shocked by his ignorance. It was explained to him that the traditional German intelligence-gathering service was the Abwehr, or Military Intelligence, which was predominantly run by the old officer class, many of whom were veterans of World War One. Following the conquest of France in 1940 the Abwehr had set up base in the Hôtel Lutetia on the boulevard Raspail in Paris, and their agents had become formidable enemies of the Resistance.[11]

But despite these successes Adolf Hitler and the Nazi hierarchy didn't trust the Abwehr and its patrician leanings. Even before the war broke out, real power had switched to the SS and the Nazi Party's own intelligence service, the Sicherheitsdienst or SD. Along with the Nazi state security police, the Geheime Staatspolizei or Gestapo, the SD came under the control of the Minister of the Interior, Reichsführer SS Heinrich Himmler, and up until his assassination in Prague in May 1942 had been run by his equally murderous deputy, Reinhard Heydrich.

The SD headquarters in Paris were in three large houses on the avenue Foch, one of the richest areas of the city. The head of counter-espionage was SS Sturmbannführer Hans Josef Kieffer, a former plain-clothes policeman from Karlsruhe who'd graduated from the Gestapo offices on Prinz-Albrecht-Strasse in Berlin. Students were warned of the efficiency of the SD wireless detection teams led by a bespectacled school inspector who, like Josef Goebbels, styled himself 'Doctor' Josef Goetz. Brevity was essential as a long

---

11 The most successful Abwehr operative in France was, ironically, not an officer but a Sergeant, Hugo Bleicher. Impersonating a Frenchman called 'Colonel Henri' he lured many gullible figures to their doom.

transmission in a large town could result in a direction-finding van arriving within 30 minutes.

There were also warnings about the gangsters and black marketeers who were leading members of the French Gestapo, or Carlingue. The worst of them was Henri Lafont, a former petty crook who, in tandem with an ex-police inspector, Pierre Bonny, ran a gang of torturers and extortionists from a house in the rue Lauriston in the 16th arrondissement in Paris. It was characteristic of the Nazis to employ local racketeers, thugs and opportunists to work on their behalf, though Lafont always claimed that he backed the Germans rather than the Resistance for no better reason than he might back the favourite in a two-horse race. A contradictory character who raised orchids and drove around Paris in a white open-top Bentley, Lafont invited rich collaborators to champagne soirées in his top-floor apartment even as his henchmen were going to work with a blowtorch and pliers in the cellars down below.[12]

One of the Gestapo's favourite tortures was the *baignoire*. Victims were immersed head first in a bath full of ice-cold water and held down until they nearly drowned. Captured British agents could also expect beatings, cigarette burns, eye gouging, having their finger nails ripped out and being suspended in agony by their fingers and toes.

The catalogue of cruelty made for grim listening and was a chastening reminder to John Goldsmith and his colleagues of the risks they had agreed to run. Over and over again the instructors impressed on them that the best way to avoid falling into the enemy's hands was to be relentlessly conscious of their own and their fellow agents' security. Goldsmith, who was more security-conscious than most, absorbed all

12 The SD officially described Lafont's activities as 'security' and he enjoyed their protection right up until the liberation of Paris in 1944.

the lessons about intermediaries, passwords and the importance of changing safe houses and only using café call box telephones.

One of John's final training assignments was a dummy mission which involved him travelling up to Newcastle-upon-Tyne where he had to hand over a letter in a café without being seen by the Special Branch officers who were there to monitor his every move. He proved adept at spotting and losing a tail and earned high marks back at Beaulieu for his self-reliance and cunning. 'To Goldsmith,' they said, 'it's just like laying out a runner for a big race.' Like Black Hawk at Aintree, they might have added, except that Black Hawk failed to complete the course.

On 8 September John was officially commissioned as a Second Lieutenant in the Army List. A fortnight later, by which time he was en route for France, he was promoted to the rank of full Lieutenant. SOE awarded officer status to all their agents leaving for the field. It provided an official stipend for the men's wives and families that continued to be paid, by bank draft, while they were away. Baker Street also retained the faint hope that if they were caught by the Gestapo and their identity revealed, being a British officer might deter the Germans from executing them as spies.

John had been earmarked to be a circuit leader while Arthur Staggs, the most convincingly French character in the group in John's opinion, was to be a courier near Paris.[13] Commissions were also given to Gilbert Norman, Jimmy Amps, Rowland Dowlen and John Young, who were all going on for further training as wireless transmitter operators at a school near Thame. A WT operator would need to be particularly self-reliant and able to cope with long periods of solitude

---

13 A circuit was a group of agents in a given area and included a leader, a courier, a wireless transmitter operator and related French contacts.

with no contacts and nothing else to do. John pictured the studious Dowlen in the role but wondered if it was the ideal job for an athletic, restless character like Norman. He was equally doubtful about Amps who was a cheery soul but still homesick and worried about his wife. But he was positively relieved that John Young was to have a job where his Geordie accent would be least likely to give him away.

Goldsmith and Young had become good friends in the nearly five months that had passed since they all set out for Wanborough Manor and John had done his best to help Young improve his French. Despite their very different worlds and backgrounds they were both grounded, realistic characters not taken in by false charm. Young and his wife joined John and Tiny for part of the men's leave in London and the quartet went racing together at Newmarket on 12 September. It was a memorable day for Young, who was a racing novice, and it was an even better one for King George VI whose filly, Sun Chariot, added the substitute St Leger to her earlier victories in the 1,000 Guineas and the Oaks. The King had won four of the season's five classic races which would have been a momentous record at the best of times let alone in the middle of a war.

On the morning of his departure, Saturday, 19 September, the firm sent a car round to the hotel to drive John to Waterloo. He was going to take a train down to Portsmouth and then join a motley collection of diplomats, couriers and servicemen for the flight to Gibraltar. He had already kissed his wife goodbye upstairs. But when he got to the station he found she had followed him on the pretext of handing him some comforts for the journey she thought he had forgotten. John had wanted an austere farewell but that wasn't Annette's style. She stood on the platform and waved and waved until his train was out of sight.

6

THE *SEADOG*

Agent Valentin, to use his new code name, was no sailor. He had even managed to feel seasick watching *In Which We Serve* with Tiny at the London Pavilion. That first night on the felucca he watched the hulls of the British destroyers receding into the darkness beneath the Rock of Gibraltar and wondered how he was going to manage. But the following day the sea remained calm and the temperature mild, and John briefly convinced himself he was in for a pleasant cruise.

As long as the weather stayed fine the passengers stayed on deck, but if another ship came close, Buchowski ordered them all below. The captain had to steer clear of the Spanish coastline as Franco's coastguards monitored foreign shipping movements and reported them to the Germans. But if the *Seadog* was to maintain its guise as an ordinary fishing boat it couldn't afford to stray too far from the recognised fishing grounds either. Buchowski, who was an expert mariner, travelled by night wherever possible, sometimes laying up during the day, and the felucca was painted with French and Spanish camouflage in case a reconnaissance plane spotted it from the sky.

As John Goldsmith now discovered, living conditions on the boat were cramped and unpleasant. The tiny galley had some coffee and stale bread but no fresh fruit or vegetables, and food was mostly eaten out of tins which were thrown overboard when they were empty. Sanitary arrangements were primitive and basically involved squatting over the gunwale and letting the Mediterranean waves slap against their bare backsides. The lavatory paper soon ran out and, as the wind picked up, their new clothes became soaked with spray which, as Sidney Jones pointed out, would be 'a dead giveaway' if any Vichy or German policeman saw them.

Buchowski, who swore constantly, alternated between moments of wild enthusiasm and suicidal gloom. The *Seadog* was meant to arrive off La Napoule on the evening of 30 September but three days out of Gibraltar they ran into a force ten gale. The tempest left the little fishing smack pitching and rolling in the swell and at one point they were all convinced they were going to die. Everyone was seasick, none more violently than Goldsmith, and for the next 36 hours the stench of vomit permeated the boat and their saturated clothing.

The felucca's engine was damaged by the storm and the bilge-pump stopped working. Buchowski repaired them both but the boat's speed was cut to three and a half knots and as a result they weren't in place off Cap-de-l'Esquillon until the night of 1 October. In the event of delay the reception committee organised by Carte was meant to return to the beach three nights running. But when Buchowski flashed his Aldiss lamp signals at the shore there was no response. Maybe the committee had been arrested or given up? Either way it meant spending another gruesome 24 hours at sea on the stinking *Seadog*.

When the same set of signals failed to attract a response again the following night it was decided that someone should go ashore and investigate. John Goldsmith, who said the smell on the felucca was the most unpleasant he'd ever experienced in his entire life, volunteered.

Around 11 p.m. he lowered himself into the boat's bobbing rubber dinghy. The crewman gave him a shove, John pushed off against the boat's side with the paddle, and he was away. Twenty or thirty yards on from the *Seadog* the shore still looked a long way off, the sky vast, and Goldsmith felt vulnerable and alone. But at least the sea was calm.

Gritting his teeth, John began paddling in the best Arisaig manner and after about half an hour he was close enough to land to see dunes and some pine trees – and, yes, emerging from behind the pines were four or five figures. This is it, he thought. Either they're from Carte or they're Germans and I'm a dead man.

As the dinghy glided into the shore he put down the paddle, stood up and stepped over the side. But in that first moment of adrenalin-charged excitement he'd forgotten the part of the briefing in Gibraltar where they'd warned him that the beaches on this part of the coast shelved steeply, and instead of shallows he suddenly found himself in more than six feet of water closing over his head. Stumbling, gasping and spluttering, he got to his feet and swore in French.

Two of the advancing men stretched out an arm to help him. 'We were expecting five. Which one are you?'

'I'm Valentin,' John replied. 'And I'm bloody wet.'

Dry clothes would have to wait. The first priority was to get the felucca inshore and land the other agents. The correct signals were flashed now from the beach. The fishing boat flashed back and within 15 minutes the little craft came puttering into view. Buchowski ran out the gang plank, down which came the Frenchman, the Pole and Fergus Chalmers-Wright and Sidney Jones carrying their own and Goldsmith's suitcases. Some other anonymous SOE agent making the home run to Gibraltar was hustled aboard and within minutes the felucca was heading back out to sea.

The reception committee divided up the new arrivals: Chalmers-Wright, the Frenchman and the Pole went in one direction and Goldsmith, Jones and their guide went in another.[14] The moon was shining, there was the clean smell of pine resin in the air and ahead of them lay an eight-mile walk to a safe house outside Cannes.

14 Chalmers-Wright made his way to Grenoble and later ended up in prison in Spain before working with Polish resistance groups in northern France. His and John Goldsmith's paths never crossed again but he survived the war and was one of the former agents who recorded an interview for the archives in the Imperial War Museum.

7

THE RIVIERA FRONT

John Goldsmith's first month on the Riviera was characterised by long periods of idleness, muddle and confusion punctuated by short bursts of excitement. He didn't realise it at the time but his experience was typical of the frustrations and insecurities felt by many agents when they first went into the field.

The Cannes safe house was called the Villa Caracasa, an attractive three-storey residence with terracotta-coloured walls and green shutters. It was surrounded by pine trees and mimosa and a gravel path in the garden led down a rocky slope to the beach. The house belonged to André Bartoli, the head of a local insurance firm and one of the Resistance leader André Girard's main lieutenants. Bartoli, who had a wife and three children, did an excellent impression of a dull, quietly bourgeois husband and father but was, in fact, a fearless patriot with a chameleon-like ability to escape detection.

Goldsmith and Jones reached the outskirts of Cannes around 2 a.m. but their guide made them hide out for another few hours as he didn't want them to arrive at the villa until after the curfew had ended. In Bartoli's kitchen, Goldsmith at last peeled off his sopping wet clothes and was temporarily kitted out in his host's best Charvet dressing gown. The new arrivals were not going to stay at the Villa Caracasa. Bartoli explained that regular comings and goings at his house would have been difficult to conceal. So after a few hours' sleep and a lunch of fish soup and fruit the two Englishmen were escorted into the centre of Cannes.

The local Carte HQ was in a beauty parlour, and while John's suit was taken away to be properly cleaned he and Sidney Jones went upstairs to be introduced to some other members of the circuit.

John was told he was to be accommodated in the home of Paulo Leonetti, a Corsican and former Mayor of Antibes who lived in Juan-les-Pins. The swarthy Leonetti, as extrovert as André Bartoli was restrained, was the town's hairdresser which was perfect cover for a *résistante* as it meant that people could come and go and talk to him in his shop without suspicion. One of his best customers was the madame of the local brothel who gave him a large jar of her home-made spicy tomato sauce every time he attended to the girls' hair. She would also pass on information about any Vichy officials using their services.

Leonetti had a wife and children, just like Bartoli, and all of their lives were at risk for harbouring British agents. But their welcome, and willingness to share whatever they had with their *en pension* guest, was as wholehearted as their detestation of the Nazis and their French sympathisers.

The Germans had officially left the Mediterranean under the control of the puppet Vichy government. But Goldsmith and Jones were warned that the Riviera was a tense, treacherous place full of spies, informants and shady characters trying to sit out the war. The tourists had gone and the restaurants were half empty but the casinos had reopened in 1941 and the salons of the grand hotels were home to a floating population of wealthy refugees from Paris and the north and swindlers and con artists trying to steal their money. Spotting foreign agents and selling them to the authorities was a profitable line. If the newcomers were going to survive in this milieu they would have to try to lose all trace of their British origins and blend seamlessly into the background.

To assist with his acclimatisation it was decided that John's spiv's suit should be packed away until needed. In its place he was given less conspicuous and more Mediterranean-looking clothing including a short-sleeved shirt and pullover, a pair of Paulo Leonetti junior's trousers worn rolled up to the knee, fisherman's rope-soled shoes and a beret. He was also found a bicycle, a natty aluminium racer with drop handlebars which he had to pay for with some of the French bankroll he'd been given at Orchard Court. His new comrades helped him rub some authentic Mediterranean grime into the notes before he handed them over.

For the first half of October John Goldsmith worked on his tan. Curious locals had been told that he was a young Parisian who had come south to avoid being rounded up for forced labour in the Occupied Zone. But Paulo Leonetti warned him that his white skin was conspicuous at the end of a long French summer. So every day for a fortnight John left the Leonetti house early and cycled off to a quiet stretch of beach where he could lie around without his shirt on. The coastline in 1942 was very different to the modern Côte d'Azur with its high-rise apartment buildings and developments and there were still numerous unspoiled coves and bays where Vichy had yet to build defences. The setting was beautiful – like the fictitious Hôtel des Étrangers in Scott Fitzgerald's *Tender is the Night*. But in the last year most of the beach bars had closed, their umbrellas, tables and chairs packed away, and despite the sunshine and the warm sea there was a melancholy end-of-season atmosphere that John found oppressive.

To help familiarise himself he dutifully bought the newspapers every morning. Not just the pro-Vichy rags like *Le Petit Marseillais* and *Le Nouvelliste* but the sporting and racing papers too. Racing had been suspended in France at the outbreak of the war but had resumed in the Paris region and at some provincial tracks in late 1940. The Nazis had helped themselves to some of the best French bloodstock including Baron Edouard de Rothschild's entire 118-horse string, which was stolen by Joachim von Ribbentrop, Hitler's foreign minister and former ambassador to London. The ex-champagne salesman was one of many Germans who enjoyed a day at the races, and meetings at Longchamp, Auteuil and Le Tremblay were enthusiastically attended by Wehrmacht officers and their mistresses.

Leading Jewish racehorse owners like Rothschild and Pierre Wertheimer were conspicuous by their absence but other French proprietors were only too happy to take part. While John Goldsmith was languishing on a beach in Juan-les-Pins, Marcel Boussac won the 1942 Prix de l'Arc de Triomphe with Djebel, the same colt that had triumphed as a two-year-old at Newmarket three years earlier.[15]

John would have loved to go racing at Marseille or Cagnes-sur-Mer but it was too dangerous. Some of the old Maisons crowd still came south for the winter, some to avoid conscription or forced labour, others because they worked for owners who were on good terms with the occupiers and were allowed to move their horses around the country at will. Not all the punters were backing the Resistance and there was a risk that John might be recognised and betrayed by someone who remembered him from the old carefree days in Paris in the 1920s and 1930s.

---

15 Boussac hitched a lift to London with the RAF in the summer of 1940 and his best stallion, Pharis, was confiscated by the Germans. But his French trainers continued to run his horses under German patronage right up to 1944.

Goldsmith didn't have a wireless transmitter. Baker Street were hopeful that his black marketeer guise would enable him to travel around freely for weeks if not months and they didn't want to compromise his status by obliging him to send his own messages. His reports to and from London were transcribed by anonymous members of Carte and from time to time he received a coded message on the BBC World Service – a line of poetry or prose alluding to an arms drop or landing – that would have been unintelligible to the Germans. There were also nocturnal briefings at André Bartoli's house. On one of these occasions John met Peter Churchill, one of the first Wanborough Manor graduates, who was already a near legendary figure in SOE. When Churchill came up the beach into Bartoli's garden he was wearing spectacles and carrying a rolled-up umbrella and Goldsmith thought he looked more like Groucho Marx than Richard Hannay.

On Saturday, 24 October, John finally encountered the artist and circuit leader André Girard who asked him a lot of questions about his background and military training. Girard, who seemed every bit as self-assured as John had been led to expect, said he'd have to think about what role the Englishman could perform and what assistance SOE could offer. In the meantime he put him in touch with yet another agent who was giving explosives and arms classes further along the coast. John sat in on the classes for a week and then started giving lessons of his own in safe houses he'd found in Juan-les-Pins and Nice. It was a momentous feeling as he unpacked his precious Orchard Court suitcase, dismantled the three Sten guns he'd brought from England and cycled with them to a blacked-out apartment where a combination of local shopkeepers, mechanics and fishermen wanted to know how to kill Germans. So impressed were Carte by John's knowledge that he was asked to write a training manual in French drawing together the lessons he'd learned at Arisaig.

Throughout this period Goldsmith and Sidney Jones, who was based further west, had avoided direct contact. Jones, who was born in Paris like John and also spoke fluent French, had been on a couple of abortive trips to Marseille where he was supposed to meet up with ex-soldiers sympathetic to Carte's plans. But the journeys had been frustrating ones involving a lot of hanging around trying to look inconspicuous, and frustration at the lack of action was almost as unnerving as the constant fear of being found out. It wasn't the same for every new agent. George Starr, a former mining engineer who'd passed through Wanborough Manor in the group after John, had also gone to the south of France by felucca. But he was routed to Gascony in the south-west and in no time was organising a network of local guerrillas and stockpiling explosives and guns. But on the Côte d'Azur André Girard kept insisting they had to wait and that no missions could be undertaken against the enemy until some decisive but unspecified moment when the rising would begin.

Eventually the boredom of clandestine life coupled with the monotony of ration-book meals got the better of Goldsmith and Jones. On the first Sunday in November they rode their bikes to a quiet restaurant overlooking the sea near Cannes. The Bartoli family joined them there, secure in the knowledge that the owner was a fellow member of Carte, and for a couple of hours they all enjoyed the kind of civilised Sunday lunch that had been commonplace before the war.

There was a dreamy, unreal atmosphere to the day heightened by the sunlight and the hypnotic sound of the sea. John was beginning to feel under-employed on the Riviera and, as he explained to the others, he was impatient to go north. But at the end of the meal

Bartoli told him that his original mission to sabotage the railway lines between Amiens and Boulogne was off. André Girard wanted him to go to Corsica instead and start a circuit up there. The French troops on the island had never surrendered their arms and the terrain was not dissimilar to the Scottish Highlands. Baker Street were enthusiastic about the idea and John was excited too and started making plans. But then, the following week, everything changed.

On 5 November General Henri Giraud was smuggled aboard a submarine near Toulon and taken to Gibraltar. The timing was highly significant. On 8 November Operation Torch, the Anglo-American landings in north-west Africa, were due to take place and the Americans wanted Giraud to take command of the Vichy troops in Morocco and Algeria and bring them over to the Allied side. The American commander General Dwight D. Eisenhower was planning to link up with the British who were fighting the Germans further east, and beyond that he was already thinking about the invasion of Italy the following year. He didn't want to have to fight the Vichy French as well if he could possibly avoid it. But Giraud – proving he could be every bit as haughty as de Gaulle – objected to the idea of British troops landing on French colonial soil and said he would agree to participate in Torch only if he was appointed commander-in-chief. It had to be explained to him that the role was already taken, so Giraud loftily declared that he would remain in Gibraltar as a mere 'spectator' of events.

Giraud's position was of keen interest to SOE F Section as well. They remained convinced he was their best bet against de Gaulle and the man to lead a military uprising in France. Now that he was in Gibraltar they felt it was more important than ever to make contact with his staff officers who had stayed behind. They would be the men who would have to liaise between the General and French units on the ground and assure the latter of SOE backing for whatever they wanted to achieve.

Giraud's escape from Königstein Castle had been organised by four senior officers led by a former cavalryman turned air force general, René Chambe. The 52-year-old, who had flown fighter planes in World War One, was now reduced to half pay and living with his elderly mother in Lyon. Baker Street wanted someone to spirit him across the Pyrenees to Gibraltar to receive written orders from Giraud which he could take back to France and use to enlist the backing of fellow officers who wanted to fight. But swayed by reports from Peter Churchill they felt the General's person couldn't safely be entrusted to Carte and André Girard. Instead the mission should be given to John Goldsmith.

While he was waiting to move on, Goldsmith had helped Bartoli with the evacuation of three Englishmen – a Colonel and two civilians – whom John assumed were working for MI6. For several nights running the trio were shunted around from safe house to safe house, supposedly waiting for a boat that never came. Finally they had to be provided with forged papers to enable them to travel by train to Lisbon via Spain, which was highly dangerous. After they'd gone, Bartoli confessed to Goldsmith that he had reservations about André Girard, who had been in charge of the escape but had bungled it, and that, more importantly, Peter Churchill had them too.

The relationship between Girard and his staff officer, Henri Frager, had become increasingly strained. Frager, an architect from Nice who'd been recruited in 1941, wanted action but Girard continued to urge delay. Goldsmith had sympathy for both men. There was always a problem for Resistance leaders contemplating acts of terrorism. Suddenly blowing up a train or a police station might just alert the enemy to the presence of a Resistance network in their midst and short-term gains could quickly be cancelled out by German retaliation at the expense of local civilians. Girard claimed to be planning for the day when there would be a mass uprising that would drive the Germans out of France altogether but Churchill agreed with Frager that although Girard talked a good game there was little evidence to back up his extravagant claims. As Bartoli told Goldsmith, Churchill was also worried about Carte's security – and with good reason.

André Marsac was one of Girard's couriers and along with Henri Frager he had been on the beach at La Napoule as part of John Goldsmith's reception committee. When the felucca didn't arrive on 30 September it had been Marsac's job to make sure the committee were in place again the following night. But due to his chaotic timing they didn't get to the beach until three hours after Buchowski had given up signalling and headed back out to sea. It was more due to luck than good management that anyone had been there to meet Goldsmith and the others the next night.

There had been another instance of Marsac being in charge of a pick-up by plane but arriving too late to reconnoitre the site. He ended up in one field with the departing agents in another and the incoming Lysander pilot, not seeing a landing signal, nearly flew away without them.

But the courier's biggest and most costly error was to write down the names of over 200 Carte members and contacts alongside their addresses and telephone numbers. Instead of memorising the list and destroying it he took it with him in his briefcase on a train journey from Marseille to Paris. Somewhere on the long ride north Marsac fell asleep, and when he woke up the briefcase was gone. He could not, or would not, admit for several days that it was lost and told Girard later that it must have been stolen. What he didn't know was that the thief was a crafty Abwehr agent who had been tailing him for days and who passed the list on to his superiors in the Hôtel Lutetia in Paris. Declining to share the information with the SD, the Abwehr spent the next month going through the list and it wasn't until the following year that the Germans moved in.

Fortunately for John Goldsmith his name was not on the list, and he didn't hear about Marsac's blunder until later. But as he prepared to travel to Lyon to meet General Chambe he was aware that, other than André Bartoli and Paulo Leonetti, his new Resistance comrades could no longer be fully trusted.

Before setting out John discarded his Mediterranean beret and pullover for his wide boy suit, now cleaned and pressed, and a pair of smartly polished low-cut shoes. The journey was to give him his first real sight of the enemy and he had to be in character. He took a local train to Marseille and then at the Gare St Charles he bought a first-class ticket to Lyon. The Paris-bound service, pulled by a hissing black Pacific class steam locomotive, was packed but he was Jean Delannoy who had money and nothing to hide and he wasn't going to stand all the way or skulk around at the end of the corridor by the lavabos.

Finding a first-class compartment with two German officers inside, John went in and sat down. Comporting his face, just like the old days when selling horses with his father in Neuilly, he wished the Germans a polite good morning in French. They nodded back, taking in his flash suit and tie. Goldsmith lit a cigarette, offering one to his fellow travellers, then settled down to read the racing paper which had a story about the Grand Prix de Marseille which was taking place at Borely racetrack the next day. Porphyros, owned by the Vicomte de Chambure and ridden by the Australian Rae Johnstone, was the favourite. John had known Johnstone in Paris before the war. He had known plenty of the other jockeys who would be riding at Borely too. Jacko Doyasbere. Roger Poincelet. Paul 'Popol' Blanc.

But as the locomotive rumbled north through Arles and Avignon, John wasn't really concentrating on racing. He was thinking about the German army. There were lots of soldiers on the train and there had been lots at Marseille station too, not just officers but ordinary ranks, and Goldsmith would see many more when he got to Lyon. He reckoned that, the officers aside, they were either in their late teens or much older and many of them looked down at heel with patches on their elbows and the seats of their uniform trousers. These weren't the bronzed muscular fighting machines he'd been led to expect, and then he realised why. The Aryans were all fighting with Rommel in North Africa or dying on the Eastern Front.

8

GETTING TO KNOW THE GENERAL

Goldsmith had memorised René Chambe's address and when he got out at Lyon-Perrache he walked to Ainay, a predominantly Catholic quarter in the city's 2nd arrondissement, looking straight ahead and walking neither too fast nor too slow so as not to alert suspicious locals following his progress.

The General had been tipped off about his impending visit but when he opened the door of his first-floor apartment and saw Jean Delannoy – and saw Jean Delannoy's tailoring – Goldsmith could feel the temperature drop. Chambe was not old but he had the clipped moustache, grey hair and stiff manner of a French officer of a much earlier era.

Drawing on his best and most formal French, John presented his own and General Giraud's compliments and informed Chambe that his old commanding officer had expressed a wish for General Chambe to join him as soon as possible in Gibraltar. They had great work to do together and John's employers, the British government, had instructed him to do everything in his power to help the General escape from France so that the friends could be reunited. The General, visibly heartened to hear Giraud's name, thawed slightly. John was offered a seat and was even introduced to Chambe's mother who stood behind her son's chair, monitoring proceedings.

'How exactly did the British intend to effect his escape?' asked Chambe. John explained that he was in touch with Captain Delmas, a Deuxième Bureau officer in Toulouse who, despite his nominal affiliation to Vichy, was sympathetic to the Allies and who could organise escapes across the western Pyrenees.[16] They would have to walk across the mountains with a Basque guide who would then rendezvous with representatives of the British Consulate in Pamplona.

Chambe laughed. Another helpful gentleman, a French gentleman, had already been to see him about an escape. To Goldsmith's horror it turned out to be André Marsac, who had been contacted on behalf of Carte by Jay Howard Benton, the US consul in Marseille, who also seemed to be very interested in the General's future. Chambe said that Marsac and the Americans had promised him a submarine or 'hydro-glisseur' (speedboat), or a felucca.

'You wouldn't like a felucca,' John assured him, and evacuation by boat was uncertain and unpredictable whereas the Pyrenees could be crossed at any time of the year. 'Even in winter?' asked Chambe. John explained that he was aware of the General's reputation as a great chasseur and countryman who was known to ride and walk the mountains in all weathers in his native Haute Savoie. Chambe seemed flattered. The Englishman was well briefed but, even so, he would need several days to think about it and if he did go it couldn't be immediately. He would need at least two staff officers to accompany him. He said this looking at his mother, who nodded her assent.

16 The Deuxième Bureau was the French intelligence agency traditionally charged with dealing with external threats.

'When would you like me to return?' asked Goldsmith. 'In a couple of days,' Chambe replied. But in the meantime John should go and look up his friend in Toulouse, the lawyer Maître René Chesnelong, who may also know about escape routes and mountain guides. While Goldsmith waited, the General wrote out a letter in a spidery hand addressed to his old companion. He also wrote down the address, which John memorised. With that it was clear that the audience was over.

Goldsmith felt sufficiently encouraged to go straight on to Toulouse. With any luck the arrangements could be made there and then and he and Chambe could be on their way out by the weekend.

It was afternoon by now, on a foggy November day, and John hadn't eaten since breakfast. Approaching Perrache station he passed the popular restaurant Brasserie Georges, which was open for business as usual. He had eaten a meal there once before the war, when returning from the races with Antoine Munat. When, if ever, he wondered, would he next sit down to a plate of coq au vin or poulet de Bresse with Lyonnaise potatoes? He had Jean Delannoy's money and he had points on his French ration card and for a moment he was tempted to go inside. But then his antennae warned him that there were too many Germans around the station and not just the young and old Feldgendarmerie he'd seen on his way up from Marseille. In Lyon he could feel the presence of plain-clothes men, Gestapo officers, their eyes boring into his back.

While buying a first-class ticket to Toulouse he was asked to show his identity card. The French official glanced briefly at the Orchard Court forgery then handed it back. Boarding the packed train, John lit a cigarette and settled down for another long, slow journey. But his mind kept returning to the subject of food, like the day of his SOE interview when Selwyn Jepson had asked him about his favourite French dishes. A perfect choucroute with ham hocks and sausage. Oysters. Bulots – or whelks. A freshly made onion tart. Real coffee. Thinking about it was a kind of self-inflicted torture but at least it helped to pass the time.

Maître Chesnelong was extremely courteous. He insisted that Goldsmith stay the night at his house and he and his wife shared with him their meagre supper. The lawyer explained that he'd had clients, including Jewish clients, who had been desperate to get out of France and who had paid large amounts of money to be escorted over the mountains. But not all the guides were genuine. Some of them were tricksters who took the cash and then disappeared or, worse, sold their charges straight into the hands of the Guardia Civil. The Spanish fascists had their own concentration camp at Miranda de Ebro and it was, by all accounts, filled with British and French escapees who had ended up trusting the wrong people. But if Goldsmith and the General needed somewhere to stay in Toulouse before setting out, the maître's home was theirs.

John thanked the lawyer for his advice. He didn't mention Chesnelong by name when he saw Captain Delmas the next day but he did press him about the reliability of his escape route. The French intelligence officer assured him that the Marie-Madeleine escape line, which was partly run by Catholic priests, was entirely reliable. It cost money, of course – the Deuxième Bureau officer had 'overheads'. But Jean Delannoy could pay, and for an agreed sum he was promised an experienced *garde forestier*, or forest warden, would guide him and his accomplice to a safe house in the Basque village of Ochagavia from where transport to Pamplona or Bilbao could be arranged.

John stayed in Toulouse for several days and while he was there the Allies landed in Casablanca, Oran and Algiers. On 11 November the Germans responded by occupying the Vichy Zone, putting an end to felucca landings on the Riviera coast. Simultaneously, Italian units invaded Corsica and crossed the frontier into the south of France. When Goldsmith travelled back to Lyon to see Chambe the train was swarming with troops. John was aware of one young Wehrmacht officer in the same compartment studying him intently. He tried to look out of the window or keep his head in his paper but eventually the German asked him his name. Then he asked where he was going. And then he asked him his business. Goldsmith, knowing that he had to play his part to the hilt, looked him in the eye and admitted with a mock-rueful smile that he worked on the black market. The German's face lit up. He'd thought as much. He was exactly the kind of man he was looking for. Might Monsieur Delannoy be able to get him some silk stockings? Not for himself of course. Jean laughed politely. No, they would be a present for someone very dear to the Lieutenant's heart and they were so hard to come by at present. Jean assured the Lieutenant that he would be happy to be of service. How many pairs would he like? Might three be possible? Of course, replied Jean, informing his customer of the going rate. The German was overjoyed, and when they got out of the train at Lyon he insisted that Monsieur Delannoy accompany him to his hotel so that he could pay him half the money in advance.

When the nervous Goldsmith finally managed to extricate himself he went into a café on place Jules Ferry and used the telephone booth to call Toto Otoviani in Nice. The Corsican promised to deliver the order to the hotel in person in three days' time and was as good as his word, collecting the other half of the fee from the German.

Unfortunately Goldsmith's second meeting with Chambe didn't go quite so well. The General had apparently chosen his two staff officers but they wouldn't be ready to leave for another month. In the interval he was going to put Carte and the Americans to the test. Walking over the Pyrenees in winter would be no casual promenade even for a chasseur like himself. So if André Marsac could arrange for a submarine to convey him to Gibraltar before Christmas, he'd take it. If not he was prepared to do it the British way in the New Year.

The frustrated Goldsmith had no choice other than to accept Chambe's decision, withdraw back south and resume his sabotage classes in Juan-les-Pins, where he found that Jean Delannoy's services were increasingly popular, not just with the locals but with the hordes of German soldiers who had now moved into the area. Some of them wanted stockings like the Lieutenant on the train, others wanted basic comforts like cigarette lighters and bars of authentic Savon de Marseille soap to replace the watered-down fakes they were given in Germany. Like Private Walker in *Dad's Army*, Jean Delannoy and Toto Otoviani supplied their every need. They handled business for the Italians too – nicknamed 'Les Pis Pis' by the French and clad in second-hand French helmets and boots – who were desperate to buy food in return for cigarettes, bicycle pumps and tyres.

Goldsmith made sure that part of his profit went to supplement the Bartoli and Leonetti family Christmases which otherwise would have been mean affairs. The rest he decided to keep to pay the guides on the Marie-Madeleine escape route when, all too predictably, Carte's efforts to exfiltrate Chambe by boat between the nights of 14 and 29 December ended in fiasco. No American submarine or speedboat arrived off Toulon or La Napoule and on one occasion Chambe was lucky to get away when the local Vichy police chief paid a surprise call on André Bartoli minutes after the General had been hurried out of the garden of the Villa Caracasa.

Chambe's view of the Americans was also coloured by their role in the Darlan affair. Admiral Jean Louis Xavier François Darlan was head of the French navy in 1939. After the armistice in June 1940 he became a leading figure in the Vichy regime, offering military assistance to Hitler, although he did manage to keep the French fleet out of German hands. By a coincidence he was in Algiers when the Americans landed on 8 November, visiting his eldest son who was in hospital with polio. Despite his record as a collaborator Eisenhower appointed Darlan the High Commissioner for Algeria. The Admiral told his countrymen to down arms and join the Allies and ordered the scuttling of the French fleet at Mers El Kebir.

Eisenhower had accomplished his main objective, but the sight of an American General dealing amicably with a former Vichy leader who was contemptuous of the British appalled elements in London. It was even more repugnant to Giraud, de Gaulle and the French Resistance who were at war with the Vichy regime. The situation took a dramatic turn on Christmas Eve 1942 when Darlan was assassinated in Algiers, shot by a young royalist who wanted to restore the French monarchy. The killer was in turn executed by firing squad two days later, taking any secrets about Darlan's death with him to the grave.

The assassination left the door open for General Giraud who had, reluctantly, allowed himself to be brought over to Algiers after the landings. The man the British labelled 'Kingpin' discovered that the Free French troops looked to Darlan for leadership, not himself. But it was Giraud who organised the court martial that tried Darlan's murderer with such speed and a few days later it was Giraud, not de Gaulle, who, with Allied blessing, was appointed commander-in-chief of all French forces in North Africa.

With many battles still to come the General needed Chambe more than ever, and in early January 1943 John Goldsmith got a message from London, via Bartoli, telling him that Chambe was now ready to leave with him and that John should begin the escape without delay. Goldsmith had no idea if he would ever see André Bartoli or Paulo Leonetti or their children again, and after three and a half months together their goodbyes were poignant ones. Especially when Madame Bartoli produced a beautiful smock dress for John's daughter Gaie, who would now be more than 18 months old. Jean Delannoy stuffed the dress in his spiv's suit pocket as he set off for Lyon once more.

9

ZONE INTERDITE

On the morning of Wednesday, 20 January 1943, John Goldsmith, René Chambe and the two staff officers left Lyon-Perrache for Toulouse. They had all bought their tickets separately and they travelled in different compartments on the same train. There was a story that when Chambe had been supposed to leave with André Marsac he had insisted on taking two trunks with him which he said contained vital papers. On inspecting the contents the harassed Marsac discovered that they in fact contained the General's dress uniforms and his collection of family silver. John had no intention of lugging the trunks over the Pyrenees and was prepared to tell the General so in no uncertain terms. But when it was time to go he was relieved to see that Mon Général had just a small suitcase, which was carried by one of the staff officers, and a knapsack or game bag of the kind any chasseur might reasonably take with him into the hills in January.

The train to Toulouse was as overcrowded as all the others had been, and not far out of Lyon there was an incident that Goldsmith knew would fascinate his SOE handlers in London. The Toulouse-bound service was held up in St Etiénne station where there had apparently been a mutiny on a troop train bound for the Russian

Front. Ordinary German soldiers, who had been told they were going home on leave, had refused to move when their true destination was revealed. As Goldsmith's train passed through there were officers with dogs and what looked like Gestapo operatives on the station platform. The more the merrier, thought John. If they're busy fighting each other in the Massif Central there'll be fewer of them hanging around the Spanish border.

When they got to Toulouse the General's aides-de-camp – a snooty pair with identikit small moustaches – were put up by Captain Delmas. At Maître Chesnelong's house, Madame served Goldsmith and the General another frugal dinner, the rations split four ways. It was all the lawyer and his wife could afford, and Goldsmith decided to leave some of his black market money behind where they would find it the next day. After the meal was over Chambe lit a cigar, suggesting that he, at least, was satisfied.

The next day, Thursday, 21 January, they took a train from Toulouse in the direction of Bayonne, getting out at Oloron-Sainte-Marie, a town south of Pau in the foothills of the Pyrenees. Their objective was Licq, a small village 25 kilometres away near the frontier in the Saison valley. The Basque guide would meet them there at ten o'clock that night and take them up over the Pic d'Orhy and through the Irati Forest to Ochagavia. The Deuxième Bureau officer in Toulouse had assured John there was very little German or French surveillance in the area and that they would be quite safe walking to Licq along the local roads. Even so, Goldsmith had decided they should spend the day in a barn outside Oloron and not begin their walk until after dark. They had water and some bread, cheese and sausage that they had been given in Toulouse, and Jean Delannoy, the black marketeer, had some chocolate bars and several packs of cigarettes. In France in the 1930s Goldsmith had only smoked about a dozen Gauloises or Gitanes a day but, to help combat the tension of life as a secret agent, he had become a 30- or 40-a-day man.

Towards the end of the afternoon Chambe took his suitcase from one of the staff officers and went to the back of the barn to change. He reappeared wearing hiking boots, knee-length socks and breeches, a thick plaid shirt and a chasseur's jacket, known as a Canadienne, which was olive green with a fur lining and fur collar. On his head he wore a felt hat with a feather in it. He looked at the two staff officers in their belted raincoats, then at Goldsmith who was still in his wide boy suit and shoes. 'Well equipped for the mountains, I see,' he remarked. 'Myself, I am like a *coq de bruyère*.' Goldsmith knew that a *coq de bruyère* was a grouse. He also thought that Chambe looked like a Tyrolean extra from central casting, but he did envy him his fur-lined coat. It was pleasant enough in the barn, surrounded by straw and the warm breath of the farm animals, but outside the temperature was beginning to drop.

At 5 p.m. they started walking along the narrow country road. They went in single file: the General at the front, followed by the two staff officers, with Goldsmith bringing up the rear. It was a frosty, moonlit night and they heard the occasional barking of farm dogs. John had been given a map by Delmas and after an hour he could see they had crossed into the Zone Interdite, which ran for 25 kilometres behind the coast. It was a prohibited area requiring special permits and if they were stopped now their ordinary forged documents would be useless. The escape line organiser had advised him which route to take and John was just congratulating himself on his Arisaig fieldcraft which had enabled them to pass the guard post undetected when, about 50 yards ahead of them, four uniformed gendarmes bicycled over the brow of the hill.

Goldsmith's party stopped, frozen to the spot. Two of the gendarmes dismounted and walked slowly towards them. They flicked their capes back as they came and John could see that they were both wearing sidearms. The leading gendarme, a Sergeant, demanded to see their papers. Nobody moved. Did they not understand that this was a forbidden area and that they required special documents to enter? Without them they would be in very serious trouble. Still they remained silent.

The Sergeant looked at Chambe. 'Your name, Monsieur.'

The *coq de bruyère* stared back at him impassively.

John Goldsmith was frantically trying to decide what to do. Unlike the policemen he wasn't armed. André Bartoli had offered him a pistol before he left Juan-les-Pins but he knew that there was a good chance of being stopped and searched on one of the train journeys and being caught in possession of a gun or a knife was a capital offence. John had learned enough from Bill Sykes about fighting with his bare hands to believe he could take out at least one or two of the gendarmes, and presumably the staff officers, and maybe even Chambe, would join in. But killing all four uniformed policemen and leaving them by the roadside would cause a hue and cry when the bodies were discovered and, even if they got away, the consequences for the local villagers would be severe. Maybe there was another way.

'Very well,' said the Sergeant, resigned to getting no answers. 'I'm afraid you will all have to accompany us back to Licq.'

The policemen, wheeling their bicycles, moved in close to the escapees, one at the front, one at the back and one on either side, and then they all started walking up the hill. Goldsmith didn't see what else they could do. Licq was where they had to go anyway to make contact with their guide and it was better to be in the company of French gendarmes than the Gestapo.

When they got to Licq, a pretty village with a river running through it and a small market square, everyone crowded into the police station. There were only two chairs in the Sergeant's office. The Sergeant sat in one of them and Chambe sat in the other, Goldsmith standing next to him. The two staff officers had to wait in the corridor. The Sergeant demanded once again to know their names and business. If they refused to co-operate, he said, he would put a telephone call through to the Kommandantur in Bayonne and the Germans would come out and collect them in the morning. John knew where that would end: jail for Chambe and his officers and a bullet for him.

He couldn't be sure whether the gendarmes were really pro-Vichy or just fonctionnaires worried about covering their own backs. Maybe he should try to pull rank. Maybe they would fall in with whatever a more senior official told them. It would be a gamble, for sure, but what choice did he have?

'I have to tell you, Sergeant,' John began, recalling the manner of a particularly patronising racecourse steward he'd known in England before the war, 'you are about to make a grave error. Not just your future but the whole course of the war could be at stake here.'

The Sergeant glared at him.

'The gentleman on my left,' continued Goldsmith, 'is one of the most important men in France today. General Giraud – you've heard of him, I imagine – has requested him to join him in Algiers without delay and we are escorting him over the Pyrenees to a safe house in Spain. You will excuse me for saying this, Sergeant, but is a mere country policeman going to intervene in a matter of such national importance?'

'What do you expect me to do?' exclaimed the Sergeant angrily. 'You are in a prohibited zone. If I don't arrest you and the Germans find out . . .' He ran his fingers across his throat. 'So much for my future.'

'I understand your predicament,' said Goldsmith. 'That is why we should refer the matter to a higher authority. I insist on seeing the Mayor.'

'Hah!' the Sergeant exclaimed to the other gendarmes. 'You hear that? He insists on seeing the Mayor. Very well, Monsieur le Comte or Monsieur le Parisien or whoever you are, the Mayor it is.'

John had won the first round.

The Mayor of Licq, Antoine Bouchet, owned the Hôtel des Touristes which overlooked the square. It was now after ten o'clock but Bouchet was still in the restaurant with his wife. The bar and dining room had an Alpine feel with wood panelling, red and white check tablecloths and chamois and wild boar heads mounted on the wall. The Sergeant hung back as if socially he didn't belong there.

Goldsmith, still acting the haughty Parisian, approached the Mayor and introduced himself and General Chambe. The Mayor, suitably impressed, stood up and shook the General's hand. Goldsmith, deciding to appeal to the man's patriotism, took the Mayor to one side and confided to him that he was a British officer on a vital mission and that it was imperative to shake off the gendarmes as soon as possible. Without hesitation Bouchet said it would be an honour to assist them. The way out was simple. He would drive Goldsmith and the Sergeant to the gendarmerie at Oloron. The Captain there would furnish them with the necessary forms on the Mayor's say-so and Bouchet would countersign them. Then when they got back to Licq the Sergeant would be off the hook and the General and his friends could be on their way.

It was a neat solution, made all the better by the large pot of beef stew, or pot-au-feu, that appeared from the kitchen before they left. John couldn't see much meat in it and it had probably been on the go for days, but it was hot, and Bouchet produced a couple of bottles of his best red wine to wash it down with.

It was 1 a.m. by the time they got back from Oloron-Sainte-Marie with the necessary documents. Goldsmith kept the originals and gave the duplicates to the Sergeant who implied he thought Goldsmith was a lucky bastard and that he'd be glad to see the back of him.

Chambe and his two aides-de-camp had been sleeping on chairs in the hotel foyer but they couldn't stay there. Bouchet warned John that the Germans sometimes turned up on Friday mornings demanding to see the hotel register, and Friday morning was now only a few hours away. The Basque guide, Elihery, was hanging around the bar, having expected to meet them there at ten the previous evening. John suspected that he was after money, and sure enough he demanded half his fee in advance, and then said it was too late to reach the frontier that night and that they'd have to wait until the following evening. Until then they could stay in a shepherd's hut above the village.

The party, five-strong now with the guide, resumed their journey, Bouchet embracing them all warmly as they left. Walking silently in the darkness they followed Elihery up the road towards Spain. From time to time one of them went on ahead to make sure there were no unpleasant surprises waiting for them around the next corner. A couple of miles outside Licq, Elihery turned off up a rocky path into the woods and after an hour's climb they came to the shepherd's hut. There was no heating in the stone shelter and nothing to sit on either. Bouchet had given Goldsmith a flask of chicory-flavoured coffee and a small hip flask containing some local digestif. John tried it and said it tasted like hair oil.

The Basque guide grinned. 'We cross at ten o'clock tonight,' he said in English.

10

ACROSS THE PYRENEES

The rocky track continued upward through thick woods and they had to duck and weave their way through the undergrowth. After an hour they came out of the trees on to a plateau. Up ahead was an even steeper climb and there was snow on the ground now as they clambered over the boulders and spurs of rock, feet slipping and sliding and loose stones falling away down the trail. From time to time they had to grab hold of a solitary tree or plant rooted into a cleft of rock or perched on a ledge. John's shoes were torn, his feet were wet and his shirt was sticking to his back but, after a day's enforced idleness in the shepherd's hut, he was hungry, not tired, and he realised now how invaluable all those hours had been hiking over the mountains around Arisaig. The General was still sprightly and upright too but the two staff officers were struggling to keep up and kept pleading for a rest but Elihery wouldn't stop. They splashed through icy water, they scrambled over ridges on their hands and knees, and at one point Goldsmith slid into a gully and found himself waist-deep in snow.

About an hour after sun-up the Basque guide finally halted and told them they had crossed the border. Everyone lit a cigarette to celebrate. 'So how far is it to the safe house?' asked John, from where, according to the Deuxième Bureau officer in Toulouse, they'd be able to telephone the British consul in Pamplona. 'There is no safe house here,' Elihery replied, 'and no telephone either.' But he was going to take them to a Spanish game warden's house near Ochagavia. The Spaniard would find them somewhere to sleep and, for money, he might be prepared to take a message to the British consul.

It wasn't exactly what they'd been promised and Goldsmith could tell General Chambe shared his suspicions that they were being fitted up. But they couldn't go back to France so what alternative did they have?

After another few miles of walking through a forest of Spanish oak, the air cold and clear and the sun rising over the mountains behind them, they came to a simple stone house in a clearing. Hare and deer carcasses were hanging from the rafters and, inside the house, the game warden was cleaning his shotgun and drinking coffee sweetened with condensed milk. While Elihery did the negotiating they all sat down by the fire and passed around a bowl of hot, sweetened coffee. Elihery told Goldsmith that the Spaniard had a pencil and paper and that on Monday he'd take a letter for them to the consul in Pamplona. Elihery explained how much it would cost and warned them that they wouldn't be able to stay in the game warden's house while they waited for a reply as mounted Guardia Civil patrols sometimes came by looking for smugglers and refugees.

After they'd finished the coffee Elihery and the Spaniard took them west for about a mile to a large cave hidden in the woods. The bedding was rudimentary and they could only light a small fire but the Spaniard would bring them food each morning. That was it for Elihery, and after John had paid him the rest of his fee, the Basque counting the notes out carefully, he wished them good luck in both English and French and started back towards Licq.

Goldsmith, Chambe and the two staff officers had to spend the next five days living and sleeping together in the cave. The Spanish game warden was as good as his word and brought them fresh supplies each day. It was good food too including cold venison, bread, coffee and a wineskin. By this time the four men were filthy, not having washed or shaved since leaving Toulouse. The staff officers wouldn't even take off their raincoats. John and the General attempted to wash themselves in a mountain stream. The water was freezing and with no soap or towels it was a brief and unsatisfying bathe.

John had written the message for the British consul, asking if he could supply them with a map and a map reference where they could be picked up from, and on the Monday morning the Spaniard had set off for Pamplona. He didn't reappear until Thursday. There was no British consul's office in Pamplona any more, he told them. It had closed. But he had paid a girl he knew to take the message to the American consul's office in Bilbao. She had set off by bus and she should be back by the weekend. In the meantime they'd just have to stay where they were.

The two French staff officers had had enough. They said they didn't believe anyone was coming to rescue them and that they were tired of living like bears in the woods. They were going to walk to Ochagavia and follow the road south to Pamplona. They expected to be picked up by the Guardia Civil and taken to the concentration camp at Miranda but they were confident that someone in the American or British embassies in Madrid would get them out. Chambe told them they were fools and that they would end up spending the rest of the war in the camp but they wouldn't listen. Goldsmith was just glad to see the back of them, and as they left he warned them that if they returned with the Guardia Civil he'd find a way to kill them both.

The rest of that day and the next day passed anxiously, but on Saturday afternoon the game warden returned to the cave with a local doctor and Anglophile who said that contact had been made with the US consul in Bilbao. The doctor gave Goldsmith a small section of map, as requested, and a map reference which was for a spot on an isolated stretch of road deep in the forest to the east. A car would be waiting there to pick them up between midnight on Sunday and 2 a.m. on Monday morning.

Dirty, exhausted and alternating between sleep and wakeful tension, Goldsmith and Chambe counted down the final 36 hours in their lair. At one point they had to lie face down on the forest floor, breathing in the scent of the pine needles, as two mounted Guardia Civil passed within 50 feet of their hideout.

On the night of Sunday, 31 January, John paid off the game warden and then, at 10 p.m., he and Chambe began their eight-mile walk. There was no snow on the Spanish side of the mountains and the going was much easier than on the way up. Thanking his Arisaig training once again, John found the map reference without difficulty, and at around one in the morning they emerged from a thicket to find a Chevrolet waiting for them a few yards away like some improbable pre-booked taxi. A man was standing beside it wearing a trenchcoat and hat and smoking a cigarette. They exchanged the password and then the man came towards them and shook hands. 'Glad to see you,' he said in an American accent. 'I'm Fuller, the American attaché. I work for Mr Hawley, the consul in Bilbao. I'm going to be your chauffeur.'

Three hours later John was soaking in an enormous hot bath in the American consul's beautiful white-walled house in Bilbao. The water was black with dirt and it took him a long time to scrub the mud and grease from his hair and nails. John shaved and dressed in the clean clothes – a conventional sports jacket and trousers with clean underwear – that had been put out for him, his own having been removed by a white-jacketed Spanish servant who had picked up his spiv's suit with a pair of tongs.

John joined Chambe downstairs for a breakfast of eggs, coffee, hot rolls and marmalade and then the two men went back up to their rooms and fell asleep. That evening a British diplomat, Mr Graham, came to dinner and congratulated them on their escape. He explained that the following morning they would be driven to the British Embassy in Madrid and then progress by stages to Seville, Gibraltar and Algiers.

When John went to bed that night there was a large whisky and soda on his bedside table and a pair of silk pyjamas lay on the turned-down sheets. Underneath the pillow was the baby's smock, now washed and ironed, that he'd been given by Madame Bartoli and which he had carried faithfully over the Pyrenees. The secret agent went to sleep clutching the child's dress like a comfort blanket.

11

TWENTY-FIVE DAYS

It wasn't until Saturday, 20 February that John arrived back in Britain and by then he was the proud possessor of a medal. As the diplomat had promised, Goldsmith and Chambe were conveyed by car from Bilbao to Gibraltar and then flown to Algiers where John handed over Chambe to the Free French. Giraud was overjoyed to see his old comrade and *copain* again and extremely grateful to the General's English saviour and guide. Just how grateful was demonstrated a few days later when John was summoned to Giraud's Algiers headquarters where, in the company of assorted staff officers and French colonial troops in kepis and knee boots, the General presented him with a Croix de Guerre. John had no uniform in North Africa so, much to his embarrassment, the medal, with its red and green ribbon, had to be pinned to the lapel of his cleaned spiv's suit.

It was considered too dangerous to fly directly from Algiers back to London so Goldsmith's journey home was via Lisbon. Like the black marketeer he'd become he bought silk stockings and scent for Tiny along with other scarce items such as coffee, chocolate and shampoo. Then he took a taxi 11 miles down the coast to the casino in Estoril and, revelling in the louche company of foreign couriers and spies, won £40 – something like £1,000 in modern money – playing blackjack.[17]

On the last leg of his journey John finally allowed his defences to drop as he imagined the long-dreamed-of reunion with his wife and baby girl. But every SOE agent returning from the field was first taken for a de-briefing, and when John's flight touched down at an RAF airfield outside Portsmouth a FANY officer was waiting to drive him straight to Orchard Court.

They were met by the doorman who had just returned from a walk in Hyde Park with Maurice Buckmaster's dog. Not normally a demonstrative type, Buckmaster was full of praise for John's achievement in getting Chambe out of France and, along with Selwyn Jepson, highly amused by the idea of the Croix de Guerre being pinned to his flash suit. They introduced him to their new commanding officer, Roger de Wesselow's old friend Colin Gubbins, who was now one of the prime movers at Baker Street. A combative Highlander with a trim moustache, Gubbins had no time for fools and dilettantes. He listened intently to John's descriptions of the chaos and indecision afflicting Carte and was thrilled that John had returned to London with Giraud's written directive to existing chiefs of the French Secret Army containing instructions to them to work in the closest collaboration with SOE.

Goldsmith had acquitted himself with distinction and was regarded as a success, that much was clear. To put the seal on it he was to be promoted to the rank of acting Captain. The not-so-good news was that Gubbins and Buckmaster wanted him to go back to France by the next

17 Ian Fleming, then an officer in naval intelligence, visited the Estoril casino in June 1941 and it gave him the inspiration for his first James Bond novel, *Casino Royale*.

moon. General Chambe, who had been appointed Giraud's chef de cabinet, had instructed Commandant Pierre Lejeune, a London-based Giraudist officer, to go to France and report back on the existing Secret Army organisation. John's job would be to accompany him as British liaison officer and technical adviser on the use of British weapons and the reception of explosives and stores.

It would be a particularly hazardous mission. 'Reception' was a euphemism for the dangerous reality of nocturnal arms drops in open country. This time John would be expected to travel all around France too, including Paris, where he would be at the epicentre of resistance but also where the Gestapo were most active.

It was a lot for him to think about as another firm car and FANY driver finally whisked him across town to the SOE South Kensington hotel where Tiny was waiting upstairs. It had been five months since he'd last seen her, listened to her voice and felt her embrace and he dreaded having to tell her that, in little more than three weeks, he'd be leaving her again. But, as so often in their life together, she was the stoical, uncomplaining one. 'Oh well,' she said as John lay back gloomily in the bath. 'If that's all the time we've got we'll just have to make the most of it.'

He gave her the things he'd bought in Lisbon. The scent, the chocolate and the silk stockings that were so hard to get in Britain. Tiny was thrilled. Annette Helen Bell Clover was good at being cheerful and brave, no matter what. But a girl still likes to have fun, especially a lovely ditzy blonde who recoiled from painting her legs with gravy browning as some women had done, and she wore John's present every day for the next fortnight.

If it was difficult enough to focus on living in the present and stop thinking about his imminent return to France it became even harder once Goldsmith saw his daughter. The thought of going away and maybe never seeing this warm little bundle again made him shiver and feel a physical pain as if a sliver of glass had been driven into his heart. Fortunately he was diverted by tales of family goings-on while he'd been away which, although farcical at times, had very nearly got Tiny and her mother into serious trouble.

Annette's devotion to her husband and concern for his welfare wasn't quite matched by a full awareness of the secrecy that was meant to surround his wartime role. Up in Cheshire with her baby, Tiny was plunged back into her mother's busy social round which included a dinner party at Foxhills to which various American officers stationed nearby were invited. It was an extremely convivial evening during which Tiny's mother talked excitedly to some of the Yanks about her daring son-in-law and his activities in France.

A few weeks later one of the Americans, Captain Bill Brown of the 1st US Armoured Division, hosted a dinner at Manchester's Midland Hotel designed to thank Mrs Clover and her daughter for their hospitality. An RAF squadron leader and his wife were also in attendance along with a couple more US Captains and a Major from Philadelphia who'd brought along his English girlfriend.

The Americans spared no expense, and as the liquor flowed there was more chat about Tiny's husband and what exactly he got up to in 'that cloak-and-dagger British show of his'. A bit squiffy and over-excited by the expansive mood of the evening, Tiny struck up a conversation with the US Major's girlfriend, Mary Stassen, who worked for the French consul in Manchester. Miss Stassen explained that she sometimes had to organise Red Cross food parcels to be sent to prisoners of war in Occupied France. At which Tiny exclaimed that she had a relation – well, to be honest it was her husband – in France and from what she'd heard he was bound to be starving and might it be possible to send him a food parcel? Butter, sugar, canned milk, that kind of thing? Mary said that it would be difficult without an address which prompted Tiny to start writing down the address of Robert Mathet-Dumaine, an old racing friend of John's who lived in Paris, but then she thought better of it and crossed it out.

Come the next day Tiny may have forgotten the entire episode and she certainly didn't try to pursue it any further. But Mary Stassen, conscious of the warning that 'careless talk costs lives', reported the conversation to the security officer at the French Consulate and, slowly but surely, wartime bureaucracy picked up on it.

On 1 January 1943 an MI5 officer wrote to a colleague expressing concern that 'Mrs Goldsmith appears to be a somewhat indiscreet person' and adding that either they or SOE should warn her 'not to advertise the fact that her husband is in British Intelligence in France and not to ask anyone for food parcels to be sent to him'.

On 10 January Tiny received an unexpected visit at Foxhills from a Lieutenant McIver who was not particularly pleasant and didn't tell her the name of the service he worked for. He asked about the dinner party at the Midland and she admitted that there had been 'some talk' about her husband. According to McIver's account she said she had probably had a bit too much to drink but she was sure the Lieutenant would understand. It wasn't easy playing Mrs Miniver day after day with an 18-month-old child to look after and no idea where your husband was or even whether he was still alive.[18] Pressed further, she admitted that the subject of her husband's role had first come up at the previous dinner party with the Americans. She said that her mother didn't know exactly what John did but that given his background in Paris she 'had probably guessed he was in

---

18 Mrs Miniver was the heroine of the popular novel and wartime film about a wife and mother valiantly holding things together on the home front.

France'. Tiny promised that she would be more careful in future but added that 'nothing whatever' would stop her mother from talking. To which McIver told her bluntly that if the authorities discovered that her mother was talking about Lieutenant Goldsmith again, Mrs Clover might very well end up in jail.

John and Tiny laughed about it when she recounted the story, and Goldsmith wouldn't have been the first husband to be amused at the thought of his mother-in-law behind bars. But MI5 didn't forget the incident and it would come up again in a more serious context in a couple of years' time.

The ten days in Cheshire soon passed. John and Tiny went riding together but there was very little hunting in the winter of 1942/43 and no steeplechasing at all. The Jockey Club had managed to get permission for another truncated programme of flat racing, beginning in April, with a 50-mile limit for stables wishing to be exempt from petrol rationing. Colts owned by the Aga Khan were the ante-post favourites for the 1943 substitute 2,000 Guineas and Derby but competition was limited and the great Fred Darling, who trained for the King, was down to just 16 horses at his Beckhampton yard.

If there were no comforting racing pleasures for John to enjoy there was, at last, a tangible feeling that Britain's wartime fortunes were on the turn. In November 1942 the British and their Commonwealth allies had defeated Rommel's Afrika Corps at El Alamein, and in January 1943 the 51st Highland Division had led the assault on Tripoli. The Axis armies had fallen back on Tunis and the route to the southern Mediterranean lay open. 'You could say that before Alamein we never had a victory,' Winston Churchill would say. 'After it we never had a defeat.'

There was an equally decisive turning point in Russia that January as 20 German divisions were trapped in the pocket at Stalingrad and 'the enemy at the gates' were wiped out. In February the Japanese withdrew from Guadalcanal in the Solomon Islands and everywhere it seemed the initiative had passed to the Allies. In Britain, fear of invasion had receded sufficiently for signposts and railway station names to be reinstated, and church bells, which would have tolled to warn of a German landing, were permitted to ring again on Sundays.

SOE F Section were already thinking about the putative landings in France, the much-heralded second front, which would not begin until 1944 but needed to be planned and prepared for with the utmost secrecy. Free French efforts centred around General de Gaulle's fledgling Committee for National Resistance led by Jean Moulin, a charismatic former *préfet* or government administrator who'd succeeded in uniting various disparate groups. As the New Year unfolded, there were more acts of sabotage against railway lines, marshalling yards and power plants. But if the pace of resistance was being stepped up so was the scale and brutality of German retaliation. There was a triple guillotine now at the Santé Prison in Paris. *Résistantes* were being shot every week at Fort Mont Valérien, and the Fresnes and Cherche-Midi prisons were overflowing with arrested suspects.

SOE's role in the struggle had entered a new phase too with women as well as men being deployed as agents in the field. Vita Sackville-West's husband Harold Nicolson, a National Labour MP, had informed Lady Astor that women were 'too intuitive' and 'ill equipped by nature' to be diplomats. But Maurice Buckmaster and Colin Gubbins felt they were very well equipped, if suitably trained, to be both wireless operators, for which there was an ever-pressing need, and couriers cycling unobtrusively from town to town. When Party 27X (one of the last groups to be mentored by Major de Wesselow) arrived at Wanborough Manor in February 1943 it included four women: Yolande Beekman, Cecily Lefort, Yvonne Cormeau and

Noor Inayat Khan. Only one of them would survive the war. Nine other women agents, including Odette Sansom, had already been sent to France between July 1942 and January 1943. But they were sent directly to the finishing course at Beaulieu and, although some of them received parachute training, they never passed through Wanborough Manor or Arisaig. Of the nine, seven of them survived.

For all the emphasis on security at the training schools and in the Orchard Court rituals there were places in London where agents knowingly rubbed shoulders with one another and emissaries from what Anthony Powell called the 'half darkness' of the secret world. One of their favourite haunts, fortunately never discovered by German intelligence, was Phyllis Gordon's club The Gaieties, which was in Berkeley Street not far from the old Berkeley Hotel.

It was there that John Goldsmith got news of his own Wanborough Manor intake. His good friend John Young had yet to be sent into the field but the moustachioed Gilbert Norman and the jockey Jimmy Amps had gone to France as wireless operators the previous October and were believed still to be there. The bargeman's son Arthur Staggs was reportedly somewhere near Paris while the former scoutmaster Rowland Dowlen was earmarked to leave on the same Lysander mission as John.

Once again Goldsmith's identity was to be Jean Delannoy, the black marketeer, but to his relief he didn't have to wear a flash suit this time. Instead he was kitted out with a smart broad-shouldered jacket, flannel trousers and a thick roll-neck pullover which he expected to come in handy on night-time expeditions to potential drop zones and pick-up points.

SOE, forever battling the disapproval of the other secret services, was continually in need of funds, so an ingenious plan had been devised whereby they would be advanced four million francs (approximately £13,000 in modern money) by the casino in Monte Carlo. A director of the Société des Bains de Mer, which ran the gaming palace, had been sounded out about forwarding such a sum until after the war was over. The director was an associate of John Goldsmith's old Parisian friend Robert Mathet-Dumaine – the man Tiny had imagined sending food parcels to the previous year. It was decided that John should take a post-dated Bank of England cheque for the amount over to France with him with a view to it being handed over at Longchamp races. The money, which would be used for courier expenses, would then be transferred from Monte Carlo to a secret SOE bank account in London.

The question of transporting the cheque was a difficult one. Eventually Orchard Court decided to make a false heel in one of John's shoes and the cheque was rolled up and stuffed inside it. Unfortunately nobody considered at the time exactly how Goldsmith was going to get the heel off again when it was time to hand the cheque over. John had also been given a letter from General Giraud to his wife which he was supposed to consider it an honour to deliver. How he transported the letter was up to him.

Goldsmith's departure was fixed for the evening of 16 March. He spent the last night and morning with Tiny at the South Kensington hotel and then, in the afternoon, a firm car rolled up to drive him and Commandant Lejeune down to RAF Tangmere in Sussex. But halfway between London and Chichester the car was flagged down by a military motorcycle messenger who told them that the weather was too foggy over south-west France and the flight was off. Goldsmith was driven back to South Kensington for an emotional reunion with his wife. The next morning he reported to Orchard Court where the air traffic controller assured him that conditions were still not suitable and that there would be no 'op' that night either.

It was a mild spring day in London and John decided to enjoy the moment and take Tiny and John Young's wife out to lunch at the Berkeley Hotel. The women went shopping first at Fortnum and Mason and by the time they joined John in the hotel bar they were all in good spirits. As the wine flowed over lunch they talked about the promising young actor James Mason who was going to play Pierre Laval in a new production by Gainsborough Films; about Dorothy Paget who had hired yet another trainer to look after her racehorses; and about Josef Goebbels' latest audacious claim that he got many of his best ideas from the BBC.

John was just enjoying a cognac with his ersatz coffee when a blushing FANY officer in uniform came hurrying over to their table. She apologised for disrupting their lunch but one of her colleagues had hazarded a guess where John might be. It was all change, she said. The weather in France had improved and they were flying that night. The Captain would have to leave for Tangmere immediately. Goldsmith, finishing his brandy, reflected that if he was going to his death at least he'd eaten and drunk well. Tiny walked with him to the door and they embraced tenderly on the hotel steps. Her husband got into the back of the firm car and moments later he was gone.

It was 25 days since he'd returned from Algiers.

12

A PIECE OF CAKE

The SOE Lysander flights to and from Occupied France and the bravery of the young RAF pilots who flew them was one of the most stirring episodes of the Secret War. The 'Specials', as they were known, were mostly conducted by members of 161 Squadron from their base at the fighter station at Tangmere which allowed deeper penetration into central and south-western France than from the heavily camouflaged Special Duties airfield at Tempsford, west of Cambridge.

The Westland Lysander had been designed in the 1930s as an RAF reconnaissance aircraft and had a short take-off and landing capability, flying at speeds of around 80mph. For wartime service all of the plane's armaments were removed and a 150-gallon fuel tank permanently attached under the fuselage which increased the plane's range from 600 to approximately 1,000 miles with a maximum of five hours' flying each way. There was a front cockpit for the pilot and a rear cockpit for two passengers who sat facing the tail.

The crucial element of the SOE Lysander missions is that they flew at night without lights or radar. The pilot had little bits of map on his lap, which often fell on to the floor, and a small torch he could shine on them, but otherwise he was totally dependent on the light of the moon. There were about 13 moons in a year and SOE's missions revolved around them. The Lysander pilots at Tangmere – and there were rarely more than three of them – could expect to fly night after night in the week leading up to the full moon and again the week after.

161 Squadron would get a briefing folder from the SOE air transport officer at Baker Street which would include a recent aerial photograph of the proposed landing area that had been taken by the Spitfire Reconnaissance Unit based at RAF Benson in Oxfordshire. There would also be a description of the landing area, supplied by an agent in France, confirmation of the number of passengers going in and coming out and details of the escorting officer who would be accompanying them to and from Tangmere.

On the proposed morning of the mission there would be an up-to-date weather forecast from Tempsford and, as long as there was no fog or heavy cloud, the operations room at Tangmere would call the firm and tell them they were happy to go ahead. That evening the BBC French-language news programmes would end with a list of personal messages including coded ones pinpointing the imminent Lysander trips. Distinctive phrases would be used, such as 'Le lion a deux têtes', which were meaningless unless you knew they referred to a particular meadow near the Loire or Saône rivers. The messages had to penetrate through heavy jamming to a portable wireless set in a barn or attic apartment where the agent transmitting was waiting to hear if the operation was on or off for that night.

John Goldsmith and Commandant Lejeune arrived at Tangmere at the end of the afternoon on 17 March. The blackthorn was in blossom and there were primroses in the hedgerows along the narrow lanes between Chichester and the airfield. Within the hour a second car arrived bringing Rowland Dowlen and Mrs Francine Agazarian, whose husband Jack was also in F Section. Dowlen was going to Poitiers to be a wireless operator for the former Bugatti racing driver and SOE agent William Charles Frederick Grover-Williams while Mrs Agazarian's destination was Paris.

The four agents were taken to the Lysander pilots' mess, Tangmere Cottage, a pretty flint-and-brick house halfway up the village street. The FANY drivers took them round to the back door where they met the NCOs, Blaber and Booker, who doubled as cooks and security guards. One of the two ground-floor rooms in the cottage was a dining room with two long trestle tables. The other one was for the operations crew and had a large map of France on the wall with known flak-defended areas marked in red. The furniture was the typical RAF wartime mixture of chairs – some comfortable, some less so – and old sofas arranged around a coal fire. Upstairs there were five or six bedrooms, exuding the atmosphere of 'a cheap Turkish hotel' according to the Lysander pilot Hugh Verity. On arrival the agents went upstairs to change into character, Blaber or Booker taking their personal belongings and locking them in a special cupboard behind the fireplace.

The escorting officer at Tangmere was Buckmaster's right-hand woman, Vera Atkins, renowned as one of SOE's strongest characters and sharpest brains. The daughter of a German-Jewish businessman who died before the war, Vera had been born and brought up in Romania, leaving for England in 1937. She had taken her mother's maiden name, and she was the closest thing to a mother figure in the F Section agents' lives. She attended the departures of all the women agents going into the field, and that night, as well as looking after 'Annie' Agazarian, she went through John Goldsmith's (or Jean Delannoy's) new jacket and trouser pockets, checking there were no tell-tale receipts or London bus tickets nestling inside.

Some agents gave Atkins power of attorney over their affairs and all of them, John included, were instructed to make a will before they left for the field. Once they were in France, Vera also wrote the monthly letters to the next of kin, reporting that 'we continue to receive excellent news' of John or Rowland or Francine or, more worryingly, that 'they were very well when we last heard'.

Like all departing agents John had been given a personal gift by Maurice Buckmaster. As long as it wouldn't compromise their fake identity, men received a pair of plain gold cufflinks and women a gold powder compact. Buckmaster hoped that the presents would be a comfort to the agents in times of loneliness and stress and remind them of the men and women thinking about them back in Orchard Court. He also reasoned that they might be able to pawn them if in need of money.

Then there was that other SOE going-away present, a phial of cyanide, which was sewn into John's lapel. For this mission he was also given a Walther P3 automatic pistol, a stack of German-issue Occupation money, several packs of Gauloises Caporal made in England and some bars of French Menier chocolate in pale green wrappers. The chocolate had been especially modified to produce a smell of garlic on the breath. Some agents went further and filled their cases with more of the devices made by SOE's equivalent of Q Branch in the James Bond novels and films. There was a fountain pen which looked harmless but contained not ink but a capsule of lethal gas. There were ordinary-looking lumps of coal which could be left on an engine footplate in the hope they'd be thrown into the boiler where they'd explode, and there were self-detonating tobacco boxes and grenades disguised as toothpaste tubes.

As the hours before departure ticked down, Blaber and Booker served everyone a special operational supper which was always a mixed grill. The pilots tucked in enthusiastically and, despite his long lunch at the Berkeley, Goldsmith did too on the basis that he couldn't be sure when he'd next get a decent meal. Some agents had little appetite but the pilots tried to relax them by talking in typical throwaway style about what they were most looking forward to when they next went on leave. Watching Phyllis Dixey and the Windmill Girls. Dancing at the Majestic Ballroom to John Allen and his RAF Orchestra.[19] Or just enjoying an evening at the Unicorn in Chichester where the landlord, Arthur King, knew all the RAF boys. For some of those about to leave these were the last descriptions of innocent peacetime pleasures they'd ever hear.

When it was finally time to go, the agents, or 'Joes' as the pilots called them, were taken out to the plane in a big American Ford station wagon driven by an army Corporal called Elston-Evans who'd been a cellist before the war. The passengers were helped up the ladder into the rear cockpit. The pilot showed them where their battered suitcases could be stored under the seat or on the shelf in front of them, fitted their parachute harnesses, plugged their flying helmets into the intercom and showed them how to switch their microphones on and off. The pilots had an escape kit on the plane including several sizes of compass and metal suppository caps containing silk maps of France. They also packed a thermos of coffee.

By 9.20 p.m. John Goldsmith's pilot, Bunny Rymills, had strapped himself into the little front cockpit, slid the roof shut and carried out all the normal checks. Then he primed the engine and started up. Happy that the aeroplane was 100 per cent he waved away the

---

19 Allen's orchestra included former members of Ken 'Snakehips' Johnson's West Indian Dance Band which used to play at the Café de Paris in Leicester Square. Johnson was one of 34 people killed when the nightclub took a direct hit from a German bomb in March 1941.

chocks, turned on to the flare path, opened the throttle fully and took off.

If agents Goldsmith and Lejeune looked back they might have seen one of the firm's cars parked on the edge of the airfield. Standing beside it would have been Vera Atkins and sometimes Maurice Buckmaster himself came down from London to see them off. Watching the little single-engine plane ascend into the sky Buckmaster, in overcoat and hat, must have resembled an anxious parent or schoolmaster watching his charges from the touchline, and offering up a silent benediction.

It was a dry, clear night with no fog or cloud and the moon was rising. Pilot Officer Rymills, climbing to 8,000 feet, left the coast behind at Bognor Regis and headed across the Channel towards Normandy. He knew to steer clear of Le Havre which was heavily defended, and as they reached the French coast he turned round to check his passengers were warm enough and to remind them to keep an eye out for German night fighters.

Up until this point the planes were still in touch with the Blackgang radar station on the Isle of Wight. The closer the aircraft got to the French landing zone, the pilot could make use of a special ground-to-air radio link made by SOE Station IX and known as the S Phone. Strapped to the operator's chest, it enabled him to communicate with the ground from about 40 miles away at 10,000 feet and from six miles away at 500 feet. Pilots tried to keep an eye out for rivers, railway lines and *routes nationales* but guiding the plane to the right spot at the right time without lights was anything but straightforward. Squadron Leader Guy Lockhart, a gambler and card player who was later killed in a Pathfinder raid on the German industrial centre at Friedrichshafen, said that piloting a Lysander always involved 'an element of cinematic stunt flying'. Another ex-fighter pilot said that coming to a Lysander after a Spitfire was 'like trying to fly a London bus' – and landing the bus was usually the most dangerous moment.

Goldsmith's and Lejeune's destination was a stretch of meadow four and a half kilometres from the village of Marnay, which was in the department of Vienne south of Poitiers. The agent in charge of the landing on the ground, Henri Déricourt, had laid out a miniature flare path consisting of three pocket torches tied to sticks and arranged in the shape of an inverted L. When the Lysander appeared, Déricourt would signal a pre-arranged Morse letter with a fourth torch. If the pilot didn't see the correct letter he had orders to abort the mission and return to Tangmere without delay. Pilots ignored that instruction at their peril.

In December 1941, Wing Commander Allan 'Sticky' Murphy landed a Lysander in a field in Belgium despite not seeing the right signal flashed from the ground. When he taxied round he suddenly came under fire from uniformed German soldiers. Turning rapidly through 90 degrees he managed to take off again and set course for home. The Lysander was not seriously damaged despite having been hit by at least 30 bullets but Sticky Murphy had been shot through the neck. He always took one of his wife's silk stockings with him as a good luck charm. He tied it round his neck to staunch the blood and, although he nearly passed out in the cockpit, he just made it back to Tangmere alive.[20]

As well as a possible ambush other hazards on landing could involve ice, mud or boggy terrain making it hard for the pilot to take off again, or a blown field that, unknown to the pilots or the reception committee, had been discovered by the Germans and planted with stakes or covered with stones.

20 Sticky Murphy was later shot down and killed over Holland on 2 December 1944.

Where there were no hitches and the landing went smoothly the pilots aimed to be on the ground for a maximum of five minutes, in which time the agents would clamber out with their suitcases and hurry into the arms of the reception committee and the outgoing passengers would take their places in the rear cockpit.

John Goldsmith's landing was the first organised by Henri Déricourt, who had himself been a barnstorming air show pilot in the 1930s and had then worked for both the French air force and commercial airlines. Married, with a flat in Paris, Déricourt was possessed of considerable brio and elan and not long after coming over to SOE he was appointed F Section's official air movements officer. Between March 1943 and February 1944 he organised a total of 17 operations involving 21 aircraft, bringing 43 agents into France and sending 67 (including himself, twice) back to the UK.

In his correspondence with London, brought out by returning pilots, Déricourt was always complaining about a lack of funding and support. British stiff upper lips infuriated him and he seemed to think SOE didn't appreciate the risks he ran on their behalf. First he had to try and find a landing field where the ground was firm, the grass was short and there were no obstacles. Then he had to arrange safe houses and transport for the agents, who might otherwise have to walk 15 kilometres to the nearest station. All in all, he said, it was 'a tough bone to swallow'.

Laudable though Déricourt's efforts may have seemed, he went on to become a controversial figure whose loyalties were in doubt. He had friends who had been Lufthansa pilots before the war and were now serving with the Luftwaffe and he was seen at the SD headquarters on the avenue Foch and talking to German officers in a nearby bar. He claimed that he kept in with his German contacts as a cover for his Resistance work, and Maurice Buckmaster felt the key to his character was money. But by 1944 there were mounting fears that his receptions were being watched and arriving agents tailed by members of the French Gestapo leader Henri Lafont's gang. SOE eventually ordered him back to London and, in the run-up to the Normandy invasion, decided it was too risky to let him go back to France. There was even talk of packing him off to a 'house in the wilds of Scotland' somewhere between Perth and Inverness.[21]

But in March 1943 those suspicions were still in the future and there was no suggestion of any double-cross as John Goldsmith's Lysander flight touched down without a hitch. Within minutes John and the Commandant, their cases stowed in the back of a truck, were riding off into the countryside on a couple of ancient bicycles. Their destination was a farmhouse that was to be their safe house until dawn.

They missed the drama of the second Lysander arrival, bringing Rowland Dowlen and Mrs Agazarian, which was 20 minutes late reaching the landing field. On touchdown the pilot, Peter Vaughan-Fowler, noticed fire belching out of the engine exhaust. As soon as the plane stopped rolling Vaughan-Fowler, who had turned off the petrol and switched off the ignition, jumped out of the cockpit, tore off his Mae West life-jacket and rammed it into the flames. It put the fire out and, to Vaughan-Fowler's intense relief, the battery was undamaged. Having dropped the agents off and picked up his passengers for the return flight, he managed to get back to Tangmere unscathed, describing the incident later as 'a piece of cake'.

Henri Déricourt might not have appreciated the RAF's sangfroid, but for John Goldsmith the camaraderie and derring-do

21 SOE/MI5 exchanges between Maurice Buckmaster and Dick White, the number two in counter-intelligence who went on to become Director General of both MI5 and MI6, are in Déricourt's file in the National Archives.

of the Lysander pilots and their world receded all too rapidly into the darkness. In its place he was back in the oppressive, clandestine atmosphere of a secret agent's life in wartime France.

13

A CITY FAR REMOVED

Goldsmith and Lejeune had brought with them a large stack of forged ration cards and torches to light the way for future Lysander missions. They stowed them in a barn at the farmhouse near Marnay and John left his Walther P3 automatic there too. Just as in the escape over the Pyrenees with General Chambe he'd decided that in an emergency he'd prefer to rely on his hands or an improvised knife or garrotte. The following morning he was driven in to Poitiers and bought a first-class ticket for the 9 a.m. train to Paris.

By 1943 the Germans had removed more than 3,000 engines and 30,000 carriages from French Railways and the rolling stock on John's train was old, and the locomotive even older. Goldsmith didn't want to travel with Giraud's letter on his person and at the start of what would be another long, uncomfortable journey he went into a cloakroom at the end of the corridor and wedged the letter behind a mirror over the washbasin. He also took the cyanide capsule out of the lining of his jacket and flushed it down the lavatory. He continued to believe it was more of a risk than a reassurance and told himself that if he got caught he wasn't going to talk, but that he wasn't going to get caught anyway.[22]

Half an hour before the train was due to arrive in Paris, John went back to the cloakroom to retrieve Giraud's missive only to find that it had slipped right down behind the mirror. It took him 20 minutes to prise it out again with a pin, journey's end ever closer and the tension mounting as other passengers, including German officers, banged on the door to demand entry.

Coming out of Austerlitz station on a damp March day, Goldsmith found himself in a city far removed from his childhood memories. Walking along the Seine past the Ile de la Cité, he noted there were still barges working downstream and second-hand booksellers along the Quais. But the sparkling, effervescent atmosphere of the 1920s and 1930s had been extinguished. There were a lot of bicycles but, with petrol now down to 2 per cent of its pre-war capacity, almost no cars. Only smoking, lumbering monstrosities known as 'gasogenes' which were powered by a gas generator with a small furnace at the back and a balloon-like container on the roof. They had a top speed of around 30mph, and shopkeepers used them to ferry goods around the city. Taxi cabs had been replaced by velo taxis, two-wheel bicycles with a wickerwork seat for the passengers that were pedalled by muscular young drivers. But there were no traffic jams because there was no traffic and it was easy to cross the road even at what should have been the busiest places.

Goldsmith passed walls plastered with lurid drawings explaining 'how to spot Jews' and black-and-red framed posters warning of the

---

22   John later told his daughter Gisele that before leaving for his first SOE mission in 1942 he flushed his cyanide capsule down a drain in London. 'Might as well kill a few rats' was his view.

latest executions. There were German control points outside cinemas and Métro stations and the café tables were empty and forlorn. Food shortages were worse than ever. Ration cards were still set at the same levels as the year before but black market prices had more than doubled. In November 1942 a kilo of sugar had cost 95 francs in the south but by March 1943 Goldsmith found it had gone up to 300 francs in Paris, and butter, cheese and coffee had gone up by about the same amounts. So-called 'days without' had been introduced with some days of the week designated 'days without meat'. Even more shockingly for a hardened *buveur* and Francophile, others proclaimed days without alcohol including wine, spirits and beer.

In the face of fuel shortages, the novelist Colette had advised her fellow citizens that wearing gold, be it rings, necklaces or bracelets, was the best way to keep warm. Less prosperous Parisians had to make do with wearing old coats, scarves and woollen gloves which Goldsmith noticed were still much in evidence, even at winter's end.

The safe house where Agent Valentin was to stay was a 1930s apartment belonging to Madame Cecily Beaufort, an old racing and polo-playing acquaintance from John's youth. It was situated in a red sandstone building at number 2 rue de la Convention, a long tree-lined street leading from Alésia to the Pont Mirabeau. The four-storey block with exterior walkways and balconies faced another identical block of flats across a small square of grass and concrete that was badly lit at night.

The ambience was not poor but neither was it Passy or Neuilly on the right bank, and it was clear to John that Madame Beaufort's circumstances had shrunk since those halcyon days between the wars. Her husband had deserted her in 1940 and her family, who originally came from Alsace-Lorraine, had lost their house and estate in the fighting. But regardless of the risks involved Madame seemed delighted to see him and was keen to introduce him to her younger brother, Georges Wall, who lived in Lorient in Brittany and had volunteered to assist the British agent in whatever way he could. Wall's first assignment was to travel down to Poitiers with a large suitcase in the guise of a travelling salesman, collect the torches and ration cards from the Marnay farmhouse and transport them to a Secret Army hideout near Clermont-Ferrand. If that mission went well Goldsmith expected to have plenty more for him to do in the weeks ahead.

On Saturday, 20 March, John crossed the river and made his way north to the more prosperous environs of avenue Marceau between avenue George V and l'Etoile. A concierge showed him up to the first-floor apartment of another old pre-war racing friend, Robert Mathet-Dumaine. The suave 43-year-old was the nephew of Comte Max de Rivaud, a leading racehorse owner and punter. The Comte and his son, the Vicomte de Rivaud, kept a mixed stable of flat racers and steeplechasers at Chantilly and Mathet-Dumaine was their racing manager, a role much in vogue in France in the 1920s and 1930s. He also ran horses under his own name.

Robert was an elegant fixture of the French racing scene. He wore a morning coat at Chantilly in June for the Prix du Jockey Club and again at Longchamp three weeks later for the Grand Prix de Paris. In August he went to Deauville sporting a white linen suit at the races by day and playing the tables in the casino by night. He was an enthusiastic gambler and one of his jobs was to place his uncle's bets for him. It was on one of the Comte's horses that John, Robert and the jockey Rae Johnstone had landed a betting coup at Longchamp in the 1930s.

The Rivauds were known as the Rubber Kings of France thanks to their family plantations in south-east Asia. Mathet-Dumaine, who

BLOWN

had been orphaned at an early age and brought up in the Comte's household, travelled the world on their behalf, facilitating deals with prospective buyers from Hanoi to Shanghai and from Detroit to Berlin. The Wehrmacht needed rubber for the tyres on their tanks and armoured cars and the Rivaud business had prospered under their patronage. What the Germans didn't realise was that Mathet-Dumaine, who had spent eight months in London in 1920 improving his English, was strongly pro-British and used his position and ease of access to offer help and information to SOE.

It was to his old friend that Goldsmith entrusted Giraud's letter to his wife along with the four-million-franc cheque made out to the director of the casino at Monte Carlo. The gentleman in question would be at Longchamp when the new season began and it would be a simple matter for Mathet-Dumaine to hand over the payment in the Comte de Rivaud's box. All the leading owners had their own box or *loge* and men of the world still settled gaming bills discreetly, war or no war.

What proved less straightforward was retrieving the cheque from the heel of John's shoe. He tried easing it open with a knife but the leather was too tough. Inserting a screwdriver might have damaged the cheque, and in the end he had to resort to a hammer and chisel supplied by Madame Beaufort. Then there was the problem of how to repair the shoe. *Chaussures* were strictly rationed and he couldn't just walk into Bally on the rue Faubourg St Honoré and buy another pair. He got round it by going to a shoe mender in Passy with a story about having caught his heel on an iron grille at the foot of a horse chestnut tree on a city street.

The next day John went to a café at Porte Maillot for a rendezvous with Commandant Lejeune. Away from the rue de la Convention he was moving around the chicest and most expensive areas of the city – districts much in favour with the Germans, including their top security personnel, as well as wealthy black marketeers and collaborators. But the political warfare tutors at Beaulieu had continually stressed the advantages of hiding in plain sight of the enemy and John Goldsmith, or rather Jean Delannoy, felt a lot more secure walking into a smart café with red leather banquettes than he would have done hanging around a bar in a poor working-class neighbourhood like Belleville or Ménilmontant.

Lejeune was well dressed and posing as the director of a textile firm with links to the Germans. He and Goldsmith drank real coffee for a change, smoked a couple of John's Gauloises Caporals and appeared to chat normally about how Monsieur Delannoy could help with orders and deliveries. The names and towns mentioned were really the locations of Secret Army groups John was to visit in the coming weeks. Once John had made contact with three or four and satisfied himself as to their requirements and readiness for the proposed uprising he was to return to Paris for another meeting with Lejeune. The Commandant would use a courier to relay the information to an SOE wireless transmitter based somewhere in the Paris region and they would encrypt the report and send it back to London. Nothing was to be written down. Everything was to be consigned to memory.

What John didn't know was that the principal SOE network transmitting messages in Paris in the spring of 1943 was the Prosper circuit and it was almost as careless of security as Carte had been in the south. The circuit was run by Francis Suttill, a barrister, who had landed by parachute with Jimmy Amps in October 1942. John's Wanborough Manor classmate, travelling under the name of Jean Maréchal, a Chantilly blacksmith, had been meant to act as Suttill's WT operator. But the reservations Lance Corporal Revay had expressed at Wanborough about the jockey's 'uncultured mind' proved well founded. Being nearly illiterate, Amps had made numerous transmission errors leading Suttill to conclude that for all his willing manner and bonhomie he was 'unsuitable for the work'. Suttill decided to make him chief of a small, isolated group of contacts to be used for minor jobs only and in the meantime he sent him back to join his wife and mother-in-law at their apartment in the 3rd arrondissement. If Jimmy was lucky he might be able to live out the war undetected.

Amps wasn't the only one of John's fellow students to be in Paris that March. One of Prosper's main wireless operators was Gilbert Norman, code name Archambaud, who had also been in the field since late October 1942. The man the others had all looked up to at Wanborough and Arisaig for his leadership and physical prowess was living in an apartment on rue de la Pompe in the 16th arrondissement not far from John's rue de la Faisanderie birthplace. But contrary to all SOE training a French courier, Andrée Borrel, a former shop assistant and nurse, was a frequent visitor to Norman's flat and the two of them and Francine Agazarian's husband Jack, another SOE wireless operator, often met and played cards together in the evening. John wouldn't have known it but it's probable that a majority of his WT messages to London between March and June 1943 were sent by either Norman or Agazarian.

In the last week of March, John took a train down to Clermont-Ferrand, meeting more Secret Army figureheads including Captain de la Blanchardie, code name l'Abbé, who was in charge of the distribution of funds. In Lyon he met Commandant Descours, code name Barman, who was to lead the 14th Division when the Liberation came, and in Vichy he made contact with Colonel André Zeller, the overall Secret Army commander in the south. For every rendezvous John used a different password. 'Avez-vous retenu la table pour M. Auguste Verlier?' he might ask a waiter in a restaurant in Mâcon. 'Oui, c'est la petite là-bas,' would come the reply. 'Pardon Mademoiselle, n'êtes vous pas une amie de Robert?' he'd ask a woman in a *café tabac* in Roanne. 'Oui parfaitement, Monsieur, je l'attends,' would be the answer.

Not all the meetings took place in restaurants and cafés. One night John was hiding in a wood near a railway line and waiting for a rendezvous with a signalman. A consignment of explosive was being moved the following night and John was there to confirm the arrangements. As he stood shivering in the darkness he lit a cigarette to calm his nerves. Moments later he heard movement on the track about 30 yards away followed by unmistakably German voices. Goldsmith had almost blundered into an enemy patrol. A German sentry demanded to know who was there. John dropped to one knee and, remembering a trick he'd been taught at Arisaig, removed a pin from the lapel of his jacket and used it to affix his smoking cigarette to the branch of a tree. Then he started crawling away on his stomach. Behind him he heard the German calling out again, and louder this time. When his demands weren't answered he fired off his rifle at the tree. The volley hit the cigarette with pinpoint accuracy but Agent Valentin was now out of the other side of the wood and running and the German never saw which way he went.

From Lyon, Goldsmith went on to similar liaisons in Marseille, Toulon, Cannes and Nice before returning to Paris on 4 April for another two-night stay with Robert Mathet-Dumaine.

To make the travelling easier John's Corsican black market supplier Toto Otoviani had helped him purchase a special season ticket called an Abonnement des Chemins de Fer which he bought at the station in Nice. It was a pink card bearing the signature and a passport-sized photograph of the holder, Jean Delannoy. He was shown a map of France with numbered districts and asked which zone he wanted to travel in. Goldsmith chose numbers 1 to 8 covering all regions from Nice to Paris. It cost 1,900 francs a month and two months had to be paid in advance but the price was not an issue for a black marketeer like Jean.

There were security advantages too. It avoided the need to buy a *fiche d'admission* for each journey from one zone to another. These passes were limited and the traveller would have to buy an ordinary ticket first and then queue up for the *fiche*, possibly under the eyes of the police, often finding at the end of a long wait that no more were being issued that day. Also when applying for the season ticket the number of the applicant's identity card was not checked and the Gestapo couldn't find out from the booking office the places the holder of an Abonnement was journeying to.

As Goldsmith criss-crossed the country that April and May, moving from express trains to branch lines and back again, he was constantly on the alert. There were often Gestapo or Vichy police checkpoints at the stations and John tried to tell himself that negotiating them was a bit like bluffing the bookies or the racecourse stewards. The corridors of the trains were too crowded for them to search every passenger effectively, and in John's experience they preferred to line people up on the platform. They were usually looking for deserters or young Frenchmen trying to evade the hated Service Travail Obligatoire. But John had a fake letter from Lejeune, in his guise as the director of the textile company, instructing him to embark on countrywide assignments on the firm's behalf and his false papers still exaggerated his age, depicting him as a war veteran too old for forced labour or the STO.

While leading his charmed life and outwardly bringing small comforts and luxuries to those who could afford them, John heard people talking increasingly openly about the war. As long as there were no soldiers around they all seemed to agree that the Germans had no chance of winning it. Goldsmith reported back to London that Hitler's occupation of the Vichy Zone the previous November appeared to have boosted Allied support in the south from roughly 40 per cent to more like 80 per cent, and Italian soldiers he met and did business with in Nice assured him they were just waiting for the British and Americans to arrive and then they would lay down their arms.

Every second French man or woman Goldsmith talked to was listening in furtively to the six o'clock news on the BBC World Service or, if they didn't understand English, to pro-Allied French-language broadcasts from London. They longed to hear news of the promised second front, daring to dream it might happen in 1943, and all of them dreaded the thought of another winter of rationing and occupation. But to soften up the Germans in advance of the eventual invasion Allied bombing raids were increasing in frequency and scope and innocent French lives were not spared.

On Sunday, 4 April, Robert Mathet-Dumaine was at Longchamp to hand over the Bank of England cheque to the director of the casino at Monte Carlo. While they were waiting for the racing to begin there was an American raid on the nearby Renault works at Boulogne-Billancourt. Some of the bombs went astray killing 300 people in total including seven spectators at the racecourse. Mathet-Dumaine had been standing on the balcony of the Comte de Rivaud's box enjoying a glass of pre-war champagne supplied by a friendly German officer. He watched in horror as terrified racegoers ran from the open-air *pelouse*, or infield, to what they hoped was the safety of the stand. When the all-clear sounded the meeting went ahead while the dead bodies were being removed from the track. The next day the Germans moved more anti-aircraft batteries into the Bois and racing there was suspended, not resuming until July 1945, although it continued at Auteuil, Maisons-Laffitte and Le Tremblay.

French anger at the inaccuracy of the Allied bomber pilots was tempered by a mounting desire to do something, to get on with it, to strike out at the enemy and do it now. But, as John Goldsmith had repeatedly been taught, random or premature action, however satisfying at the time, might only alert the enemy to resistance in their midst. The consequences for individuals were often fatal and could also threaten the very unity and structure that would be vital once the second front finally arrived.

Most Secret Army groups saw the sense of John's advice but one sceptical Commandant near Lyon refused to proceed with further liaison with SOE without a demonstration of the effectiveness of their weapons. He literally wanted a big bang both to boost morale and enhance his reputation in the eyes of his men. Goldsmith reluctantly agreed to lay something on. Drawing again on his Arisaig training and days planting explosive in the railway cutting outside Morar, he spent two weeks reconnoitring a stretch of line about 20 kilometres from Lyon. When he showed the Frenchman how much of the almond-scented paste he intended to use the old soldier was scornful and refused to believe that such a small amount could cause any damage worth bothering about. But on a moonlit night in late April, Goldsmith patiently attached his time pencils in three places, each about five yards apart. He and the Commandant then retired to the safety of an old Simca that John had borrowed for the evening and which was parked about 50 yards away.

The Commandant, head out of the car window, waited disbe- lievingly for something to happen. The only sound was a night-time breeze rustling the poplars lining the road. Five, ten, fifteen minutes passed, and the Frenchman was just about to start berating Goldsmith when there was a sudden flash of light followed by what sounded like a crack of thunder rippling over the fields. The Commandant was ecstatic. The Englishman's plasticine toys had worked after all and the Commandant could lay claim to a genuine act of sabotage. He was so excited he wanted to jump out of the car and run up to the railway embankment to inspect the damage. Goldsmith, mindful that they'd probably woken up every German in the neighbourhood, had to physically restrain him.

The following day friendly railway workers reported back that they had successfully blown up more than 30 yards of track, halting all services on the branch line and all movement of German goods and ammunition. The proud Commandant acclaimed Agent Valentin as his new best friend and John took some satisfaction from knowing that he'd followed the Bill Sykes Arisaig training manual to the letter. But he also knew that the track would be repaired in a week and that some innocent local in the area would probably be interrogated by the Gestapo and shot.

As the days lengthened and the weather warmed up the increasingly desperate French population slowly realised that there would be no second front that year after all. Meanwhile German security measures against the Resistance intensified, beginning on 16 April when the Abwehr – who were still active despite the SD – finally rolled up Carte. The congenitally reckless André Marsac was one of the first to be arrested and taken to the Fresnes Prison in Paris. Even then a wily German interrogator continued to play a double game, convincing Marsac that he was an anti-Nazi Wehrmacht officer and that if Marsac could provide him with the names of more circuit members in south-eastern France he'd be able to help them. The gullible Marsac, fooled too by a French turncoat who'd gone over to the enemy, co-operated, and among the next wave of arrests were the SOE agents Peter Churchill and Odette Sansom.

The Carte leader and dreamer André Girard escaped to England while André Bartoli, whose wife had bought John Goldsmith's daughter the pretty smock dress, managed to disappear with his family. The insurance salesman re-emerged months later living as a harmless water colourist in Antibes. The hairdresser and former Mayor of Antibes-Juan-les-Pins, Paulo Leonetti, furiously denied any knowledge of Resistance activity and such was the strength of his personality that the Germans believed him.

The wreckage of the Carte circuit was taken over by Girard's former henchman, the architect Henri Frager, who attempted to rebuild it under a different name. But, unbeknown to SOE, the Abwehr were on Frager's tail too, though it would be another 12 months before they brought him in.

Goldsmith witnessed one of the consequences of Marsac's folly and Carte's demise first hand. On his way to a covert meeting in Lyon in late April he saw a member of de Gaulle's Committee of National Resistance throw himself out of a first-floor window. The Frenchman's torturers, still hoping to extract more information, rushed out into the street in an attempt to revive him but, after getting briefly to his feet, their victim collapsed and died. His body was dragged away in front of a crowd of silent but hostile onlookers.

With every train journey and every new arrival in a new or familiar town John could sense that danger was close at hand. There were stoppages on all the trains now between Lyon and Marseille, with services delayed for up to four hours as a result, and double the number of German soldiers on the platforms. Increasingly wary of using familiar safe houses, John decided it was better to get as close up to the enemy as he could. He slept some nights in a Turkish bath in Lyon, surrounded by steaming, sweating Wehrmacht officers clad only in towels. Others were spent in a Maison de Passe in Paris where prostitutes rented rooms by the hour and their German clients automatically assumed that any flash Frenchman patronising the same establishment as themselves had to be a collaborator rather than a patriot.

The only way to survive, John decided, was to shut out every association with his real self and blank all thoughts and recollections of his wife and child. John Gilbert Goldsmith had become Jean Delannoy in thought as well as deed, by day and by night and it was Delannoy not Goldsmith, he told himself, who took a lover in Toulouse. She was the wife of a French officer who had disappeared in 1940 and was believed to be in a POW camp in Germany. John never knew her proper name and she never knew his English name. It was against SOE advice to strike up a relationship with a woman but it was a predominantly sexual affair with few revelations of past histories. The tension and fear experienced by people living on the edge in wartime could be a potent aphrodisiac that pushed couples together sometimes for no more than a night or an hour or two at best. In a blacked-out spare bedroom in a strange house, England and family seemed far away. For the first time the normally optimistic John, now waiting for the sound of a car pulling up outside and a sudden knock at the door, was beginning to think he would never see them again.

There were scares on an almost daily basis, some of them supplied by his own side. On one typically slow journey back to Toulouse from Lyon the train halted for several hours in open country. Bored passengers, Jean Delannoy included, opened the doors, climbed down on to the cinder track and walked up and down beside the stationary carriages, talking and smoking cigarettes if they were lucky enough to have any. All of a sudden the crowd parted and Goldsmith found himself face to face with a fellow SOE agent. Brian Rafferty was a bright, charming, Oxford-educated linguist who had some Irish blood in him and had been recruited into the firm a few months after John.

To Goldsmith's horror, Rafferty broke into a grin, punched him on the shoulder and started to say, in English, 'Well, fancy seeing you again—'. Conscious that there were German troops on the train and maybe plain-clothes Gestapo operatives too, Goldsmith responded angrily in French. 'I think you must be mistaken, Monsieur,' he said. As Rafferty hesitated, John fixed him with a blue-eyed unblinking stare. It was a look that said 'be careful you bloody fool or you'll get us both killed' and, after a moment, the Irishman, muttering a brief 'Pardon Monsieur', moved away. Goldsmith walked slowly in the opposite direction half expecting to hear an order to halt and turn around. He paused deliberately to finish his cigarette, looking out across a field at twilight, then returned to his compartment.

Fifteen minutes later the train journey continued and John never saw Brian Rafferty alive again.

14
AVENUE FOCH

On Friday, 18 June, Jean Delannoy bade his French mistress farewell and took a train from Toulouse to Paris. His original travelling companion, Commandant Lejeune, was in Brittany and expected to be exfiltrated back to England the following week. In his place was another Giraudist officer, Commandant Pierre Du Passage, code name Pepé, who wanted Goldsmith to help him check out a Parisian address that had been used as a letter box by numerous SOE and Secret Army members, including Lejeune.

The letter box was in fact a black market restaurant near the Gare St Lazare run by a French NCO, code name Marion, who'd escaped from Germany with Lejeune in 1941. As well as supplying forged ration cards the bistro acted as a place where Lejeune could leave communications for other Secret Army organisers passing through Paris and they could leave information for him.

'Marion' was suspicious of two letters a stranger had left at the restaurant and that were supposedly from Lejeune to Du Passage on the one hand and to a young Parisian banker's son and Secret Army member called Guillaume Lecointre on the other. The stranger said he had been asked to pass on the letters by 'Archambaud', which was the SOE code name for Gilbert Norman, and that they contained further details of planned drop zones of weapons and ammunition to Secret Army groups.

Marion was right to be concerned. The restaurant was blown and had been for weeks due to the lax security of the Prosper circuit and its agents. Francis Suttill, Jimmy Amps, Gilbert Norman, Andrée Borrel and others had all used the house of a confidante called Germaine Tambour who had been arrested in late April. Information obtained then had led the Germans to Marion. They had also intercepted wireless messages sent by Norman and Jack Agazarian on behalf of no fewer than 24 different agents, including Commandant Lejeune, and the SD had begun dropping off bogus messages at the bistro in the hope of snaring more victims.

Fortunately for John Goldsmith, the enterprising Guillaume Lecointre bicycled over to take a look at the restaurant on the same day that John and Du Passage were on the train up from Toulouse and, from his vantage point across the street, Guillaume actually saw Marion being taken away by two men in plain clothes. Forewarned, Goldsmith and 'Pepé' steered clear, but it was vital for them to establish a new address to receive communications between Paris and Secret Army commanders in the south.

John didn't mention any of this when he went back to stay with Madame Beaufort in her apartment on the rue de la Convention. Over the weekend of 19/20 June he was waiting for her brother Georges Wall to return to the flat so that he could give him a message to take to a Giraudist unit in Lyon. Wall was supposed to get back on the Sunday but Madame Beaufort informed John that he'd been delayed by train cancellations and German security checks and wouldn't be able to join them until Tuesday evening, 22 June. She suggested a totally new meeting place, a small café-bar on the rue de la Boétie off the Champs-Elysées. If things went well and Wall had made progress in the south, John might be exfiltrated back to Britain by the end of the month.

Goldsmith had all of Monday and Tuesday daytime to kick his heels in Paris. The weather was hot and sunny and rather than sit around in Madame's drab apartment John took himself off for a nostalgic walk around some of his old childhood haunts across the river. He paused wistfully outside the locked entrance to Auteuil racecourse. Robert Mathet-Dumaine's gelding Kargal had won the 1943 Grand Steeplechase de Paris there earlier in the month. A bumper crowd had come to watch and, according to a report John read in the *Petit Parisien*, betting turnover was higher than in 1939 suggesting that some of the capital's hard-pressed citizens had turned to gambling to try to supplement their income.

Before he walked on John made a mental note to ask Robert if he could train Kargal and race him in England when the war was over. Maybe he would be another Black Hawk or, better still, maybe he would be a Cheltenham Gold Cup horse. It felt like a fine, positive note to focus on.

Going down into the Ranelagh Métro station on the Monday afternoon he recognised a young woman whose family had lived in Passy before the war and been good friends of his parents when they'd lived nearby. He caught her eye and they started to chat. She remembered him all right, and although he didn't tell her why he was in Paris he could see she'd guessed that he must be a British officer in disguise. Despite that, and in spite of the risks of associating with him, she invited him back to the family home for supper where he was welcomed with a few quizzical looks but no questions and enjoyed a few precious hours of almost normal life. Taking care to leave in time to catch the last métro, John decided that the next day he would go and explore Neuilly.

The following morning the temperatures were soaring and Goldsmith took his jacket off and swung it over his shoulder in an almost 1920s mood of summertime jollity as he made his way to Jim Pratt's stable yard off the rue Perronet. To his astonishment nothing seemed to have changed and the old man, who must have been in his eighties now, was there himself in the back yard trying to persuade a fractious mare to submit to the attentions of a stallion.

A young stable lad, who appeared to have been kicked by the mare, was rolling around painfully on the ground. 'Don't just stand there, get the shackles on her!' Pratt yelled in French. Jean Delannoy, suddenly back in the role of John Goldsmith the horse dealer's son, did as he was told and after about half an hour's strenuous effort the mare was anchored and ready for the stallion who, by now beside himself with excitement, performed his role with gusto.

It had been hot, dusty work, and after the stable lad had recovered and the horses been taken back to their boxes John followed Pratt into the shade of the house and they drank a glass of wine together sitting at the table in the kitchen. Jim never mentioned the war, and if he was surprised by John's sudden reappearance, an Englishman in Paris in 1943, he gave no indication. He asked no questions and John volunteered no answers. They just talked about racing and the victory of Le Verso, owned by the Comte de Rivaud, in the Prix de Diane at Le Tremblay the previous day and about the frustratingly truncated wartime programme. It was as if they were back in the owners and trainers bar at Longchamp 11 years before and John had just popped out between races.

When they'd finished their wine and John got up to leave, Pratt shook him by the hand. 'Give my regards to your father,' he said.

John promised he would, though Jack Goldsmith was now living near Didcot and his only son had no idea when, or if, he'd ever see him again.

Maybe nostalgic thoughts were still on Goldsmith's mind as he walked down the Champs-Elysées from l'Etoile early that evening and turned left into the rue de la Boétie. Maybe his normally security-conscious mind wasn't quite as sharp as usual as he went into the small and unremarkable café-bar that Madame Beaufort had recommended.

It was one of the detested *jours sans*, or days without. John sat at a table in the corner and ordered an orange juice. It was a couple of minutes after 7 p.m. Georges Wall and Madame Beaufort were meant to meet him there at seven. Maybe they were running late? John lit a cigarette and started reading through an evening paper. From time to time he looked around at the other customers. There were only a few of them. A couple of young lovers sitting on bar stools. A workman leaning against the counter. An elderly couple with a basket of fresh vegetables who looked as if they had just returned from a visit to the country.

The clock behind the bar ticked round to half past seven. Still no sign of Wall or Madame Beaufort. Agents were told that if they were at a rendezvous and the other person hadn't arrived after five minutes they should get up and leave. But, for whatever reason, that hot Tuesday evening John Goldsmith stayed put and it was nearly eight when he finally threw a coin down on the saucer and got up to go.

Just as he reached the door a black Citroën Traction Avant pulled up outside. As John hesitated, four men in hats and light summer suits got out and walked across the cobbles towards the café. Goldsmith knew immediately who they were and he knew they were coming for him. 'German police,' said one of them in French. He was a big redheaded man wearing a cream fedora and two-tone shoes. He put his shoulders back so that John could see the holster beneath his jacket. 'Come with us please.' They didn't bother with warrant cards.

John looked left and right but the pavement was blocked. He turned back, desperately, towards the café and realised with a sinking heart that he had never bothered to check if there was a back entrance. The proprietor and the other customers were watching. John nodded at them stupidly. It had finally happened. After more than three months living under cover and on his second mission to Occupied France they had got him.

'They' – the Gestapo.

Two of the men took him by the arms and hustled him into the back seat of the car. John felt something hard and unyielding jamming into his back and, looking round, saw a Schmeisser machine pistol just like the one he'd test-fired at Wanborough Manor. The two men sat on either side of him, John squeezed uncomfortably in the middle, and a sly-looking character, who reminded Goldsmith of a bookmaker he'd known before the war, took the wheel. Sitting beside him in the front seat was the redhead who was clearly the leader of the group. The ginger-haired chief lit a cigarette for himself and the driver and then the car reversed out into the Champs-Elysées, turned left and headed back up the road towards l'Etoile. After rounding the Arc de Triomphe they accelerated down a wide ceremonial boulevard with vast houses back from the road on either side. At the bottom was the Bois de Boulogne.

Just before the roundabout at Porte Dauphine they pulled over to the right where the road was bordered by a lawn and some shrubs. The Citroën's driver stopped in front of one of the big houses and sounded the horn. After a moment a pair of black wrought-iron gates opened automatically and, when the car had driven through, they shut heavily behind them. John didn't need to be told where they were. It had been described to him so many times he could have drawn a map. The house was number 82 to 84 avenue Foch. The Paris headquarters of the Nazi Sicherheitsdienst, or SD.

The prisoner was marched up three or four flights of stairs, passing open doors and rooms cluttered with telephones, maps and wireless headsets. Goldsmith remembered that the third floor was home to Dr Josef Goetz and the wireless section. In one of the rooms he saw a group of smartly dressed young men and women sitting at desks behind typewriters, smoking cigarettes and passing reports on to a uniformed officer.

The bigger rooms on the fourth floor looked like someone's private apartments. They all had elegant period furniture and double windows with magnificent views out over the avenue. There was also a private office with a Louis XV armoire and a map of France on the wall behind the desk.

John was taken on up to the fifth floor, into a bare unvarnished room with a carpet and about half a dozen chairs. There was a large wooden table with a telephone on it and an old copy of Bottin, the Paris telephone directory. There were no table lamps. Only a bright overhead electric light. John realised that the ungilded surroundings were not so very different to the room near Baker Street where he had first met Selwyn Jepson the previous year. 'Fifty-fifty' the weasel had said. An even money chance of coming back alive, and John had taken the odds.

Very well then, he thought, heart pumping. They're under starter's orders.

The redhead in the hat ordered Goldsmith to empty his pockets. They took away his identity card, in the name of Jean Delannoy, his work permit, ration book and certificate of demobilisation, all of them forged by SOE, and his railway season ticket. Then they sifted briefly through his wallet which contained 27,000 French francs (roughly £100 in modern money) – loose change to a black marketeer. What they didn't discover was a small piece of paper hidden in a pocket in the waistband of his trousers and concealed by his brown leather belt. On it was the name of a counterfeiter in Lyon who, in receipt of a pre-arranged message on the BBC, would exchange English currency into French Occupation money at the rate of 300 francs to the pound. John had intended to pass the name and the message on to Georges Wall who was meant to collect the money en route to Lyon and hand it over to Secret Army commanders for the acquisition of black market petrol and goods. But Georges Wall had never turned up for their meeting. The SD had come instead.

Goldsmith was told to sit in the chair in front of the desk. Nobody asked him any questions. Not yet. Neither did they tell him why he'd been arrested. His jailers just stood and sat around the room, looking bored and chatting to each other in both German and French. The redhead was still wearing his hat but he'd taken off his jacket and loosened his top button. John noticed he was wearing a loud, painted lady tie. He must have seen too many American gangster films, John thought. Or more probably he was a member of Henri Lafont's gang, the French Gestapo, or Carlingue.

Goldsmith was allowed to smoke and he worked his way steadily through a whole packet of Gauloises. When the ashtray was full one of the SD men emptied it. As the glow of the long summer evening gradually faded outside, John was thinking of where he would like to have been on a night such as this. Sipping wine and discussing form in Jim Pratt's kitchen. Eating supper with his parents in the rue de la Faisanderie when he was a boy. Or just at home in England with the horses and his wife and child.

John Goldsmith.

Above: Annette.

Left: John, Annette and Gaie with John's DSO outside Buckingham Palace, February 1946.

Above: Arisaig House.

Below: John and Annette at home in Oxfordshire before the war.

Above: Major Roger
de Wesselow.

Below: Colonel Maurice
Buckmaster.

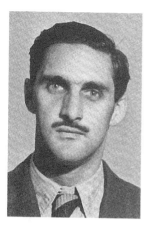

Left: Gilbert Norman.

Right: Camille Rayon.

Left: André Bartoli.

Below: A Paris café restricted to German military personnel.

Above: Parisians queuing for bread during the Occupation.

Left: German soldiers in the grandstand at Auteuil racecourse.

Left: German officers and a glamorous French companion at Auteuil. May 1943.

Below: The Paris-based officers of the Sicherheitsdienst or SD. Hans Josef Kieffer is in the front row, fifth from the left. The man in the glasses, front row, second from left, is the wireless expert Dr Josef Goetz.

COUR DES SAUSSAIES

A German military band marching through Paris.

A German sentry and a French gendarme in the road outside the Hôtel Continentale, Paris.

John Goldsmith's return to the Hôtel Continentale, March 1969. He is looking at the ledge along which he climbed.

Resistance members sabotaging the Marseille–Paris railway line. August 1944.

A Maquis band studying the mechanisms and maintenance of weapons dropped by the RAF.

A Lysander waiting on the ground at RAF Tangmere.

Above: Maquis members preparing an ambush.

Below: General Charles de Gaulle in front of the Arc de Triomphe as he begins his walk down the Champs-Elysées. 26 August 1944.

Below: Gaie and Gisele in 1949.

When he said he needed the lavatory he was taken to a bathroom at the end of the corridor. It had bare walls and the tiled floor was dirty. There was a toilet bowl with no seat, a washbasin and a large bath in the corner. John wondered if this was where they subjected prisoners to the *baignoire*. He couldn't stop thinking about the details. First they filled the bath with cold water. Then they stripped the victim, bound his hands and feet together and perched him on a board. Then they began to ask questions. If they didn't like the answers they tipped the board so that he fell head first into the water. They left him there until he nearly drowned. Then they dragged him out, gasping and spluttering, revived him with a shot of hot coffee or brandy, and started again. To someone like John, who had a phobia about water, the idea of being immersed in a bath unable to breathe was terrifying.

When he was sitting in the chair again in front of the desk he tried to think who could possibly have betrayed him. Jim Pratt? Never. The family in Passy? Surely not. Maybe Pepé or Lejeune had been caught and interrogated and had cracked under pressure. What about Madame Beaufort and Georges Wall? Maybe they hadn't turned up to the meeting because they'd already been arrested. Maybe the SD had them in another room in this same building. Maybe they had been tailing them for days, waiting for them to lead them to him.

It was after 10 p.m. when a man in plain clothes finally walked into the room and took the seat on the other side of the desk. The other four stood up smartly when he came in and arranged themselves in what seemed to be a routine formation. One of them went and stood on John's left-hand side while the big redhead took up a position just behind him on the right. The man behind the desk was about five feet ten inches tall and 40 years old. He was clean shaven and rather plump with hair *en brosse* and an oval face, and he was wearing a smartly pressed brown lightweight suit with a light brown shirt and tie. As John sat there he took a pen and some papers out of his inside pocket and shuffled them around on the desk, a bit like a bank manager about to refuse a loan. Then he took out a handgun and put that down on the desk next to them.

'I'm sorry I kept you waiting so long,' he said quietly. 'I was at dinner when I was informed of your arrival.' He spoke French but with a strong German accent. 'Herr Vogt will translate for us if needed,' he added, pointing to a tall, broad-shouldered man with a face like a boxer who had accompanied him into the room.

John said nothing.

The man sat back in his chair and stared at him. 'So,' he said eventually. 'Jean Delannoy.'

'You know my name,' said John in his faultless French, 'but I can only call you "Monsieur". That doesn't seem right.'

The man leaned forward for a moment. 'I am only a simple soldier of the second class,' he said. He looked up at Vogt and the others and smiled. One of them smiled back. Then he turned back to John. 'My name is Kieffer,' he said. 'Sturmbannführer Josef Kieffer. I am the head of counter-espionage here in Paris.'

'Pleased to meet you,' said John, doing his best to sound confident.

'Are you sure of that?' asked Kieffer. He put his fingertips together and studied John intently. 'You don't look much like a Frenchman, do you?' His tone was confidential, almost friendly.

'My name is Jean Delannoy,' insisted John, trying to effect an air of injured innocence. 'I am a dealer, a general dealer, and I admit I do a bit of trading on the black market.'

Kieffer shook his head. 'We know all about you,' he countered. 'You were sent by Colonel Buckmaster at Baker Street. You are an English officer working against the Germans with subversive organisations.'

Again John angrily protested that he was nothing of the sort. He was Jean Delannoy, born and bred in Paris, as his papers would show. Kieffer picked them up and started reading. As he did so he made notes in the writing pad on the desk. After about 20 minutes he consulted with Vogt. Then he pushed the documents away.

'Useless,' he announced. 'Forgeries, all of them. We know you are an English officer. Now tell me your rank.'

Again John reiterated his French name and cover story.

'Very well,' said Kieffer. 'Where were you before the war broke out?'

'Here in Paris,' John replied at once.

'You claim to have been in the army,' Kieffer continued. 'What unit?'

John had an answer ready.

'Where?' asked Kieffer. 'Sedan? Alsace? Or just a barracks in the suburbs?'

John had an answer for that too. These were explanations he'd gone through many times at Beaulieu.

Kieffer listened to him indulgently then looked at his watch, excused himself and got up and left the room. John was left on his own for about half an hour. The others all stayed where they were. When Kieffer returned he was rubbing his hands. Unbeknown to John, other suspects were being arrested across the city at that very moment.

'Now then,' began Kieffer, sitting down again. 'You say you were born in the rue de la Faisanderie. So tell me something about your supposed early life.'

John went into detail about his father's horse trading and the stable yard in Neuilly and the apartment and the schools he went to. Kieffer wanted to know where he'd been at the age of 14. Then he wanted to know where he'd been at the age of 24. John's real-life

Parisian biography was running out now and it was becoming harder to answer the questions convincingly. Why hadn't they done more work on that at Beaulieu?

'You realise that I only have to send someone down to the rue de la Faisanderie to check this out?' said Kieffer pleasantly.

John understood all right. His father had left Paris before the war and the stable was long gone but it wouldn't be hard to find a few neighbours who remembered the English family who had once lived there.[23]

'Come along,' said Kieffer. 'I know this is a cover story. A child could see through it. You are an English officer sent by Baker Street. Now tell me your rank.'

John said nothing. All of a sudden the big redhead dealt him a stinging blow to the head. John was momentarily blinded and he almost fell off the chair, coughing and retching. Kieffer shuffled his papers around as if he found the whole thing slightly distasteful.

'Are you aware we had you tailed all day yesterday?' he said when John had recovered. 'We know you went to Neuilly.'

'Nonsense,' began John, 'I never left—'

The redhead hit him again, in the same place. Then the man on his left joined in. All told they hit him about half a dozen times, always on the side of the head rather than the face, and in the ribs and kidneys.

John was holding on to the table now. His eyes were shut and the pain made it difficult to breathe but he was determined not to let them hear him cry out.

Kieffer leaned forward again. 'You know what happens to our agents when they are picked up by the War Office?'

---

23 John's parents had moved back to England after the Munich crisis in 1938 and his mother Florence died in the UK in 1942.

John did know. They weren't released and sent home. They were tried under the Treachery Act and then hanged at either Wandsworth or Pentonville or, in one exceptional case, shot at the Tower of London.

'Here we have special men who can extract information,' Kieffer continued. He nodded in the direction of the redhead, who clicked his knuckles. 'But if you talk and admit that you are English and tell me your rank I promise you that you will not be harmed.'

It was Kieffer's favourite tactic. To try and draw the prisoner into a pact in which he'd admit certain things in return for a promise of protection. John didn't believe the promise. He'd been warned at Beaulieu to expect just such a line and to recognise it as a treacherous deceit. But he'd also been taught how important it was to play for time and avoid being taken straight to a cell in the place des États-Unis or to the Fresnes or Cherche-Midi prisons. Once he was behind bars, in leg irons, it would be almost impossible to escape. His only chance of getting away was to try and come up with some delaying tactic. He had no idea what that might be, but then Kieffer himself gave him an idea.

'Why not just admit it?' the German persisted.

'Admit what?' mumbled John.

'Admit that you work for Colonel Buckmaster and that you were parachuted into France to spy on us.'

Parachuted? thought Goldsmith. He hadn't been parachuted. He'd been flown in by Lysander. Maybe Herr Kieffer didn't know as much about him as he was pretending. Maybe he wasn't quite so confident either. What was it he'd said earlier? 'I am only a simple soldier of the second class.' John lifted his head to face his interrogator and decided he was looking at a man who was more insecure than his smart clothes and haircut and swagger job description might

133

suggest. A Nazi bureaucrat who hadn't been born into the Prussian officer class but maybe wished he had been. A man he might be able to flatter and deceive.

Even though his lips hurt and his throat was burning, John asked for a cigarette. When they gave him one he blew a smoke ring with as much nonchalance as he could muster. Then he looked Kieffer in the eye and admitted he was a British officer. Kieffer smiled. He asked again for John's correct name and rank. John gave it to him. Kieffer wrote it down. The Captain had seen sense. Now perhaps further unpleasantness could be avoided. Kieffer wanted to know how often John had been in France and how he had got there. Goldsmith, lying inventively, agreed that he had been dropped by parachute and had landed near La Rochelle. He added that he had arrived in March and gone straight to Paris, which would corroborate any information given them by Georges Wall if he was already in custody.

Kieffer got up and left the room. When he returned he was carrying a book with photographs of suspects, all of them French. He showed John the pictures and asked if he knew any of them. Goldsmith recognised Commandant Lejeune and saw that there was a picture of his wife Arlette there too. Kieffer pressed him to identify them. John feigned confusion.

Kieffer wanted to know the names of 'all the subversive people' John had met in France and the organisation he worked with. John told him he'd been working mostly in the south and gave him the names of Carte members he knew to be either already under arrest or safely out of the country. Carte was so completely blown John calculated there was no more damage the Germans could do to it. Kieffer shook his head. He said he knew all about Carte and that they had been on to them for months. The Captain would have to do better than that. John claimed that he'd been told to try to pick up the pieces after Carte's downfall which made his recent return to Paris more plausible. He said that he hadn't been able to accomplish much and was finding it hard to make contacts.

Kieffer asked John for the names of his commanding officers in the UK. John said he'd never been told any of their names. He said he'd been recruited by an anonymous Colonel from the War Office and that subsequent arrangements had all been made by courier.

Kieffer shook his head again. 'We know all about the training schools,' he told John. 'We know all about Scotland. We have a man in Orchard Court.'

John said nothing and tried to look as if he'd never heard of Orchard Court.

Kieffer then asked him about his regiment back in England and John said he was an officer in the Tank Corps. The German wanted to know about the Valentine tank. What arms did it carry? 'A two-pounder and a Sten gun,' replied John, which was a lie. It carried a Bren gun.

Kieffer returned to the subject of John's mission. Who had accompanied him to France? Who had he met, and where were they now? John must give him names. Goldsmith frowned. The Sturmbannführer was asking him to betray his friends which was a terrible thing. How could he expect such behaviour? Would he, Herr Kieffer, a 'fellow officer and gentleman', ever consider such disloyalty if their situations were reversed? Of course he wouldn't. So he must put himself in John's position. How could he ask him to do it?

Goldsmith's reference to Kieffer as an officer and gentleman was a calculated ploy. Kieffer wasn't a gentleman, John guessed, but he'd like to be one and would be rather pleased to be described as such by his English prisoner. It seemed to work. Kieffer's expression softened and once again he leaned forward confidentially and assured John that if he talked he would not be harmed. He would have to be detained until the war was over but that was all. Still playing for time, Goldsmith said that he was tired and confused and would have to think about it.

'You know that you will have to tell us eventually,' said Kieffer. 'Tomorrow or the next day or the day after that. We are in no hurry. But everyone talks in the end.'

John found himself thinking of the bath along the corridor. He looked Kieffer in the eye. He said he'd told them as much as he could for now. But maybe after a night's sleep he'd be able to tell them more.

'Excellent,' said Kieffer, his face brightening. 'Do you like champagne?'

John stared at him. It was the last thing he'd expected to hear. He almost wanted to say 'but it's a *jour sans*'. Instead he nodded.

'I thought as much,' said the German. 'Then we will share a bottle.'

Instructions were issued and within a few minutes Vogt had returned with a tray bearing a bottle of Vintage Krug and two glasses. Goldsmith wondered if it was from Kieffer's personal supply or whether they just kept a few cases sitting around the building. Kieffer opened the bottle and poured.

'Santé,' he said, with no hint of irony.

'Salut,' replied John.

Goldsmith half expected the wine glass to be smashed from his hand by the redhead in a version of the old double act routine he'd heard about at Beaulieu. But Kieffer wanted to chat. He presumed John had been to a traditional English public school? John reminded him that he had been born and brought up in Paris. But he was a member of a gentlemen's club? 'Of course,' John lied. Kieffer also asked him about the war. How did John think it was going?

'You are not strong enough to win,' John answered honestly.

'You must not say that,' chided Kieffer. 'You must say that we are strong enough not to lose.'

While refilling John's glass like a genial host he explained that Germany expected to reach a compromise with America and then they would fight the Russians together. But no compromise was possible with England, he added. It was regrettable but true. John said nothing and drained his glass. Kieffer had already finished his. The other four looked enviously at the empty bottle.

John yawned. Kieffer put his gun back in its holster and his pen back in his pocket.

'It is late,' he said, 'and we are both tired. My men will take you to your hotel.'

'Hotel?' John thought he must have misheard, and the disbelief showed on his face.

'Oh yes,' confirmed Kieffer, enjoying himself. 'We are playing a little game. Tonight, as a British officer and gentleman, we will put you up in a hotel reserved only for German officers. It is all arranged.' His expression darkened. 'But please remember. Tomorrow morning we will be back to collect you at 10 a.m. You are a brave man. But I want names. I have the men and I have the means to make you talk . . . and I will not hesitate to use them. Goodnight.'

Kieffer swept his papers off the table, got up and left the room, Vogt following him. Within five minutes John and his four guards were walking back down the stairs. This time the bookie and the redhead both drew their guns as they pushed him into the car. As they drove out through the wrought-iron gates it was a little after midnight. Agent Valentin had ten hours in which to escape.

15

THE GETAWAY

Five hours later John was 60 feet up on the ledge outside his bedroom on the third floor of the Continentale Hotel. Flat against the wall in the shape of a cross, leading with his left foot, with his chin pointing in the same direction and his belly button rubbing against the brickwork. It was as perilous a scenario as anything Richard Hannay ever encountered and, to begin with, John Goldsmith was, literally, paralysed with fear.

While lying on his hotel bed earlier and waiting to make a move he had been worrying about all the contacts he had made in the last few months and all the people who had helped him. He thought again of the *baignoire* and the three guillotines at the Santé and the firing squads and prayed that his friends wouldn't be caught and that he wouldn't betray them. What he didn't know was that the Secret Army officers were safe but that the SD had moved in on the Prosper network that night and arrested most of them, including Gilbert Norman and his courier Andrée Borrel. But even if John had known, there was very little he could have done to help them now, and when he got out on to the ledge he found he needed all his strength and courage just to save himself.

Moving very slowly he counted 15 steps as he edged towards the drainpipe and the ledge running at right angles to the one he was on. To get round to that side of the building and the open window beyond he would have to step across the gap. But when he tried to stretch out a leg it shook uncontrollably for several minutes, and at that moment he would have pushed the odds on his survival out to 500–1. He knew that if he didn't move soon his knees would give way, he would lose his balance and he would fall.

Raging at himself to get a grip, he finally managed to force his left foot on to the sill and drag the right foot over behind it, one hand still hanging on to the drainpipe. After a few moments to steady himself, he started to edge along again towards the open window. He had to pass two other bedroom windows first, their blackout curtains closed, and from one of them came the sound of loud German snoring. When he got to the room with the open window – which had a light on too, in contravention of all air-raid precautions – he saw to his relief that it was not a bedroom but a small kitchen and that it was empty. The light came from a stove in the corner on which someone – a night orderly maybe, or a batman – had been making coffee.

Goldsmith eased his way in through the window as quietly as he could and collapsed on the floor, shaking with relief. When he got up and tried the handle on the door he discovered it was not locked. John went out into the corridor, shutting the door softly behind him. He turned right and then right again into the corridor on which his own room had opened. He pulled up sharply. The orderly who had been sitting on a chair outside John's room was dozing and he had turned round so that his sleeping face was pointing in John's direction. Heart pounding, John turned round and retraced his steps, going right round the other way to reach the staircase behind the orderly's back. He tiptoed down the stairs, passing no one on the way. The orderly on the second floor had gone and he could see that the orderly on the first floor was also asleep.

John reached the hall where he'd been brought in the night before. The chairs in the foyer where the German officers had been sitting were empty. There was still a scent of cigar and cigarette smoke in the air but John couldn't smell leather boots. He could see one orderly at reception but then he turned round and went into a small office behind the desk. John was about to hurry across the foyer to the front door when he heard footsteps coming up a corridor behind the stairs so he dived to the left through some swing doors and found himself outside in the courtyard.

He realised he'd come out of the side entrance of the hotel. On his left were the glass windows of the palm court. On his right were a series of tall pillars fronting the rue de Castiglione. Hiding himself behind one of the pillars he spotted two sentries. Instead of one walking one way and one the other they were patrolling together. As he hid behind the pillar and counted they walked past him, taking 30 seconds to reach the rue de Rivoli, where they turned around, and 60 going back to the rue du Mont Thabor. John waited until they had passed him again, going right up towards the Tuileries Gardens, then ducked out from behind the pillar and started walking down the street to his left. Nothing happened. There were no shots and no commands to halt. When he reached the corner he turned left again and started sprinting as hard as he could. He ran along the rue du Mont Thabor until he came to a left turn into the place de la Concorde. The curfew must have ended because there were a few bicyclists around now and sleepy pedestrians on their way to work.

Standing beside the entrance to Concorde Métro station was a solitary gendarme. The Resistance and Secret Army contacts John had made had all told him that most *agents de police* of the rank of

Sergeant or below hated the Germans and would help you if they could. It hadn't been like that with the Sergeant in Licq but maybe it would be easier in Paris. John went up to the policeman and asked him if he was a good Frenchman. The gendarme looked John up and down, taking in his collarless shirt and his shoes without laces. 'If you are,' John continued, 'give me five francs and don't ask any questions.' The gendarme put his hand in his pocket, took out a handful of coins, gave them to Goldsmith and then turned and walked away.

A few minutes later John was on a métro surrounded by early risers. He kept his face down, praying that there would be no German control points at the other end. Changing at Motte Picquet, he rode another train out to Porte d'Auteuil. While walking up the boulevard de Montmorency, not far from Auteuil racecourse, he was acutely conscious of his shabby appearance but nobody stopped or challenged him and at 6 a.m. he arrived safely at Commandant Du Passage's sister's house. It was an address he was only meant to use in a dire emergency and the convention was that he should telephone ahead first. But the Commandant's sister, roused from sleep and fearing the worst, quickly grasped the situation. She arranged for a message to be sent to her brother, who had been in Burgundy, warning him not to return to Paris. Then she found John socks, shoelaces, spectacles, an old jacket and a beret and guided him through the waking streets to a smart basement flat on the avenue Victor Hugo, a wide thoroughfare that was only a few blocks away from the avenue Foch.

The apartment belonged to Edouard Grosval, a brave, intense young man who had a wooden leg having had his right leg smashed by a German shell on the Meuse in 1940. Indifferent to his handicap, despite the constant pain, Grosval acted as a Paris courier for Giraudist officers like 'Pepé' and Lejeune. After listening to John's incredible story and examining his face and body to make sure he wasn't more seriously injured, he produced coffee and thimblefuls of vintage cognac to accompany a breakfast of garlic sausage and bread. Then he strapped on his wooden leg, warned John to stay exactly where he was and under no circumstances to answer the door, and went off to try to find out if anyone else in their group had been arrested and to alert them if they hadn't.

When Grosval had gone, John tried to sleep on the couch in his sitting room. But his mind kept returning to the ledge outside the hotel bedroom and Sturmbannführer Josef Kieffer and the interrogation in the avenue Foch. He imagined the surprise and incredulity of the redheaded thug and his accomplices when they arrived at John's room in the Continentale at eight o'clock to find him gone. He imagined Kieffer's fury at having his entertainment spoiled and then his embarrassment when it became known that he'd allowed a suspect to get away. The Wehrmacht officers who witnessed John's arrival at the hotel would have known that he was a spy and they would talk about it. It gave John considerable satisfaction to think that he'd fooled them. But he also realised that his life was now in danger as never before. There would be a hue and cry and a hunt and a price on his head, and if the Gestapo caught him a second time there would be no mercy.

When Grosval returned that evening the news was grave. During the night, while John was being questioned by Kieffer at the avenue Foch, the Germans had made dozens of arrests. Gilbert Norman and Andrée Borrel had been taken at their apartment in the rue de la Pompe while the Prosper circuit leader, Francis Suttill, had been trapped in his hotel room at St Denis at 9 a.m. Jimmy Amps, the jockey and 'imperturbable beast', had been arrested at his wife's house at the same time. Norman was believed to be under guard at the avenue Foch while the others were in the Gestapo prison on place des États-Unis, not far from the avenue Marceau. It was lax security that had brought about Prosper's downfall rather than a traitor in their midst, but in John's case the finger of suspicion was pointing firmly at Georges Wall who had not returned to his sister's apartment on the rue de la Convention.

Grosval explained that he too was under suspicion and being watched by members of the French Gestapo, who were only round the corner on the rue Lauriston. From John's description of the redhead with the fedora, Grosval thought it highly likely that he belonged to Henri Lafont's gang. Former pimps, gambling racketeers and hired guns, they were the public face of the SD and he had frequently seen them swaggering around the neighbourhood. In the circumstances it was vital to find John another hideout as soon as possible.

The man who came up with the perfect safe house was the banker's son Guillaume Lecointre, who arrived at Grosval's flat on the morning of 27 June. He brought two bicycles with him, one for himself and one for John. The two Frenchmen dressed Goldsmith up again in the jacket, beret and spectacles and then Guillaume and John set off for the left bank, crossing the river at Bir Hakeim near the Vélodrome d'Hiver, the bicycle stadium where thousands of French Jews had been rounded up in 1942 before being transported to Auschwitz.[24]

There hadn't been time yet to provide John with a new identity card. He had no documents on him of any kind and he knew that if he was caught it would be the end. Guillaume, radiating the confidence

---

24 Over 12,000 French Jews, including more than 4,000 children, were rounded up on 16 and 17 July 1942 and held at the stadium. The Paris police participated in the arrests. The captives were later transported to Auschwitz by train. None of the children survived.

of a young man whose family used to be conveyed around Paris in a chauffeur-driven Lancia, rode 30 yards ahead of him. If he saw a control point or a road block coming up ahead, he would suddenly stop or veer off left or right, giving John a chance to follow.

Feeling painfully conspicuous in his beret and glasses and having difficulty handling the bicycle, which had been designed for a much shorter man, John envisaged oblivion rising up to greet them at any moment. But ahead of him Guillaume continued to pedal along in a relaxed manner in the bright sunshine as if he was out for a pleasant Sunday morning constitutional.

It was about half past twelve when they passed the Ile de la Cité and turned right off the Quai la Tournelle into the narrow entry of rue Cardinal Lemoine. Ahead of them was the boulevard St Germain, behind them was the river, and on their left was the Tour d'Argent which was one of the oldest, most famous and most expensive restaurants in Paris. A uniformed doorman in a peaked cap was standing outside and a chauffeur-driven Mercedes had just arrived, discarding a group of smartly turned-out Wehrmacht officers who were greeted warmly by the staff as the doorman showed them inside. Ignoring the Germans, Lecointre stopped his bike outside a side door a few yards down on the left and indicated to John to follow suit.

Nowadays the flats above and behind the Tour d'Argent are used by the restaurant, but in the 1940s they were still private apartments with their own entry and stairwell. Guillaume led the way up the narrow staircase until they came to the landing on the third floor where he rang the bell of apartment number 6. The door was opened by the owner, Madame Tantzy, a 35-year-old Romanian actress who was prepared to offer John sanctuary for the next month. Her apartment was larger than Grosval's right bank basement. There was a sitting room, kitchen and bathroom, Madame Tantzy's bedroom, and what she described euphemistically as the box room. Not much larger than a clothes cupboard, this was to be John's quarters which he had to share with Madame's Siamese cat Laszlo and Laszlo's litter tray.

Madame Tantzy, who was what used to be called a fine figure of a woman, was a charming if rather exhausting host. A relentless talker with an extravagant manner and a Mittel-European accent, she told John that she hated the Germans who had ravaged her country, and that she felt especially tender towards British agents with young wives and families. Hour after hour she regaled him with tales of the old days in Bucharest and Prague and together they shared memories of the cabarets and night club entertainers of Paris in the 1920s.

Madame Tantzy had a gentleman friend, Monsieur Henri, who was over 60 but still dapper and well preserved. As he explained to John, he hated the Germans too, and understandably, having had a testicle shot off by them in World War One. Not that this appeared to have diminished his ardour. On alternate days he would arrive for lunch, always bringing a few little delicacies that he had somehow managed to acquire on the black market. After the meal, which John shared with them, the couple would retire to Madame's bedroom leaving John shut up in the box room with the cat.

Goldsmith was warned on no account to leave the apartment but, to satisfy his curiosity about the outside world, he sometimes peered around the curtains to watch the customers coming and going at the Tour d'Argent. The owner, André Terrail (who had also built the Hôtel George V), had created a fabulous menu and ambience in the top-floor dining room overlooking the Seine and Notre Dame. Wehrmacht and Luftwaffe officers turned up most nights of the week, and on Tuesdays and Thursdays John noticed distinctive groups of plain-clothes men in smart lightweight suits and hats. Gestapo, no doubt about it, and John wondered if Kieffer was among them, enjoying the pressed duck and the famous vintages in between torture sessions at the avenue Foch.

At least Georges Wall wouldn't be gifting him any more victims. Guillaume Lecointre, making a fleeting visit to the flat to check that all was well, told John that the Resistance had staked out Madame Beaufort's apartment on the rue de la Convention and when Wall finally returned on 4 July they had abducted him. Under 'questioning' he had admitted selling John to the Germans for 300,000 French francs (the equivalent of £1,000 in modern currency). He said his sister desperately needed the money as she had no other way to make ends meet, but Guillaume's colleagues showed no mercy. Wall was handed over to the Communist Francs-Tireurs Partisans and shot the same day.[25]

If Goldsmith thought the dramas he'd lived through in recent weeks would be enough to get him swiftly exfiltrated back to England, he was mistaken. With vital planning still to do before the second front the following year, Baker Street had more liaison work for him in the south. A courier, Nicole, who was the daughter of one of the directors of Guillaume's bank, came to the apartment with John's new identity card and other forged papers. His new cover was to be that of a respectable businessman who'd been ill in Paris and needed to go to the country to convalesce. To fit the part, Guillaume and Nicole bought him a new suit and shoes as well as a sober shirt and tie.

---

25 The FTP were the military wing of the French Communist Party's resistance movement, renowned for their toughness and discipline. A *tireur* was a rifleman in the Revolution.

One morning Monsieur Henri arrived and handed John a pack of cigarettes he'd been given by a market trader at Les Halles. Inside one of the Gauloises was a thin strip of paper bearing the name of a country town near Vichy, St Germain des Fosses, along with the code name of the man who would meet him there. Monsieur Henri had looked up trains. John was to leave from the Gare d'Austerlitz at ten o'clock on Monday, 27 July.

Monsieur Henri drove John to the station himself in a little three-wheeler that barely went faster than a milk float. Before they left a weeping Madame Tantzy had hugged John to her ample bosom and presented him with a black trilby hat she said had once been her father's. She thought it would go perfectly with his costume as a man of commerce.

As he mingled with the crowds under the high glass roof of Austerlitz station, remembering happy pre-war journeys on the Sud Express to Biarritz and Hendaye Plage, John became aware of plain-clothes men standing by the barrier. The suits and hats looked familiar, and for a minute he thought his tormentor with the red hair was waiting for him. Then all of a sudden a squad of German soldiers pushed their way through, scattering onlookers this way and that. Goldsmith and other travellers surged forward in their wake and the tide carried him on to the platform undetected and on to the train.

He'd purchased a first-class ticket and settled down into a compartment with what looked like innocuous fellow passengers. But just as they were about to leave another well-dressed businessman squeezed into the seat next to him. He drew John into conversation about the weather, the war, rationing and the black market. As they were chatting away, John noticed a large gold signet ring on the forefinger of the man's right hand. It was in the shape of a *croix gammée*, which was what the French called a swastika. 'Are you German by any chance?' John asked. 'For your French is perfect.' The man admitted that he had been born in southern Germany but had lived in Paris for 15 years and currently worked for a government department. Goldsmith had a good idea which one.

After about 20 minutes John got up and excused himself, saying he was going to see if he could find a friend who was meant to meet him on the train. He walked right down to a packed second-class compartment at the back and stayed there, nerves fraying, for the rest of the journey.

Changing trains at Vichy he hoped he'd left the Gestapo officer with the swastika ring behind but, when the local train disgorged him at St Germain des Fosses and there was no one there to meet him, he feared the worst. But then a dusty old Renault came barrelling up the station approach and screeched to a halt on the gravel. A man got out wearing plus fours and a cap. Smiling broadly, he walked up to John, exchanged the password and ushered his recovering 'city cousin' into the front seat of his car. 'Sorry I'm late,' he said. 'A difficult birth. Cigarette? I know I need one.'

The beaming French gentleman was Dr Costes-Broussard, code name Le Toubib or 'The Medic', and he was a country physician. With a profession that gave him the perfect excuse to travel all around the region and the petrol to go with it, he was also the leading non-military figure in the Giraudist Secret Army of the south.

16

LONG WAY HOME

Everything that John Goldsmith did during his period of 'convales-cence' was intended to build up the readiness of the Secret Army for the moment when the second front would finally begin. The French men and women John worked with no more knew the exact date of the invasion than he did. But they understood that every parachute drop and every directive from London and from General Giraud's headquarters in Algiers was designed to bring the eviction of the Germans a step closer.

During the months of June and July there were no parachute drops in the Zone Sud due to the short nights but in August there were 25, each of them comprising eight containers of arms and ammunition flown in by the RAF. The extra Bren guns, Sten guns, revolvers and wireless sets were badly needed. John estimated that there were around 32,000 Giraudist 'effectives' in the south, including 12,000 in Lyon and 3,000 in Toulouse. Some of them had guns that they'd retained in 1940 or seized from the Germans in guerrilla raids but they were desperate to receive more from London.

Sir Arthur Harris, head of RAF Bomber Command, had been resisting attempts to divert planes and air crew from the saturation bombing of German cities. Harris was contemptuous of SOE, describing it as 'amateurish, ignorant and irresponsible'. But acts of sabotage could be a lot more precise than aerial bombardment and kill fewer innocent civilians too. The passionate lobbying of men like the legendary RF Section agent Wing Commander Forest Frederick Yeo-Thomas, better known as Tommy or 'The White Rabbit', persuaded Churchill that if the invasion was to succeed, more arms had to be dropped to the Resistance from the air. The radio reports of John Goldsmith, both before and after his capture in Paris in June, helped to bolster those arguments.

Goldsmith and Costes-Broussard reconnoitred landing grounds together in the doctor's Renault, scouting out fields and meeting the reception committees who were all recruited locally and regarded as trustworthy men with essential local knowledge. John radioed back to Baker Street that he could see little advantage in replacing them with new faces flown in from outside.

Once landed, the British weapons were removed on lorries, of which the Secret Army had plenty along with ample supplies of petrol. Goldsmith reported to London that some 50,000 litres had been hidden in the south by August 1943. As for the guns, they were all oiled and packed in cases so that they wouldn't deteriorate if not required until the spring of 1944.

Goldsmith also sent back intelligence on the Garde Mobile, paramilitary reserve units that had been created by the Vichy regime, supposedly to maintain order alongside the Gendarmerie. From the summer of 1943 they began to be used in offensive operations against the Resistance in the Midi (all of southern France from the south-western shore to the Pyrenees, Languedoc, the Côte d'Azur and the Italian frontier on the Mediterranean). But John's assessment of their GHQ in Vichy was that their officers were almost entirely pro-Ally, some for patriotic reasons, some to save their own skins. The one exception was their Commandant, General Perrett, but he was dismissed by Le Toubib as 'a collaborator who will be liquidated on D-Day'.

The Garde had light machine guns, revolvers, hand grenades and motorbikes and sidecars, all of which, John observed, would come in extremely useful to the Resistance once the rising began. By 'Resistance' Goldsmith and Costes-Broussard were still thinking of the Giraudist resistance, tough military types that they expected to take the lead in any action. By contrast, the Gaullist Committee for National Resistance, which was also organising secret armies and arms dumps, was seen by SOE as primarily a political body that was already thinking of the future governance of France. In June the CNR had suffered a devastating blow when its leaders were arrested and Jean Moulin, a potential post-war Prime Minister, brutally tortured to death. By the time of the invasion John Goldsmith expected the Gaullists and the Giraudists to have merged into one body, which was an accurate assessment, except that John still fondly imagined that it was General Giraud who would take the lead.

By late August John's 'convalescence' had come to an end and, knowing that the Gestapo had posted his name and photograph all over France, SOE were anxious to pull him out. But the way home was not easy. Buckmaster wanted to get him on one of Henri Déricourt's Lysander flights but they couldn't be sure when a seat would be available and they couldn't organise it while John was still in the south. To be ready to move as soon as the signal came through he would first have to return to Paris where he would be most at risk.

Feeling every inch a wanted man but trying not to look it, John dressed again in his sober businessman's suit with Madame Tantzy's father's black trilby and a pair of spectacles and, on the morning of 3 September, boarded a train at Vichy. At four o'clock that afternoon he was met at Austerlitz station by his old friend Robert Mathet-Dumaine who had the Rivaud family Packard waiting outside. The car was a conspicuous statement of wealth and privilege and they attracted some abuse and resentful looks from hungry, oppressed onlookers. But, as so often in John's clandestine life, taking the smart, expensive option, even though it meant close proximity to the Germans, was much safer than scurrying down the steps into the Métro and heading for a one-room apartment out beyond the Gare du Nord.

Robert, comfortably placed thanks to a new contract with the occupiers, drove them back to his apartment on the avenue Marceau, which was to be John's refuge for the next fortnight. The flat was at the heart of the smart neighbourhood around l'Etoile and the avenue George V that was known as the Nazi Triangle. Stretched out on the window seat in Robert's first-floor sitting room, John could see staff cars driving past every day taking German officers to lunch at Prunier where they could sample the best new-season oysters from Marennes and the Oloron Basin. For most shriven and despairing French citizens, Paris that September was sadder and more miserable than ever, a city of empty food shops and acorn coffee and wooden-soled shoes. But for a secret agent like Goldsmith and a double agent like Mathet-Dumaine, maintaining an appearance of profitable collaboration was the way to survive.

The two men attempted to keep tension at bay by talking for hours on end about horse racing. John formally asked his friend if he'd send him Kargal to train after the war. Of course he would, Robert replied, and they'd win many races together. John was touched by Robert's faith in the prospects of an Allied victory, not to mention their chances of both living to see it. But he was also intrigued by his belief in the likely superiority of French bloodstock in peace-time Europe. Thanks to German patronage, French racehorses had enjoyed an uninterrupted supply of the best oats and straw throughout the hostilities whereas many of their English counterparts had been on short rations, just like the humans who looked after them. What a difference that might make when the money was down.

After a week, John's orders came through from London, passed on to Mathet-Dumaine by one of Guillaume Lecointre's couriers. On the afternoon of Friday, 17 September, John was to take a train to Angers, some 200 miles south-west of Paris. A contact would be waiting for him there with a bicycle and together they would ride seven miles to Henri Déricourt's escape field, code name Indigestion, north by north-west of the village of Villeveque.

Feeling jubilant at the thought of going home and being reunited with his wife and daughter but also fearful of another betrayal, John was driven back to the station in Mathet-Dumaine's Packard. Ten hours later he was one of a group of half a dozen men in coats and hats clutching small suitcases and huddling in the lee of a hedgerow on the edge of a vast moonlit field. Déricourt and his reception committee, more than 20 of them in total, some of them armed, had shepherded them from a warm farmhouse down dark lanes and cart tracks to the landing area. The escapees saw the stakes driven into the ground to mark the places where the men with torches would stand to flash the correct signal to the approaching Lysander pilot. Two Lizzies were due to land, bringing three agents in and taking two planeloads of passengers out again.

John's fellow travellers were Ben Cowburn, a fiercely brave Lancastrian and former oil technician who was completing his third SOE mission, Henri Déricourt's second-in-command Rémy Clément, who was going over to Tangmere for a flying course, an escaped Polish POW, a young RAF tail-gunner who had been shot down over Troyes, and Guillaume Lecointre, who had been meant to leave from a field near Compiègne the previous night and was a last-minute addition to the party.

As the group looked on anxiously, their suitcases now stacked up ready for embarkation, the moon illuminated the water meadow ahead of them. When they heard what sounded like a loud trampling from the far side of the field their French guardians crouched down and grasped their rifles, the safety catches off. But the shapes emerging out of the darkness were not the Gestapo but French cows lumbering slowly in the opposite direction to the incoming flight path.

Goldsmith, concentrating hard and feeling the adrenalin pumping, could hardly believe that two British aeroplanes could land safely and take off again fewer than ten miles from Angers and its Wehrmacht garrison. But Déricourt, whose SOE code name was Gilbert, and Clément seemed totally at ease, for reasons that would have horrified John if he'd known about them. There was some talk among the group about the fate and whereabouts of other agents the two air transport officers had handled. In particular John was disturbed by rumours that his old Wanborough Manor and Arisaig classmate Gilbert Norman had succumbed to Kieffer's and the SD's blandishments while in captivity at the avenue Foch. There were suggestions that he may have given away the names and contacts of dozens of other members of the Prosper circuit.

Déricourt and Clément admitted they were both suspicious of Agent Archambaud, as Norman had been known, and hinted that they might be able to say more if they had the time. But all of a sudden there was a faint buzzing overhead and then a few minutes later the first Lysander appeared, dropping towards them like a bird out of the night sky. The signals were flashed, the torches lit, and the plane landed, taxied, turned through 180 degrees and came to a stop opposite the waiting huddle.

John felt French hands on his back urging him forward over the wet grass. He saw the arriving passengers as they were helped down the ladder and handed their suitcases. A woman brushed his arm as they passed. The 32-year-old Yolande Beekman was one of the steadiest and most capable students to pass through Wanborough Manor where she had been in Major de Wesselow's final mentoring group. She had gone on to do special training as a wireless operator and was going to work around St Quentin in Picardy. But an SD direction-finding team would catch up with her the following January and, almost a year on from her night-time arrival near Angers, she and three other women agents would be shot at Dachau.

Despite three men being crammed into each Lysander's rear cockpit where there was really only room for two, John would remember 'Operation Milliner', as his escape was known, working seamlessly. He put it all down to Henri Déricourt's expert direction. Like all the others he was blissfully unaware that, to protect himself and his Paris wife, Déricourt was indeed working hand in hand with the SD. They allowed his departing flights to go ahead, taking agents out of France, but in certain cases they monitored the landings and tailed incoming agents almost from the moment of their arrival. Henri Lafont's gang, including the redheaded bully who'd arrested John in June, lurked near the landing grounds, and on one occasion Josef Kieffer was there too, watching from a safe distance. The Germans knew an Allied invasion was coming soon and Kieffer may have believed that, sooner or later, Déricourt would bring in English officers with precise details of the date and location. It was later thought that the SD were near Villeveque and watching Operation Milliner on the night of 17 September 1943.

Déricourt may not have told them that Jean Delannoy was one of his outgoing passengers but, helped by Gilbert Norman's captured radio set, he as good as betrayed many others straight into the Germans' hands.[26]

The pilot who flew John Goldsmith, Ben Cowburn and Rémy Clément back to England was Wing Commander Bob Hodges, who went on to become an Air Chief Marshal. The second plane was piloted by Flight Officer Jimmy Bathgate, a young New Zealander with a fair moustache. The journey was completed in under two hours with only light flak over the French coast and no sign of any German night fighters. When they arrived at Tangmere, Vera Atkins was there to greet them, sharing the station wagon with Corporal Elston-Evans. They were all driven back to the cottage in the village where the NCOs, Blaber and Booker, cooked them a breakfast of bacon and eggs and coffee with fresh milk that was better than anything John had tasted for the last six months.

Their personal effects were retrieved for them from the cupboard behind the fireplace, John imagining the people who would never be coming back to reclaim theirs, and they were given time for a quick shower and shave. Then the uniformed FANY officer arrived, ready to drive them up to London and a de-briefing with the management at Orchard Court.

Just as he had been in February, John was greeted warmly by his commanding officers. 'I can't understand Goldsmith,' joked Selwyn Jepson. 'He always comes back looking better than when he went away.' There was only praise too from Maurice Buckmaster who told

---

26 Another theory, advanced after the war, is that Déricourt was not a double but a triple agent working for MI6. In this scenario the secret intelligence service were supposedly paying him to co-operate with the Germans as a way of diverting them from the Allies' real invasion plans.

John that the grateful French had awarded him a Palme to go with his Croix de Guerre. But after John had recounted the details of his arrest and extraordinary escape from the Hôtel Continentale in June, along with Kieffer's comment about having a man at Orchard Court, he was warned that MI5 would want to talk to him too. He had been temporarily in German custody and admitted having passed on some names, albeit blown, and information to his interrogators. The British security service would want to satisfy themselves that he was still their man and not in fact a double agent who had been turned while in captivity.

MI5's attentions were pressing and not entirely friendly but Buckmaster intervened to insist that for the next fortnight the returning Agent Valentin should be left in peace with his wife and family. At the end of the afternoon John was chauffeured back to the SOE South Kensington hotel where Annette was waiting for him. He had lost weight. He looked drawn and tired. But, to the surprise and great joy of both of them, he was still alive.

That night a short message was broadcast to France on the BBC World Service. 'Jean de la Lune a rejoint Annette et Gaie,' intoned the announcer. 'I repeat: Jean de la Lune a rejoint Annette et Gaie.' The message told Robert Mathet-Dumaine and Edouard Grosval, Madame Tantzy and Monsieur Henri, Dr Costes-Broussard and everyone else who had helped him escape that John Goldsmith was safe and back home with his wife and child.

The dangers they had risked on his behalf had not been in vain.

17

LONDON TO ALGIERS

John spent the first part of his leave at Foxhills, Annette's family home up in Cheshire. His mother-in-law was keen to show him off and one night there was a dinner party at the house of her neighbour, Lady Daresbury, where John's friend and fellow trainer Rip Bissill was also a guest. To Bissill's amusement the hostess, spurred on by Mrs Clover, told everyone present that John parachuted in and out of France whenever he felt like it. The Germans, she claimed, were powerless to stop him.

Goldsmith may have blushed at Lady Daresbury's exaggerations but hers was not the only English voice he heard brimming with superficial optimism. Ribbentrop's Mercedes, in which he'd been driven around the country when he was the German ambassador to London in the 1930s, was up for sale. The auction was seen as a symbol of the reckoning that would overtake all the Nazi leaders when the war was won. Following the success of the Dambusters raid the RAF were celebrating a 'lock-busting' raid in Holland, and in Italy, Allied forces were pressing north around Naples and Salerno, the newspaper coverage blissfully ignorant of the bloody fighting that lay ahead.

The landings in Italy might have been the big show in autumn 1943 but planning was now under way at the highest level for Operation Overlord, the projected Allied invasion of France in the summer of 1944. On 20 September Churchill returned from Canada and the Quebec Conference with Roosevelt at which the two leaders had begun to discuss specific details of what would become the Normandy Landings. The Prime Minister's train arrived back at Euston at 9.30 p.m. As he got out on to the platform, smoking an enormous cigar, the blackout was temporarily lifted and the whole station bathed in light. Every porter, guard and ticket inspector gathered round to applaud as the PM, giving them his trademark V for Victory salute, was ushered through the crowd to his car.

Churchill's grasp of theatre and the capacity of a vivid image to uplift and inspire was unsurpassed. It was at the heart of his endorsement of SOE. But when John Goldsmith reported back to Orchard Court, the news of his colleagues and former classmates still in France was anything but inspiring. Jimmy Amps, whose hopes of quietly living out the war with his French wife and family had been cruelly dashed, was in the Fresnes Prison in Paris, in the same cellblock as the former scoutmaster Rowland Dowlen, who had radioed back news of the first wave of Prosper arrests. An SD wireless detection finding team had tracked him down in August. The cockney bargee's son Arthur Staggs was still at large somewhere in the north. But the fatally indiscreet Brian Rafferty, who had crossed John's path on the train journey outside Toulouse, had been caught on his way to a parachute drop and was also in the Fresnes.

The Germans pursued radio operators relentlessly and many more of them were rounded up in the wake of the Prosper disaster. In October the luminously beautiful Noor Inayat Khan, one of the four women who had flown out together from Tangmere that summer, was betrayed in Paris and taken to the avenue Foch. Then the next month, John Goldsmith's great friend John Young was trapped in a sawmill he was hiding in near Lons-le-Saunier in the Jura. Between May and November the good-humoured Geordie with the shaky French accent had sent 88 messages back to London. With him at the time of his capture was Diana Rowden, a 28-year-old courier who had gone into the field on the same Lysander flight as Noor in June. The sequence of disasters culminated at the end of November when Sidney Jones, the Elizabeth Arden rep who had gone to France by felucca with John in 1942 and shared that sunny Sunday lunch with him and the Bartoli family outside Cannes, was arrested in Paris.

Unless they could escape the prospects for all these captive agents were bleak, though so far there was no indication that any of them had cracked and told the Germans what they wanted to know. The case of Gilbert Norman was more perplexing. Agent Archambaud, the inexhaustible athlete and self-appointed leader of the group at Wanborough Manor and Arisaig, was apparently alive and well and living at 82 avenue Foch. Messages smuggled out of the Fresnes said that newly arrested agents had seen him there when they were brought in for cross-examination by Kieffer and that Norman had encouraged them to talk, telling them that resistance was futile as the SD knew everything.

Norman had apparently hidden his wireless set in a house belonging to the parents of a French comrade. When he turned up there with three Germans in plain clothes the French family were horrified and initially imagined that the SD men must have been bribed or won over. But when Norman asked them to hand over the transmitter to his new companions they charitably assumed he was giving up 'the small people' in order to 'save the important ones'.

An impression was building that Norman was a traitor, but the cruellest aspect of his story had not yet been revealed. As a prisoner under duress he had sent London a radio message omitting his usual security check and substituting a pre-arranged false check that should have alerted the firm to the probability that he had been captured and that his wireless set was blown. But the SOE F Section chief Maurice Buckmaster had radioed back that Archambaud should 'stop fooling around' and go back to using the proper check next time he was transmitting.

It was one of Buckmaster's biggest mistakes of the war, and it was Gilbert Norman's tipping point, especially when he had to watch Dr Josef Goetz, master of the 'Funkspiel' or Radio Game, playing his wireless set back to Baker Street repeatedly over the next few weeks using the usual security code. London's replies detailed forthcoming Lysander missions and parachute drops and the orders and whereabouts of many agents already in the field. In their own time the SD arrested them all, finally convincing Buckmaster that Norman was 'a goner' and 'probably a double agent'.

John Goldsmith, unaware of the whole story, was shocked by Norman's apparent betrayal of his colleagues. But, though never less than loyal to Buckmaster and the firm, he was also angry that someone like the jockey Jimmy Amps, despite being nearly illiterate, had ever been considered for the job of a wireless operator, and he was weighed down with sadness over the fate of John Young. In the circumstances it was a relief to go racing.

On Saturday, 18 September, the day of John's return to Tangmere, thousands of spectators, many of them in uniform, packed into Newmarket's July course to see the 1943 substitute St Leger. Those bookmakers who'd continued trading throughout the war reported that over £2 million (£40 million today) was bet on the race, much more than the last pre-war running at Doncaster in 1938, and that £100 cash bets were commonplace on course. The bookies had to pay out over £100,000 (£2 million at current rates) on the result as Lord Derby's filly Herringbone, given a brilliant ride by Harry Wragg – who was nicknamed 'The Head Waiter' – came late and snatched the prize on the line.

Interest in the Turf was booming, reflected by the soaring prices paid for yearlings at the Newmarket sales. High rollers, including not a few who had profited from the black market and seemed inured to wartime losses, were gambling on the value of their new colts and fillies climbing sharply once the conflict was over. The upbeat mood continued on 2 October when Ascot staged a special meeting that had been officially sanctioned by George VI. Up until 1939 there had only been one fixture a year on the Heath, the four-day Royal meeting in June. Traditionalists argued that further racing would be a dilution of Ascot's position and prestige but the King didn't share that view and was more than happy for a touch of democratisation to lift battered wartime spirits.

The main features on a seven-race card were substitute versions of the Cambridgeshire and Cesarewitch, the two legs of the so-called Autumn Double, traditionally run on Newmarket's Rowley Mile. So popular was the event that 15,000 racegoers, including John and Annette Goldsmith, found a way to get there even though petrol rationing meant that no more than 200 of them arrived by car. Some came in horse-drawn vehicles, shooting brakes and dog carts while others relied on the normal Southern Region train service from Waterloo.

There was no royal enclosure, this being a democratic Ascot, and 30 shillings would buy you entrance into the main grandstand. The champagne flowed with 1929 Bollinger and Veuve Clicquot selling at 70 shillings a bottle, or £80 in modern money. There were over 100 bookmakers in the ring and thanks to the presence of scores of servicemen and women, including Americans flush with funds, not to mention off-duty factory workers, there was a record turnover on the Tote.

The society columnists, far from redundant in time of war, were out in force and the *Tatler* correspondent alighted on the smartly uniformed John Goldsmith and his wife who were photographed for the magazine's next issue. 'People there' said the caption under the picture. 'Everyone was delighted to see Captain John Goldsmith who used to train some good jumpers before the war. He was racing for the first time this year, having had many adventures as a paratrooper. Mrs Goldsmith, who was a bright figure in emerald green, has been doing stable work for John Beary.'

For Tiny, the day at the races offered a rare chance to dress up, to laugh, to chat, to see old friends, to have a drink and a bet and to escape, even briefly, the crippling tension of being a secret agent's wife. Tension that, according to the prevailing code of behaviour at the time, she was meant to rigidly suppress and control.

If her husband found it faintly surreal to feature in *Tatler* a few months after his 'many adventures' with the Gestapo he was too polite to say. And by the time the Ascot issue was on the news stands he'd been back to Orchard Court to hear what they had in mind for him next. MI5 were still asking questions about how he came to spend a night in the Hôtel Continentale but John was told the supporting testimony of Guillaume Lecointre and reports radioed from France by Colonel André Zeller, Dr Costes-Broussard and Commandant Lejeune should be enough to shut them up.

The idea of Kieffer having a man in SOE was worrying Buckmaster and Gubbins though. Was it Gilbert Norman or Henri

Déricourt, they wondered, or was it just an SD bluff? The situation was made more complicated by Norman's Christian name being the same as Déricourt's code name. Intercepted German intelligence reports frequently referred to 'Gilbert', but which one were they talking about?

It was in the months following that Buckmaster, and his MI5 and MI6 counterparts, decided they could no longer safely use Déricourt as their air movements officer. As far as John Goldsmith was concerned, though, the firm regarded him as a distinguished and highly valued agent who was 'brave, likeable and imposing'. But, as Buckmaster explained, he was so blown in Paris and the north of France that they couldn't risk sending him straight back there. So for the time being they were posting him to the SOE station in North Africa, code name Massingham, which organised arms drops and covert operations in the Mediterranean theatre.

On 4 November Captain Goldsmith said goodbye once more to Annette and Gaie and at dawn the next day his RAF transport plane landed in Algiers. The Club des Pins at Guyotville, about 13 kilometres west of the city, was a once-elegant French beach club surrounded by pine trees and date palms. In the 1930s it had been a favourite watering hole of rich colonial residents seeking a bit of exclusivity away from the heat and dust of the capital. In keeping with their penchant for taking over large, comfortable country houses, SOE had decided that the Club would do very nicely as their North African command, communication and training school, and Massingham had set up shop there in 1941.[27]

27 It was a recurring wartime joke that the acronym SOE really stood for the 'stately 'omes of England', and they favoured similar accommodation overseas.

By the time John Goldsmith arrived, almost three years of war had left the buildings looking rather shabby and down at heel. The net on the tennis court was sagging, the pool needed cleaning and paint was beginning to peel off the villa walls. But it was from this faded colonial setting, with its terrace overlooking the Mediterranean, that SOE and their French, Canadian and American allies planned acts of sabotage and weapons drops in Italy, Sardinia, Corsica and the south of France. There was an old commercial airfield adjoining the Club and the flying time to Provence and the Côte d'Azur was less than from England. At the beginning the station's efforts had been hampered by a lack of planes and resources. But, as the tempo inexorably increased in the countdown to 1944, so too did the supply of money and aircraft to support the southern arm of the liberation.

The commanding officer at Massingham, Lieutenant Colonel Douglas Dodds-Parker, described the Club as 'a playboy's paradise'. The fine weather, very different to the rain and mist at Arisaig, made it easy to practise beach landings and parachute drops, and the clear skies meant that supply planes could fly to France in all seasons. Civilian exercises were carried out in Algiers itself and, at the day's end, British officers could relax with a sundowner around the pool. But beyond the Club walls the political situation in North Africa was anything but straightforward.

From October 1943, the head of Massingham's French section was Lieutenant Commander Francis Brooks Richards who had previously been running SOE naval missions from Cornwall to Brittany and Gibraltar to the Mediterranean coast. The main task facing the adroit Brooks Richards was to manage the transfer of SOE's support from General Giraud to General de Gaulle, who had supplanted his older rival since arriving in Algiers in June. The merger of the two Resistance Secret Armies was happening just as John Goldsmith had expected it would. But, although Giraud didn't finally give up 'the unequal struggle' until the spring of 1944, it was de Gaulle – still haughty and obstreperous but by now a skilful political operator – who had become the dominant figure.[28]

It was an extremely delicate situation with the potential to embarrass the British government right up to Churchill himself. Maurice Buckmaster would later say that, despite backing Giraud for so long, SOE F Section switched their support to de Gaulle's FFI, or Forces Françaises de l'Intérieur, to avoid causing a split in the Resistance. But, as John discovered, almost every branch of the French military in Algiers seemed to be at odds with someone or other and it was only the strength of de Gaulle's personality that kept the whole thing together. The Gaullists were still suspicious of the British. The Giraudists distrusted the Gaullists but also felt the British had let them down. The remnants of the Vichy regime's officer class loathed the British and were suspicious of the Gaullists who, for their part, would have loved to put the Vichy officers up against a wall.

In John Goldsmith's eyes the one characteristic all these Frenchmen shared, Algerian Pieds Noir included, was a contemptuous disdain for the local Arab population whose yearning for self-determination would erupt eventually in a savage colonial war.[29] But fortunately for John, his dealings were not so much with the French military as with individual French agents, many of whom had backgrounds every bit as diverse as their British counterparts. It

28 Giraud had directed the liberation of Corsica in September/October 1943 but the following April he retired. M.R.D. Foot, writing in *SOE in France*, felt that Giraud was too closely identified with 'the established order' whereas de Gaulle offered a break with the past.

29 The Algerian War lasted from 1956 to 1962. The Pieds Noir, or Blackfeet, were people of French descent who had lived in Algeria for generations. Many of them returned to mainland France when Algeria became independent.

was John's job to go through their cover stories, brief them on what conditions to expect in the field, covering everything from *jours sans* (days without alcohol or meat) to buying train tickets and acquiring black market food and clothing coupons, and supervise their parachute and explosives training.

British officers at Massingham slept four in a room but at least they had their own mess and orderlies who waited on them. French agents completing their training had to sleep in huts and queue up for their meals at the cookhouse. Social and recreational amenities for the French were almost non-existent and many of them attempted to inoculate themselves against the boredom by escaping into Algiers where every imaginable pleasure and perversion could be indulged in. On more than one occasion John had to drag an agent out of a brothel in the middle of the night and drive him back to the airfield, pale and hung over, where a Halifax or Lysander was waiting to take him on a pre-dawn flight to Provence.

To make life more tolerable, John got Brooks Richards' permission to convert a number of beach bungalows into private rooms for resting or waiting agents, and servants were provided. Goldsmith also cut a deal with a local wine grower whose son was a French officer. The vineyard owner supplied the base with crates of good wine at a discount in return for a share of the scarce bread made by Massingham's Spanish bakers. By March 1944 the tennis court had been refurbished and agents could play basketball and go riding in the surrounding countryside. There were even Saturday night dances, attended by eager young women from the other services, with music provided by a jazz band that had once played with Django Reinhardt and Stéphane Grappelli in the Hot Club de France.

The ambience may have been more agreeable but there were no illusions about the job Massingham's agents were being trained to do. The long struggle to evict the Nazis from the occupied countries was reaching its climax, and John Goldsmith was about to play a crucial part in the denouement. In the summer of 1944 the French would settle their accounts with the Germans, but first they had to be persuaded to join arms with one another.

18

MAQUIS

On 6 June 1944 more than 150,000 Allied servicemen came ashore on the Normandy beaches – Utah, Omaha, Gold, Juno and Sword. Over 4,000 of them died on the first day and, by the end of the Normandy campaign in August, total Allied casualties would amount to over a quarter of a million killed, wounded and missing in action. It was brutal, attritional fighting that dragged on for weeks. Cherbourg held out until 26 June, and it wasn't until 21 July, the day after the abortive July Plot against Hitler in Berlin, that Caen, or the obliterated rubble that remained of it, fell to the British.

In the days and nights leading up to Operation Overlord the BBC broadcast hundreds of cryptic messages to France, phrases and lines of poetry that were intelligible only to the *résistantes* and SOE circuits listening in to them. The years of planning and the scores of dead agents were finally to be vindicated as dozens of SOE circuits went into action, carrying out acts of sabotage and disrupting rail traffic and communications. The most conspicuous successes were in the south-west where, partly thanks to the efforts of George Starr's guerrilla band, the 2nd SS

Panzer Division, Das Reich, were delayed by two weeks in their attempted journey from Toulouse to reinforce the Normandy bridgehead.[30]

But the Allies weren't aiming only to hit the Germans in the north. A second amphibious invasion, Operation Dragoon, was planned for August in the south. In advance of the landings it was the job of SOE Massingham in Algiers to strengthen those Resistance groups that were most likely to be able to harass the enemy, cut off reinforcements and impede their withdrawal north. The passage of the Rhône valley from Avignon to Valence was going to be a key battleground and waiting for the Germans in the high country east of the river were going to be the most famous of all French Resistance groups.

In some rural corners of the Midi and south-eastern France the very word 'Maquis' still brings tears to old eyes. The name, supposedly Corsican in origin, refers to the rough bush, the scrubland or garrigue, in which the bands of armed guerrillas lived and hid out. Whereas *résistantes* in towns and cities stayed in houses and apartments and had outwardly normal jobs by day, the Maquis were outliers like the Confederate guerrillas on the Missouri–Kansas border during the American Civil War.

The Vichy regime had unintentionally contributed to the rise of the Maquis thanks to the infamous Service Travail Obligatoire which Pierre Laval had made compulsory in February 1943. To avoid being rounded up and sent to work in Germany, hundreds and then thou-

---

30   One of the worst atrocities of the war took place on 10 June 1944 in Oradour-
     sur-Glane in the Limousin region north of Toulouse. Frustrated by persistent
     Resistance activity in the area, the 2nd SS Panzer Division destroyed the village
     and murdered 642 of its inhabitants. On de Gaulle's orders the village was never
     rebuilt but left as a permanent memorial to the victims of the Occupation.

sands of young men took to the hills and woods, arming themselves as best they could and vowing not to return to their homes until the occupiers had been defeated. Clad in little more than a pair of trousers, an open-necked shirt and a beret with a Sten gun or old hunting rifle slung over their shoulders, the Maquis were brave and often careless of their own safety.

They weren't a national organisation. There were dozens of different Maquis groups, some of them only really interested in liberating their own departments. Brimming with local knowledge, they could cause serious problems for the Germans. But for the purposes of Operation Dragoon, they needed to be properly armed and unified and told to play to their strengths. It was not for them to confront the enemy en masse or in the open; they could leave that to the incoming American and Free French armies. Their role would be to hit and run, to wound and to harass and then to fade back into the landscape, like the Native American Indians harrying the US Cavalry.

Whereas Vichy dismissed the Maquis as outlaws, de Gaulle and SOE saw that they were ideally placed to collect and hide stores of parachuted arms. But although some groups were properly clothed and organised, others were hungry and untrained. There were Gaullist Maquisards, Giraudists, nationalists, royalists and Communists and the latter were suspected of keeping weapons for themselves to use in some future civil war inside France. SOE and de Gaulle agreed that, for the invasion to be a success, it was vital for these disparate elements in Provence and the Vaucluse to be brought together. To achieve that, Massingham decided to launch Operation Orfroi, an inter-Allied mission, one month ahead of Dragoon. Politics dictated that a Frenchman, the Gaullist officer Commandant Gonzague Corbin de Mangoux, should lead it. But the second-in-command, and the man charged by the British with 'obtaining the maximum effort from the forces of resistance', was John Goldsmith. It was to be his third and final mission for SOE and it would draw on everything he had been taught at Wanborough Manor and Arisaig and all that he had learned during almost three years of war.

John's orders were to get the Gaullist Forces Françaises de l'Intérieur and the Communist Francs-Tireurs Partisans in particular to agree to have one military chief. Whoever was appointed would take priority when it came to receiving and issuing arms and, as long as that condition was met, SOE would supply them with the necessary funds to improve their food, shelter and clothing. To make the job easier, Massingham had decided that John should work as closely as possible with an FFI officer called Camille Rayon who was felt to have sufficient influence to make the Maquis leaders co-operate. In June, Rayon was flown over to Algiers from the Vaucluse to spend several days at the Club des Pins and be apprised of SOE's intentions.

Thirty-one years old with dark black hair, blue eyes and what John Goldsmith called a 'face like a wolf', Rayon was a 'Grand Patron' of the Resistance. Born in Biot in the Alpes-Maritimes, he was running a bar in Antibes when the war broke out. A passionate anti-fascist, he'd spent some time in Munich in the 1930s in Tyrolean disguise attempting to hatch a plan to kill Hitler.

After the humiliating French surrender in June 1940, Rayon escaped to Britain via Spain and was recommended to SOE for paramilitary training. A supporter of de Gaulle from the outset, he'd been parachuted into Provence several times and by 1944 was one of the General's FFI staff officers with special responsibility for all arms drops, evacuation of Allied airmen and subversive actions in seven departments on the east bank of the Rhône. He commanded a force of a thousand men based around the village of Lagarde on the Albion plateau. It was arid, hilly country stretching from Céreste overlooking the Luberon Valley to Forcalquier and its lavender fields, and villages like Banon and Sault under the shadows of Mont Ventoux – the so-called Beast of Provence. The town of Apt was 26 kilometres to the south and Avignon, the administrative centre of the Vaucluse, was the same distance away on the banks of the Rhône.

Rayon, code name Archiduc, was lean, hard and charming, a man of seemingly inexhaustible energy and verve. He made an instant impression on the French-speaking British SOE agent and the feeling was entirely mutual. Massingham could send him any officer they wanted, Rayon joked to Brooks Richards, as long as his name was John Goldsmith. He even secured John's promotion from the rank of Captain to Major, and when Goldsmith set out to follow him a month later he wore his RAC battle dress jacket rather than the civilian garb of a spy.

On 11 July Commandant de Mangoux was flown into the Vaucluse by Lysander. Five nights later SOE dropped a wireless operator. Then on the night of 18 July John Goldsmith left Algiers in a Halifax bomber accompanied by a French Canadian Major from Montreal and two FFI officers. When John had said goodbye to Tiny in London the previous November he had assured her that he was only going to Massingham in a training role. She had stoically endured the weeks of nagging anxiety during his two tours of duty as an undercover agent but this time, he promised, there would be no service in the field. It was just a desk job. A piece of cake, as the Lysander pilots might say. Yet here he was about to parachute back into Occupied France and honestly, truthfully, it was a thrilling sensation. There would be none of the loneliness and tension of going solo as he had done in 1942 and 1943. This time he was going to join the Maquis and the FFI and, before it was all over, he was going to fight the Germans at close range.

There was no moon but the weather was fine and dry with no cloud and John had what he called excitedly 'a wonderful trip'.[31] The Halifax crew were on their seventieth and final operational mission and had all the experience in the world. The RAF despatcher ushered John through the hatch at 600 feet, his chute opened without a problem, and he floated effortlessly to the ground exactly on target. The landing zone, code name Armateur, was one of two on the plateau near Camille Rayon's camp outside Lagarde and Archiduc was on the ground himself with the reception committee.

As John got out of his parachute and harness, Rayon's men moved quickly and efficiently to unpack the containers of arms that had been dropped from the sky after the four officers. First they loaded them on to a cart and then into a lorry waiting under the trees. Everyone seemed to know exactly what to do and where to go and John was struck by the contrast with the chaotic melodrama of Carte's receptions on the Côte d'Azur in 1942.

Within half an hour, the French Canadian and his two colleagues had been whisked away in different directions and John was sitting in Camille Rayon's powerful grey Citroën – no worries about petrol for le Grand Patron – as they sped down a dusty white track leading ever further into the interior. Their destination was an abandoned farmhouse where, just like in Juan-les-Pins in 1942, John was told to take off his uniform and swap it for a simple shirt and a pair of old trousers. Bed was a wooden bench in a ruined barn lit by oil lamps, but an exhilarated John Goldsmith lay down under a blanket that smelled of horseflesh and tobacco and slept like a baby.

The world he awoke to the next day was a place of brilliant sunshine and clear Mediterranean light filtering through the rafters

31   John Goldsmith de-briefing, National Archives.

of the barn and the branches of the trees. Looking around him he could see that some of Rayon's men had made improvised tents out of tarpaulins and empty weapons crates while others had slept on the ground in the ruined outbuildings. Breakfast was strong black coffee, a hunk of bread and a cigarette.

Camille Rayon returned at 8 a.m., seemingly untroubled by so little sleep, and in the still fresh July morning the pair of them set off in his Citroën to begin a tour of neighbouring Maquis bands.

In the cultivated country below the plateau there were lavender fields and fig trees as well as more scrub oak and garrigue. As they raced along the chalk tracks and unmarked roads the scents of lavender and thyme mingled with the eye-watering smoke from Rayon's Gitanes Maïs or yellow paper cigarettes. They swept down into valleys and crossed ridges, passing more abandoned houses and farms, and from time to time they saw Maquis look-outs, young boys in berets maybe no more than 16 or 17 years old, crouching by the side of the road, revolvers in their belts and a Sten gun balanced on their hip.

Any unease John may have felt about the likelihood of a British officer persuading the various guerrilla chiefs to unite under one command was dispelled by the total confidence of his French host and driver. Arriving in Camille's company immediately vouchsafed John's credentials. It also helped that, unlike some other British intelligence officers in the south, he spoke fluent French in a tone that was blunt but never patronising.

The first leader John met was the Forces Françaises de l'Intérieur Lieutenant Colonel, Philippe Beyne, whose men were camped on the lower slopes of Mont Ventoux. The former Montélimar tax collector was a 48-year-old veteran soldier who had fought with the 152nd Infantry Division, the Red Devils, at Colmar in Alsace. The Colonel was an honourable socialist and patriot and his military record made him the obvious choice for the role of commander-in-chief. He listened patiently to their request and then invited them to stay to lunch which they ate outside at a table in the shade. They had thick slices of *sanglier*, or wild boar, with bread and red wine and Beyne discoursed gravely on whether de Gaulle or the Communists would form a government in France when the war was over. John Goldsmith, listening to the cicadas and watching the lizards warming themselves in the sun, tried to imagine what peacetime life would be like back in England if he lived that long.

Over the next few days Goldsmith and Rayon visited Louis Malarte, an Avignon dental surgeon, and Jean Garcin, code name Commandant Bayard, who were the heads of the Groupe Francs based in the village of St Christol near Apt. Then finally they made contact with Commandant Lombard, head of the Communist Francs-Tireurs Partisans. The FTP were the most suspicious of SOE's intentions and they wouldn't let John and Camille come right into their camp. Instead Lombard and three lieutenants emerged suddenly out of the woods, bandoliers across their chests, looking like a cross between Mexican bandits and chasseurs on a Sunday morning hunt.

The early years of the war had been uncomfortable for the hard left who were constrained by the Molotov-Ribbentrop Pact, Moscow's temporary non-aggression pact with Berlin signed in August 1939. But once the Germans invaded Russia in the summer of 1941 the Communists in France established themselves as some of the toughest and most disciplined Resistance fighters while professing little love for the British and Americans. Remembering his political warfare lessons at Beaulieu, John told them that SOE had absolutely no interest in their differences of opinion with other guerrilla groups and how they shaped France when the occupiers were gone was entirely their business. All SOE wanted was to work with them in the most effective way possible to destroy the German armies in the south. If they and Malarte and Bayard agreed to accept the overall leadership of Colonel Beyne, the Patron would straight away give them enough arms to supply 400 of their men and more would be dropped nightly in the run-up to Dragoon. To John's delight the FTP, like the Groupe Francs and all the other Maquis leaders, agreed to the plan.

Each evening John and Rayon went back to the camp on the plateau. Dinner was a mixture of olive oil and garlic enlivened by whatever stray bird or feathered or furry creature the Maquis had managed to trap or shoot in the surrounding woods. In winter life in the hills had been hard, but going hunting on hot summer days reminded John of the poaching expeditions at Arisaig – except that these were conducted in 30° heat.

Every night between 19 July and 14 August there was another parachute drop bringing tins of petrol and cases of guns, ammunition and stores. A plane could carry a dozen containers at a time. One load might comprise 50,000 rounds of ammunition and 240 Bren and Sten gun magazines; another might have three dozen Lee Enfield rifles or American carbines, bazookas and their rockets, explosives and their fuses and field dressings. Rayon continually implored the wireless operator to radio Massingham and ask them to send an RAF plane. The British pilots came in low and invariably hit the target whereas the Americans were jumpy and flew too fast and dropped their parcels from too great a height. Sometimes their containers would come smashing and splintering into the trees, scattering their contents all around, and once they dropped a consignment of Mills bombs on the main street in Apt.

The Maquis' preparations were almost complete but the guerrillas were continually warned not to come out too soon or try to engage the Wehrmacht head on before the Allies arrived. Rayon's disparate troops, putting dissension to one side, obeyed the directive faithfully. Unlike the Maquis on the Vercors Plateau 50 miles to the north who bravely, foolishly and tragically tried to fight a pitched battle with the Germans in late July. The uprising was brutally suppressed by the SS and the French fascist Milice resulting in more than 800 Maquisard and civilian deaths.

Camille Rayon was furious when he heard the fate of his impatient neighbours. 'The fools. Why didn't they wait?' he kept saying to John Goldsmith. But even Archiduc and the English Major made mistakes. Not long before John arrived in the Vaucluse, a young French agent, code name Noel, had been parachuted in from Algiers but had missed the landing zone. Several weeks later Camille's men found him wandering in the garrigue about seven miles south of their camp. Noel claimed that he'd been trained at Massingham and told to make contact with the Vaucluse Maquis. He said that Commandant Goldsmith would know all about him.

Noel was taken to a café in Apt where both Rayon and Goldsmith came to interrogate him. John indeed recognised him and told Camille that he believed he was genuine. Rayon suggested contacting Massingham all the same to check his story but Goldsmith knew the Algiers station was overrun with messages going back and forth about the imminent invasion and wouldn't welcome unnecessary enquiries. Rayon was still unsure and refused to take Noel under his command. But he did offer him to a Communist FTP splinter group who he thought would keep an eye on him. The young Frenchman joined the cell outside Apt run by a Jewish architect called Max Wedermeyer. Two nights later he slipped out of their camp, stole a bicycle and rode into Avignon, returning at dawn with a platoon of SS who were able to sneak up on the unsuspecting FTP. The heroic

Wedermeyer and his comrades fought to the last, like El Sordo's band on the hilltop in *For Whom the Bell Tolls*, but 25 of them were killed along with 17 of Rayon's men whom he had sent to strengthen the group.

John Goldsmith felt mortified for failing to check out Noel's cover with Algiers. Le Grand Patron said he didn't blame him but Goldsmith could sense his rage. Within 36 hours Noel had been tracked down and shot dead in Marseille, but then on 4 August the Germans struck again. A teenage member of Rayon's Maquis left his post on a Saturday night and went into Avignon to see his girlfriend. Indiscreet chatter in public places alerted the Gestapo who tailed and abducted him. The next day the Germans threw the boy's body out of a car at a crossroads near Apt. When Rayon and Goldsmith saw it the corpse was barely recognisable. Both his eyes had been gouged out and his testicles had been cut off and shoved into his mouth.

Archiduc's retaliation was ruthless. Rayon and his Marseille gangster bodyguard kidnapped the French mistress of the Avignon Gestapo chief and the mistress's mother. He drove them up to the camp near Lagarde, arriving in the evening. The bodyguard got out and Camille told John Goldsmith to get in the car with him. The two women were tied up in the back. Camille drove further into the hills, finally stopping at the end of a rutted track leading into deep woods. He had a loaded pistol in his belt and he took another one out of the car's glove compartment and gave it to John. While Rayon dragged the younger woman into the woods on the right, John Goldsmith steered her mother into scrub on the left. John knew exactly what he was meant to do, and as the older woman knelt down, praying frantically, he pressed his gun against the back of her neck and pulled the trigger. As she fell forward he heard a second shot from the other side of the track.

It was a shocking moment. There are no scenes in John Buchan where Richard Hannay shoots an unarmed woman in cold blood. The 50-year-old, not a German soldier or a Gestapo chief, was the first person John Goldsmith had actually killed. But he understood the shooting was a test. The last one he had to pass in Camille Rayon's eyes. The final proof he was not an English outsider but a Maquisard as committed as the rest of them. It was war, said Rayon. The two women had been sleeping with the enemy and the younger one's lover had savagely mutilated and murdered an adolescent boy. But Goldsmith saw that for le Grand Patron this was not a hot-headed or emotional act. It was calculated. Camille would ensure that the Gestapo chief in Avignon received a message informing him of the fate of his mistress. The Germans would then come after the Maquis of the Vaucluse, which is exactly what Camille Rayon wanted them to do, and when they had placed their heads in the noose, Archiduc would have them.

19

MONT VENTOUX

The Allied invasion of southern France began in the same fashion as the Normandy Landings with an aerial bombardment and heavy shelling by the warships of the Western Fleet. An airborne task force had been dropped behind the landing zone in the early hours of 15 August, securing the strategic village of Le Muy which was about 25 kilometres inland from Fréjus. Then from 8 a.m. three American infantry divisions – the 3rd led by General 'Iron Mike' O'Daniel, the 36th and the 45th – went ashore at St Raphael, St Tropez and Cavalaire-sur-Mer. They were followed by the French 1st Armoured Division led by General Jean de Lattre de Tassigny, a flamboyant and aristocratic cavalryman and future Marshal of France. Among the senior officers at his side was General René Chambe, returning home for the first time since his escape across the Pyrenees with John Goldsmith in January 1943.

A total of 94,000 men and 11,000 vehicles were part of the initial landings. There was heavy fighting on Camel Red Beach at St Raphael but elsewhere the German coastal forces fell back surprisingly quickly.

The American commander, General Alexander 'Sandy' Patch, a veteran of Guadalcanal, discovered why when he received vital intelligence from Bletchley Park in England. The Ultra code break-ers had analysed and deciphered Enigma messages from Hitler's high command to his forces on the Mediterranean. Gradually retreating before the Allied advance in Normandy, the Germans were planning to set up a new defensive line from Sens in Burgundy to Dijon and the Swiss border. The Wehrmacht had been ordered to withdraw all their troops from the south other than the 11th SS Panzer Division who were to act as a rearguard for the retreating German army in the Rhône Valley. Patch decided he would try to block that withdrawal. He ordered the airborne units to guard his right flank between Fayence and La Napoule – where Agent Valentin had first come ashore in 1942 – and let the French swing left towards Toulon and Marseille. Meanwhile the Americans would 'thrust north' up the Durance river into Upper Provence and attempt to make contact with the Maquis.

Colonel Philippe Beyne's men had already been engaged in a series of short, sharp actions leading up to Dragoon. Motorcycle scouts had been picked off on the D543 road from Apt to Sault and a day later a lorry was fired on and five German soldiers killed. The occupiers responded with a punitive attack along the same road, briefly occupying Sault where five French hostages were shot. On 8 August Beyne trapped a small detachment of Panzers in a deep ravine south of the Château de Javon. Thanks to Camille Rayon's arms caches, Beyne's men had machine guns and grenades and the Nazi tanks were all put out of action in 12 minutes.

The successes were heartening but the German 19th Army Command in Avignon now had their eyes on the Albion Plateau and were less than a day's march away from Rayon's airstrips, Armateur and Spitfire. Fearful of another Vercors disaster, le Grand Patron sent John Goldsmith back to Algiers by Dakota on 12 August to brief them on the imperative need for more Bren guns and anti-tank weapons to keep the Germans at bay. This time Massingham complied straight away and on 13, 14 and 15 August there were successive heavy arms drops with planes coming and going by night and day.

D-Day in Provence was also John's 35th birthday, and he spent it back in the Vaucluse returning on one of the many flights bringing in new military advisers including an American who enraged Camille Rayon by taking a bath both morning and night and using up a disproportionate share of the available water. Not that any of the guerrillas had much time to wash. From the 15th onwards all the Maquis leaders Goldsmith and Rayon had met began blowing up bridges and railway lines, liquidating Garde Mobile units and piling further pressure on an already demoralised enemy.

The German General in command of the 19th Army was the 52-year-old Friedrich Wiese, a decorated veteran of the Russian Front who had been one of the conquerors in May 1940 when France was overrun in five weeks. Now he had to try to organise an orderly retreat towards the Vosges Mountains. He had originally hoped to hold the strategic gap at Orgon where the Durance flowed towards Avignon, but when that fell he saw it was vital to keep open an escape route across the plateau north of Mont Ventoux in case the southern roads were all lost.

On 19 August Rayon received intelligence from his spies in Avignon. The local Gestapo chief, vowing revenge for the killing of his mistress, had persuaded Wiese to send a 1,000-strong column up on to the Albion plateau. The objective was to clear out the Maquis and open the way for a full withdrawal, and the expedition would set off on 22 August taking the narrow D942 road that ran from Apt up into the foothills around Sault. At a hastily arranged meeting with

Beyne, Malarte and Lombard, le Grand Patron urged them to mount an ambush and Philippe Beyne agreed. He thought he knew exactly the right place to block the German advance.

The rough country south of Sault was textbook guerrilla warfare terrain. On the lower slopes the D942 was lined with thick undergrowth – a jumble of trees, rocks and thorn bushes that would offer perfect cover. Then as the road climbed higher the sides got steeper and, on the point of breasting the ridge, there were more boulders and rocky outcrops that could hide an anti-tank gun. Beyne and Rayon had three of them, and by dawn on 22 August they were dug in near the Armateur airstrip in camouflaged positions. Further down the hill there were Bren and American Thompson sub-machine guns, and at the bottom hundreds of Maquis armed with Sten guns and grenades were hiding in the woods like the Sioux and the Cheyenne waiting for Custer at the Little Bighorn.

Halfway up the hillside in the trees beside the road was Camille Rayon in dusty army fatigues and a French paratrooper's red beret with the ribbons hanging down the back. By his side in his RAC battle dress jacket was Major John Goldsmith, husband, father and English racehorse trainer and gentleman gambler who had never been shot at before.

It was another brilliant Provençal morning. By 10 a.m. the sun was high in the sky and John could hear a faint droning sound in the distance as the first German tanks reached the bottom of the incline. There were 12 of them, Panzer Mark IIIs, at the head of a convoy of 36 vehicles, the tanks followed by motorcycles and troop carriers, the German soldiers standing up and holding on to the sides of the open lorries.

Obeying Beyne's and Lombard's and Rayon's orders the Maquis held their fire and waited until the tanks had got right up to the edge of the plateau a mile away. Then the anti-tank guns and the Bren guns opened up, the booming explosions echoing back down the slope to where John Goldsmith was waiting anxiously. It later transpired that several of the German tanks got stuck in the narrow defile and were unable either to reverse or turn around. Rayon's heavy weapons destroyed them, palls of black smoke drifting over the countryside accompanied by the stench of cordite and burnt rubber. Some of the troop carriers had tried to overtake the abandoned tanks but then they too came under fire from the Maquis machine-gun nests, and soon dozens of Germans were running and scrambling back down the steep track. When they reached Rayon's vantage point in the trees he opened fire with his Sten gun and suddenly all the woodland and garrigue was crackling with rifle fire.

John Goldsmith quickly discovered that a Sten was every bit as unreliable as he'd been warned. Discarding the jammed and useless gun he started running down the hill through the trees, going parallel with the road and hurling grenades one after another at the German trucks. He was as accurate and deadly as a top Test match cricketer throwing the ball in from the covers and, convulsed with that maniacal mixture of fear and adrenalin unforgettably described by Siegfried Sassoon in *Memoirs of an Infantry Officer*, he was shouting out in English at the top of his voice, 'Come on then you bastards! Come on! Come and get it!' Camille Rayon, amused but also worried that John would stop a bullet, told him afterwards that he was behaving 'like an old woman in red drawers'.[32]

Rayon was adamant that every German they killed now was one less to fight later and he and Goldsmith tracked some of the

---

32 *Accidental Agent*, p.176.

survivors into the undergrowth. Before the morning was over John finally got to use his Commando knife, the Bill Sykes design he'd first handled at Arisaig, and it was quick, bloody and lethal work.

Two hundred and fifty Germans were killed or wounded that day and all of their tanks were immobilised. The remainder of the column retreated back to Avignon. The Maquis didn't lose a single man. Neither did they take any prisoners. John Goldsmith would never forget the blazing August heat, the cloud of smoke and dust that obscured the sun and the sound of his French allies going among the German wounded and finishing them off with a single shot.

The ambush on Mont Ventoux was the climax of John Goldsmith's war and the culmination of everything he had trained to do with SOE. It also came within days of momentous steps in the liberation of France. On 24 August the Germans abandoned Avignon and, amid much rejoicing, Philippe Beyne's Forces Françaises de l'Intérieur entered the city. On the 26th Toulon fell to General de Lattre de Tassigny, and the following day Marseille surrendered. A telegram sent by de Lattre to Charles de Gaulle on 28 August informed him that 'as of D Day +13 the only Germans left in my army's sector are either dead or captive'.

The battle of Provence was over. On 3 September Lyon was liberated, and on 10 September the first American units from the south made contact with General George Patton's Third Army which had launched its Normandy breakout the month before.

Paris had been liberated on 25 August. As General Philippe Leclerc's 2nd Armoured Division fought their way up the rue de Rivoli the staff of the Hôtel Continentale hung white sheets out of the bedroom windows to show that they were friendly. The next day de Gaulle walked up the Champs-Elysées at the head of a million people, having been proclaimed head of the Provisional Government of the French Republic.

On 28 August it was announced that all members of the FFI – 'combatants without uniforms' – would officially be incorporated into the Nouvelle Armée Française. De Gaulle warned them that there was still much fighting to do and the Germans would not be completely driven out until March 1945. But before then the French had begun the equally satisfying business of settling accounts with one another.

On Boxing Day 1944 the heads of the French Gestapo, Henri Lafont and Pierre Bonny, were executed by firing squad at the Fort Montrouge in Paris. The ex-policeman Bonny went to his death tight-lipped but the gangster Lafont, enjoying his Death Row infamy, claimed his right to a last cigarette and maintained he was just a street boy who'd been trying to stay alive.

Hundreds of other collaborators faced summary justice in the 'Épuration Legale' that swept the country in the next few years. Some of them were indisputably guilty, like the Milice leader Joseph Darnand and the Belgian Georges Delfanne, who claimed to have invented the *baignoire*. Politicians were among their number, like the Vichy Prime Minister Pierre Laval, who was shot at the Fresnes in October 1947 insisting that all he had done was try to save France from even greater destruction. Marshal Pétain was also tried for treason and sentenced to death but spared by de Gaulle on account of his age and status as the hero of Verdun.[33] The Marshal was instead incarcerated in a fort on an island off the Atlantic coast,

---

33 Pétain commanded the French 2nd Army at the Battle of Verdun between February and July 1916. He was regarded as one of the more successful military leaders of World War One and was made a Marshal of France in 1918.

and died there, aged 95, in 1951. But there were no arrests among the *beau monde* of the French racing community even though many of them had spent every Sunday fraternising with the Germans at Longchamp and Auteuil.

The most brutal treatment, or 'Épuration Sauvage', was reserved for the hundreds of ordinary women who had their heads shaved for sleeping with the enemy. Some of them were prostitutes who had entertained the Wehrmacht as they would anyone else who could afford to pay. But the great majority had been alone and vulnerable without food or money and had done the only thing they could to survive.

No doubt the mistress of the Avignon Gestapo chief and her mother would have said the same thing had they lived. Their deaths went unrecorded, with neither ceremony nor investigation. Their judge and jury Camille Rayon went back to Antibes in 1945 to begin a dazzling career in business.

But what of his English friend and fellow assassin, the much-travelled SOE veteran John Goldsmith? What did the future hold for him?

20
TERMINATION OF ENGAGEMENT

John returned to London at the end of September 1944 and on the 28th he was de-briefed as usual at Orchard Court. He was generous in his praise of Rayon and his fellow French Resistance leaders who, he said, were 'all absolutely top class from the word go'. Thanks to Archiduc and his contacts and his grey Citroën, John had been able to achieve in weeks what might otherwise have taken months to accomplish and he felt privileged to 'have had the good luck to work with them'.[34]

Baker Street was equally enthusiastic. The British General Henry Maitland-Wilson, Supreme Allied Commander in the Mediterranean, had told Brooks Richards that Maquis activity in the Vaucluse, co-ordinated by John Goldsmith, had reduced German military effectiveness at the time of the invasion by as much as 40 per cent.

John went off on his by now customary two-week leave with Tiny and Gaie, wondering what the war had left for him. SOE F Section operations in France may have been drawing to a close but the conflict with both Germany and Japan was far from over, and

34 National Archives.

at his de-briefing Goldsmith had expressed an interest in going to the Far East 'if there was anything doing'. Instead he found himself posted to Sunningdale golf course in coniferous Surrey.

The Allies had yet to discover the scale of the subhuman butchery that had been taking place in the concentration camps in Germany and the east. But as their armies crossed the Rhine they became extremely worried about the fate and condition of their prisoners of war. The Nazis were recognised as no respecters of the Geneva Convention and there were fears that, with the conflict lost, their captives would be harmed or killed or would simply disappear en masse.

A plan was drawn up for a multi-national unit to be parachuted into Germany to secure the POW camps and ensure the safety of the men inside them. The Special Allied Airborne Reconnaisance Force, code name SAARF, was to be drawn from all the Allied countries and include SOE and American OSS (Office of Strategic Services) agents as well as members of the SAS and the US 82nd and 101st Airborne Divisions who had been some of the first Allied troops to drop into Normandy on D-Day.

In keeping with SOE's predilection for conducting affairs from comfortable premises in the country the headquarters for Operation Vicarage, as the mission was to be known, was the clubhouse at Sunningdale. Several large stockbroker houses in Wentworth were also requisitioned.

The plan was for SAARF to operate in teams of three, comprised of two officers and a radio operator all of the same nationality. A few parties were parachuted into Germany in April 1945, but by then the advancing armies had already liberated most of the camps and there was never a wholesale deployment. Even if there had been, John Goldsmith wouldn't have been part of it. Despite training diligently among the pine trees, fairways and bunkers, his active participation in SAARF had been blackballed by MI5.

The almost constant bickering between the traditional security services and the upstarts in Baker Street had been a recurring theme of the secret war. MI5 already had a rather jaundiced view of John based on Tiny's indiscretions at the American party in Manchester's Midland Hotel. In January 1945 another MI5 officer, Major Roche, was deputed to review John's security clearance for Operation Vicarage and this deskbound official decided there was something not quite right about John's account of his escape from Paris in June 1943. 'Experience of such cases makes me very unwilling to say that such an escape, extraordinary though it may seem, is impossible,' he graciously allowed. But he still questioned how John had managed to end up spending a night in a German officers' mess in a room with a private bathroom. The possibility that sheer chutzpah and nerve had enabled him to find his way out of a tight spot was not considered.

It was characteristic MI5 suspicion of SOE and their methods and a reflection of the shifting emphasis as the Cold War began. Setting Europe ablaze with acts of Buchanesque derring-do may have struck a chord in 1940, but it was no longer fashionable. Roche admitted that, where Goldsmith was concerned, his was just a personal view and 'only the result of my reading of the case and not based on any knowledge of the handling of the matter'. But the residue of suspicion that dripped into John's file was enough to have his security status for the prisoner of war missions downgraded.

Another MI5 officer conceded that John had shown 'great initiative in his work in France' and that SAARF may 'have in mind for him a role where you would feel justified in taking some security risk in order to obtain the benefit of his initiative. But from a strictly security point of view he cannot be graded as being recommended.'

John Goldsmith never saw his MI5 file and probably wouldn't have thought much of it if he had. He never went to Germany either, but in April he had a third and final run-in with the security services. This time he got into trouble for a conversation that was overheard in a pub near Reigate. 'I have heard that a man called Captain Goldsmith, described as tall and very good-looking, has been telling civilians that he was dropped in France on several occasions during the Occupation,' complained a Major Cussen. 'Should it be investigated by MI5 or SOE?' In the event it was investigated by neither and was of negligible interest to Buckmaster and Gubbins who, that same month, recommended John for a DSO. 'In the face of constant difficulty and danger and with repeated experience of the hazardous nature of his work,' read the citation, 'Major Goldsmith never flinched from prosecuting his voluntary missions with the highest qualities of leadership, organisation and courage.'

On 30 April Adolf Hitler committed suicide in the bunker in Berlin and a week later Germany surrendered. By the end of August Britain had elected a Labour government, the atomic bomb had been dropped on Hiroshima and Nagasaki and John Goldsmith had signed his 'termination of engagement' with SOE. The firm's F Section, RF Section and every other section was disbanding and what remained of it was to be absorbed into the secret intelligence service MI6. The offices in Baker Street and the country houses, including Wanborough Manor and Arisaig, were returned to their former owners and the flat at number 68 Orchard Court was put on the market. Maurice Buckmaster would soon return to work for the Ford Motor Company in Dagenham. At least he was alive.

Vera Atkins was determined to discover what had happened to the F Section agents who had never returned and in early 1946 she was attached to the British War Crimes Unit working in Germany.

Over the course of the next 18 months her unflinching determination to uncover the truth yielded conclusive proof that 117 of the 118 missing operatives had died in captivity.

In December 1941 Hitler had issued the Nacht und Nebel ('Night and Fog') decree. It not only mandated the death penalty for all enemies of the state in the occupied territories but proclaimed that every trace of their existence should be erased so that their relatives would never know what had become of them. Before the liberation of Paris in the summer of 1944 British, French, Polish, Dutch and all the other foreign agents held in the Fresnes and other prisons were shipped east to concentration camps. Most of them were transported by train from the Gare de l'Est, handcuffed and crammed into a wagon with no water or sanitation and no room to sit or lie down.

For John Goldsmith's former colleagues it was the final stage of the long journey that had begun in the back of the army truck riding in the spring sunshine to Wanborough Manor in April 1942. Of the six of them who had gone to France only himself and Arthur Staggs had survived. The cockney bargeman's French accent had proved every bit as foolproof as John remembered. Arrested in Paris in December 1943, Staggs had managed to convince the SD he was an innocent workman with no connection to SOE and had found his way to the Pas de Calais where he was taken in by a local Resistance group. But awaiting the others was a slow death, malnourished and in rags, in camps that were the very incarnation of hell on earth.

There were two major purges. The first took place in September 1944 and among the victims were Gilbert Norman, John Young and Sidney Jones, who were hanged at Mauthausen in Austria. Six months earlier Norman had tried to escape from the avenue Foch in the company of Noor Inayat Khan, his value to Kieffer and the SD having steadily diminished once SOE realised they were being duped and that his radio reports could no longer be trusted. Following the failed breakout Agent Archambaud was treated very differently and sent to join the other captured agents in the Fresnes.

Norman's hanging, and that of Young and Jones and the others the next year, was not done the British way. They weren't weighed and measured for the drop. They were hung from a hook on the wall and left to strangle, and some reports say that the nooses were made of piano wire, as in the executions of the July plotters in Berlin. Jimmy Amps, Rowland Dowlen, Brian Rafferty and Jack Agazarian were part of a second group that died in similar fashion at Flossenburg in Bavaria. Their deaths took place on 29 March 1945, less than a month before the camp was liberated.

Francis Suttill, the head of the Prosper network, was shot at Ravensbrück. The architect Henri Frager, Carte's number two, was decapitated at Buchenwald. Noor Inayat Khan was shot at Dachau with Yolande Beekman in September 1944, and Diana Rowden, who had been caught in the Jura sawmill with John Young, was killed by lethal injection with Andrée Borrel at Natzweiler Struthof in July of the same year.

The next of kin of the executed agents all received a personal letter from Vera Atkins beginning with the same sombre words: 'It is with the deepest regret that I have to inform you of the death of . . .' and so on. The families were assured that the camp officials responsible for the deaths 'will be tried as war criminals and the charge is murder'.

Some of the SOE agents who survived were treated with scarcely credible animosity by Charles de Gaulle. The buccaneering George Starr, for example, who had ended up leading a 2,000-strong Maquis near Toulouse, was told in person by the General that he was a mercenary who had two hours to get out of France. But de Gaulle could show appreciation too. In January 1946 he approved the award of the Chevalier de la Légion d'Honneur to Major John Goldsmith, and the decoration was officially presented on 21 February.

By the time John was shaking hands with the French ambassador the elation of August 1944 and May 1945 was long gone and both France and Britain were suffused with post-war gloom. The dangers of the past six years may have passed but so too had the excitement while the deprivations continued in the shape of yet more rationing and shortages. French reconstruction was plagued by the bitter political differences between the Gaullists and the Communists. The situation got so bad that the General, not uncharacteristically, threatened to resign three times in three months.

Britain was undefeated but insolvent. The 1945 election result had committed the nation to an ambitious social revolution and Clement Attlee's government were pressing ahead with idealistic plans for a National Health Service and a welfare state. But the public finances were as pot-holed and ruinous as the bomb-damaged wreckage in central London. Some people dreamed of a better life elsewhere, like the 1,000 British GI brides who met Eleanor Roosevelt in Leicester Square prior to setting off for new homes in the US. Some resorted to low-grade black marketeering, hoarding petrol coupons and nylons. Some even attempted to amuse themselves by sending fan letters to Hermann Göring who, along with other leading Nazis, was on trial for war crimes at Nuremberg.

It was as if the long-suffering public, plunged back into a colourless world of bread rationing and power cuts, yearned for an 'intermediate state' in which they could retain some of the exuberance of wartime life without the same risks.[35] Restless ex-RAF pilots, like

---

35 See *The Spivs*, David Hughes, p.104, and *Age of Austerity*, Penguin Books, 1963.

Freddie Page in Terence Rattigan's *The Deep Blue Sea*, raced cars at 100 miles an hour down the Great West Road or flew illegal immigrants to Palestine but, in the late 1940s and early 1950s, many thousands of otherwise hard-working citizens experienced their thrills through betting and racing.

The very fact that horse racing had continued throughout the war, albeit on a much-reduced scale, was a testament not so much to the lobbying skills of the Jockey Club as to the tolerant views of assorted government ministers and the active support of the former Premier who owned horses himself and had always been sympathetic to a gamble. Among the scores of demobbed racing figures returning to their old jobs were owners, trainers, jockeys and journalists like the diminutive Geoffrey Hamlyn, who was the official starting price reporter for the *Sporting Life*. The ineffably charming Hamlyn, who died in 1994, had been an intelligence officer with the 159th Infantry Brigade and over the course of his 50-year career in journalism he would glean more intelligence about the betting ring and its leading protagonists than any man alive.

When Hamlyn went back to work in 1946 he was struck by two things: the vast crowds of people at the big race meetings at Aintree, Epsom and Ascot, and the fact that while the economy may have been officially on its uppers the racecourses were awash with black market money. There were almost as many shady characters around as on the Riviera in 1942. With no costly overheads like betting tax or betting levy to pay, the bookmakers were prepared to play for high stakes and all sorts of mavericks and chancers, including returning POWs who had spent time 'in the bag', were at large and looking to make a profit.

It was a situation that was very much on John Goldsmith's mind as he settled back down to civilian life with his wife and daughter. If he was going to make a living in post-war Britain, John urgently needed horses to train and owners to pay for them and he started thinking about the conversations he'd had with Robert Mathet-Dumaine when he'd been on the run in Paris in 1943. His friend had continually stressed the health of French bloodstock due to the patronage racing had enjoyed under the Germans; a state of affairs, he'd argued, that would result in the predominance of French stables after the war. It was a view shared by the splendidly gruff *Sporting Life* correspondent Colonel E. E. Wilford who observed in October 1945 that 'the Boche encouraged racing by all means in their power during the occupation and there were plenty of oats to be had when things were at their worst in the UK'.

Suppose John could get his hands on a string of fit French horses. Imagine the damage he could do. But to really make it pay he would have to deploy some of the nerve and cunning he had shown in France during the war. Aside from events like the Derby and Royal Ascot, the great majority of races then, especially over the jumps, were worth very little. The only way for a stable to make ends meet, let alone show a profit, was through betting. So horses had of necessity to be campaigned selectively so as to maximise their odds and their chances when the money was down.

What John needed was a patron, a gambling owner with the money to buy a dozen good prospects and the patience to hold his fire – like the Maquis on Mont Ventoux – until just the right moment. And in the summer of 1946, he found one. A former RAF officer who was also a rich London bookmaker and punter prepared to bet the house on a good thing.

A Parisian upbringing and a familiarity with the Turf's guileful ways had ideally equipped John Goldsmith to become a wartime secret agent. Now perhaps his French contacts and the lessons he'd learned with SOE would help him pull off some of the biggest betting coups in the history of British racing.

21
THE MAYFAIR BOOKIE

The Friday Novices' Hurdle, Division Two, run at Windsor on Friday, 1 March 1946 was not the most prestigious contest but it provided John Goldsmith with his first winner of the post-war era. The horse, appropriately enough, was called Maquis, and he was a four-year-old French-bred gelding owned by Mrs Rosemary Upton. After a couple of unplaced efforts in similar races earlier in the year he triumphed by four lengths at odds of 4–1 and winning bets were struck. For topical or sentimental reasons, John may well have backed the winner of the first race too – another recent French acquisition, ridden by Fred Rimell, saddled by Dorothy Paget's new trainer, Fulke Walwyn, and called Giraud.

The former Secret Army General after whom the horse was named had displayed some interest in the Turf in retirement, though nothing like as much as the former Resistance sympathiser Robert Mathet-Dumaine who, along with his patron the Vicomte de Rivaud, remained at the heart of the Paris racing scene. At the beginning of 1946 the Vicomte had given John Goldsmith a boost by sending him his grey steeplechaser Jalgreya. The ten-year-old had some useful wartime form in France and there were hopes that he might be good enough for the big races at Cheltenham and Liverpool. He finished a close second in a three-mile chase at Windsor in February and was backed to go one better in a similar event over the same course and distance on 2 March. But the conditions were atrocious that day and he was caught out by the slippery going and came down at the water jump.

John stuck to his plan to run the grey in the Cheltenham Gold Cup on 14 March and he'd hoped to be represented by Robert Mathet-Dumaine's Grand Steeplechase de Paris winner Kargal too. That had been the plan the two friends discussed when John was on the run in Paris in September 1943. Mathet-Dumaine was still enthusiastic about the idea but, on the day Kargal was due to have his final prep race at Auteuil, the meeting was snowed off and in the end the French champion remained at home in his box.

The 1946 Festival played to huge crowds undeterred by the threat of more snow, frost and fog. The North Sea had frozen over off the Suffolk coast, the Minister for Fuel and Power, Emmanuel Shinwell, was warning of further gas and electricity cuts, and the Chancellor Sir Stafford Cripps had exhorted the nation to embrace 'hard work' as 'the only road to prosperity'. Punters were looking for a more direct route and they thought they'd found it in the shape of the Aly Khan's classically bred French colt Wood Note, whose original target had been the 1945 Derby. Injury curtailed his flat racing career but he'd since joined a top jumps stable and over the winter he was a 'springer' in the Champion Hurdle market. Despite having never yet jumped an obstacle in public he was backed to win over £10,000 (£370,000 in 2015 money) at 33–1. But as was the case with so many 'ante-post' plunges, or bets struck before the event, he had another setback and was forced to miss the race.

Dorothy Paget's Distel won the hurdling blue ribbon at odds-on, and in the Gold Cup Jalgreya was no match for the great Irish steeplechaser Prince Regent who was owned by the glamorous punter Mrs J. V. 'Pat' Rank, sister-in-law of the film mogul J. Arthur Rank. But the grey horse had his day eventually, landing a three-runner race back at Cheltenham in April and following up in an amateur riders' contest at Fontwell Park the next month. Each time the Goldsmith/Mathet–Dumaine stable money was down.

The yard hit the target again at Wye races on 6 May. The pretty East Kent course, one of the smallest in the country, held all its meetings on Mondays, which was the same day as Ashford Market. The costermongers and street traders, their pockets bulging with black market cash, went on to the races after work and in the 1940s there were dozens of bookies in the ring at Wye waiting to accommodate them.

The strong betting market was exactly what John Goldsmith wanted as he was hoping to get a decent bet on a sure thing at short odds. The horse's name was Santac and he was a 15-year-old veteran with good form at Cheltenham before the war. John had seen him win a selling chase at Wincanton in April and had claimed him in his wife's name for 100 guineas at the post-race auction. His objective at Wye was another modest race, the Tonbridge Selling Chase over two miles, and there was never a moment's worry. Santac strolled home by ten lengths at the prohibitive odds of 8–15, which meant you would have had to put on £15 to win £8, or £150 to win £80, and so on. But, as John believed the odds should have been more like 1–10, or ten to one on, the bet was well worth it.

John and Tiny had slipped impressively into the roles of the thrusting trainer and his wife and were beginning to attract a following. 'They were a very glamorous couple,' remembers John's good friend Gerry Albertini, himself a charming gentleman gambler of the old school. 'She was extremely pretty and he had such magnetism. Mind you, when he looked at you with those blue eyes, well, it quite made you shudder.'

The friendship between Goldsmith and Albertini was bonded by their shared passion for the Turf but they approached the business of finding winners with contrasting means. Gerry was also tall and good-looking with dark hair and a moustache that lent him an uncanny resemblance to the actor David Niven. His family had made fortunes in American railroads and tobacco and his grandparents were the original owners of number 82 avenue Foch, the house in Paris that the Gestapo took over when the Germans invaded France and the location of John's encounter with Josef Kieffer and the SD. Gerry's grandfather was sculpted by Rodin but he gave the bust to his Russian caretaker Valkonski who escaped from Paris with it in 1940 and ended up in London as the landlord of the Bunch of Grapes on the Brompton Road.

Having completed his formal education at traditional English boarding schools, Albertini was now deploying some of his inheritance in his battle with the bookies. Mr and Mrs Goldsmith's ambition was to hit the bookmakers too but, without Gerry's resources, their wagers were only £20 and £50 a time (£1,750 maximum in today's money) not a 'monkey' (£500), let alone a grand, and they were still some way from the big time.

Then on 31 May they went to Salisbury races and met Percy Thompson. In a gambling fraternity not short of high rollers Percy was as big as they come. The 41-year-old, who'd served in the RAF during the war, was a traditional boards bookie, meaning he stood on a box in the ring, chalking up the odds on a blackboard and accepting cash bets that were recorded by a clerk writing them down in pencil in a big ledger. Thompson, who traded on the same scale as

William Hill and Max Parker, had the number one boards pitches, making him the first bookmaker you saw when you entered the ring from the Members' Enclosure at the big courses in the south and at tracks like Liverpool, Lincoln and Manchester.

Geoffrey Hamlyn remembered that when Percy first started bookmaking in the 1930s he electrified the ring with the scale and audacity of his trading. 'He'd tap his board before each race and call out "Any horse to win £5,000" [£175,000 in modern money],' recalled Hamlyn in 1994. 'If he had a losing race he'd just tear off the tissue [the sheet with the runners and riders on it] and move on to the next one. He showed no fear.'

The size of the bets that Thompson struck were all of a piece with his way of life. He wore snap brim trilby hats, hand-made shoes and tailor-made suits woven from the finest cloth. He had a fleet of cars including a Daimler and a Rolls-Royce and when he went up to Aintree for the Grand National meeting he always stayed at Manchester's Midland Hotel (where Tiny had been entertained by the Americans in 1942), booking an entire floor for himself and his staff. He sometimes took his mistress with him taking care to ensure she was every bit as well dressed and kitted out as he was. Benno Miller, a Bond Street commission agent who placed bets for wealthy owners in return for a percentage or commission when they won, recalls Thompson 'buying his lady a diamond ring as big as the one that Edward VIII gave Mrs Simpson'.

Percy lived in a capacious flat in Aldford Street in Mayfair and had off-course credit offices at numbers 32 to 34 Regent Street and at Mitre House on the Western Road in Brighton where 'clients visiting the south coast can telephone their instructions'. The organisation, claimed Percy, was 'at the service of all Sportsmen' and the off-course team – which included his brother Warwick – would man the phones each day, taking bets from regular clients and relaying the business back to their men on the track.

Geoffrey Hamlyn said that Thompson was impressively numerate with a proper grasp of mathematics and percentages but that he also liked to 'take a view about a horse or a race' and back his judgement accordingly. Sometimes that view depended on the inside information he received, be it from the trainers and jockeys who looked after his horses or from clients with contacts in other yards. One of his closest confederates was his brother-in-law, the Derby-winning jockey Charlie Elliott. A brilliant and inspirational rider who excelled in the biggest races, Charlie was also a compulsive gambler. Since 1935 he had been based in France riding for Marcel Boussac and, like a good spymaster, Percy Thompson paid him well for all the latest news of French form and running plans.

Robert Mathet-Dumaine and the Vicomte de Rivaud were two of the French owners who had accounts with Thompson and the ever loyal Robert testified to the bookie that there was no better man at training a horse to peak on a given day than the ex-SOE agent John Goldsmith. None tougher either, or less likely to grass up a plot to the enemy.

Percy had remained earthbound in the RAF and had great respect and envy even for men who had seen action. He was impressed by the stories of John's war behind the lines and decided he was the man to plan his betting ring battles. The two of them had just seen an Irish-bred horse of Percy's called Osberstown finish fourth in a small race at Salisbury. Percy felt the gelding might do better with a change of scenery and asked John if he'd take him. Goldsmith's view of training was never rigid or hidebound. He was always prepared to try an unconventional approach, and for Osberstown he recommended a stint on the beach at Bognor Regis. Freshened up by the sea air and working on the sand, Osberstown came third at Nottingham in late June, second to one of Dorothy Paget's horses at Brighton on 6 July, and then won a mile and a half amateur riders' race back at Salisbury on 11 July. He was returned at 13–8 and, in betting ring parlance, Percy Thompson 'filled his boots'.

The bookmaker said he'd like to buy up to 20 horses, experienced types capable of competing both over jumps and on the flat, that he could run and bet on in races in the south. Some of them he would register in his own name. Some would be partnerships. A delighted John Goldsmith said that France was the place to find them if they wanted to get an edge but that if he was to be involved his stable staff, including his head lad, known as 'old Orbell', would have to be included in the profits when the horses won.

Thompson gave him his blessing, and that summer John crossed the Channel, money in hand, and began to fill his order book.

22

A SILENT KILLING

Everywhere you looked in 1946 it seemed that racing's bigger picture had taken on an emphatically French hue. At Epsom in June an estimated crowd of half a million people saw the 50–1 outsider Airborne win the Derby for an English yard. But in many of the top races it was fit, strong and blue-blooded French horses who led the way.

At Royal Ascot runners owned by Marcel Boussac finished first, second and third in the Gold Cup and, tipped off by Charlie Elliott who rode the winner, Caracalla, Percy Thompson had them in the correct order. Boussac ended up in second place behind the Aga Khan in the 1946 list of leading owners in Britain. Gallic stables won a total of £40,000 worth of prize money that season (£1.4 million today) and British owner-breeders had to endure the mortifying sight of the Grand Prix de Paris winner Souverain routing Airborne by five lengths in the King George VI Stakes at Ascot in October. Perhaps it was just English sour grapes but the manner of Souverain's victory attracted much comment afterwards in the press room and betting ring, not all of it complimentary.

The French colt was trained at Chantilly by Henri Delavaud and part-owned by the ebullient Louis 'Lulu' Chataignoux, who was an inveterate punter. If the Occupation had been the equivalent of a four- or five-day race meeting you would say that Lulu had managed to come out ahead. He landed some hefty bets at Ascot helped by rumours beforehand about Souverain's well-being and him being supposedly off colour after a bad Channel crossing; stories which helped his odds drift out to 11–2 on the day of the race at which price his foxy French connections stepped in. When Monsieur Delavaud was confronted afterwards by suspicious English journalists he was all smiles. 'Ahah,' he said. 'Our little horse woke up this morning and recovered his best form just in time.' No doubt just 'a happy and fortuitous coincidence' as one correspondent put it. But in private there were mutterings that Gallic trainers must be giving their horses some kind of dope or cocaine-based supplement to make them run faster and they were suspected of acquiring it from the Germans during the war.

The dastardly French were at it again at Newmarket the following Wednesday where Monsieur l'Amiral, trained by Emile Charlier but ridden by Britain's Harry Wragg, took the Cesarewitch by three quarters of a length. The two-and-a-quarter-mile race, named after the official title of the eldest son of the Tsar of Russia, is one of the oldest and most eccentric contests in the calendar. It begins in Cambridgeshire and ends in Suffolk and the first mile is invisible from the grandstand. Nowadays big TV screens relay the action from the outset but 70 years ago an account of the early stages depended on the subsequent reports of a few windswept correspondents standing on top of the Saxon earthwork known as the Devil's Dyke.

The main attraction of the Cesarewitch was that it was a massive betting race, much more so than today, with big fields and countless wagers struck weeks and even months in advance. There was no public gamble on Monsieur l'Amiral, who was returned at 33–1, but his owners, the expatriate Englishmen 'Hans' Barnard-Hankey and Captain Ian Henderson, backed him to win a thumping £80,000, or £2.8 million in modern money.

Regardless of the run of French victories horse racing had never been more popular in the UK. Over 100,000 people flocked to Newmarket on Cesarewitch day – their biggest ever crowd on the Rowley Mile – and the sport's hold on public consciousness was underlined by the front page of the following morning's *Daily Express*. The news of Barnard-Hankey's spectacular coup shared top billing with a report of the execution of Ribbentrop and nine other Nazis at Nuremberg and the suicide of Hermann Göring hours before he was due to hang.

It would have been understandable if John Goldsmith had felt some satisfaction on reading that Allied justice had caught up with the likes of Ernst Kaltenbrunner, Heydrich's successor as supreme head of the Gestapo and SD and the man ultimately responsible for the torture and death of scores of SOE agents. But, 18 months after he had walked out of Orchard Court for the last time, John was reminded that the firm had had to battle treacherous and reprehensible Frenchmen as well as Germans. And that whatever Boussac or Lulu Chataignoux had done in the war, there were some French racehorse owners and collaborators who could not be tolerated at any price.

John's moment of revelation came at Hurst Park racecourse on the banks of the Thames on Saturday, 9 November. It was a damp, misty autumn afternoon, the wet leaves around the paddock mingling with the discarded fag packets and pages of form. Six competitive races had drawn a big crowd and all the top bookmakers were in attendance.

John Goldsmith had two runners. One of them was owned by Percy Thompson. The other one belonged to an overweight black marketeer called Javier Cruz-Valer. The plump Frenchman had been a commercial traveller in the 1930s working for the Parisian department store Bon Marché. During the Occupation he had branched out into a profitable sideline manufacturing coffins and selling them to the Wehrmacht, and he was a good friend of the chocolatier Marcel Pupier, who also did business with the Germans. At the height of the Épuration the pair were called before a tribunal who decided their collaboration was of the passive kind, earning them heavy fines rather than an appointment with a firing squad. Cruz-Valer managed to arrange for his bill to be paid off in instalments but he thought it tactful, if only temporarily, to move his racehorses across the Channel.

John didn't much like the coffin salesman and felt that his wartime record stank, but his training fees would help to pay the stable lads' wages and keep the Sparsholt yard afloat. So he had taken delivery of a horse of Cruz-Valer's called Urgay, formerly trained by Marcel d'Okhuysen, president of the French Trainers' Association. The four-year-old colt had shown good form in Paris in 1945 but, to maintain the pretence that Cruz-Valer was no longer the owner, he had been re-registered as the property of Madame Pierre Lafarge, a friend of the Comte de Rivaud.

John formed a plan for Urgay not dissimilar to his strategy with Osberstown. He gave the colt a couple of preliminary runs at Ascot and Newmarket, where he finished second in the Jockey Club Cup – a high-class race – and then entered him in a valuable two-and-a-half-mile event to be run at Hurst Park. The horse had been almost as fat as his owner when he first arrived in England but after five months in John's care he had reached peak fitness and was as good a bet as he ever would be.

According to the accepted racing etiquette of the times, the owner's money should have gone on alongside a wager on behalf of the stable to reward the trainer and his staff if the horse won. But Cruz-Valer, who flew over from Paris the night before, was as devious as any Vichy or Gestapo double agent. When he met up with John a few hours before racing he refused to say if he was backing his horse or if he wanted it stopped so that he could get better odds next time out. All he would say was that he would go and stand on the course by the gate where the runners came out from the paddock. If his hat was under his left arm when Urgay came past, the jockey should ride to win; but if he was holding it under his right arm, the jockey should wait for another day.

Goldsmith was disgusted. He knew that what Cruz-Valer really wanted was to get his money on at the bigger price and only then, when the odds had collapsed, would the stable be permitted to place a bet. It wasn't the way a gentleman behaved and, as John watched the fat man waddling off to the paddock, something in him snapped. Cruz-Valer reminded him not of Camille Rayon, André Bartoli or Paulo Leonetti but of the worst kind of Frenchman, the types that had colluded with the Nazis, profited from the oppression of their fellow citizens and betrayed hundreds of them, as well as British agents, to their deaths.

The Dawkins Memorial Stakes was due to start at 2.15 p.m. By two o'clock Cruz-Valer had left the saddling-up area and lumbered off to the gate out on to the course. As soon as he'd gone John hurried over to the bookmakers' pitches and asked William Hill for a private word. If there was any money for Urgay today, John said, Hill was to lay him and keep on laying him – meaning he should keep taking bets on the horse without worrying about hedging his liabilities elsewhere in the ring. 'Bill' Hill absorbed the news with a look but no comment, as did Percy Thompson when John sought him out on the boards.

Goldsmith then hastened back to the paddock where Urgay was completing a final lap before going down to the start. The jockey, George Bridgland, was a hard-bitten old professional. John told him that, as he went out on to the course, he might see Monsieur Cruz-Valer doing odd things with his hat but that he should ignore them. Most importantly of all, whatever he did in the race, he should not win. Bridgland, who had seen it all and knew the ways of the world, just nodded.

When John reached the viewing terraces he could see Cruz-Valer down among the bookmakers. 'The bastard,' thought Goldsmith. 'He's putting his bets on at the last possible moment so that we can't get on even if we wanted to.' The Frenchman's conduct may have been intolerable but watching the race was a pleasure. They used to say that the best jockeys at stopping a horse were the best jockeys and George Bridgland finessed it to perfection. Urgay, whose price tumbled from 7–1 to 5–2 at the off, the owner's money down, was in third place entering the home straight but then 'he was unable to go with the leaders', as they say in the formbook, and 'ran on at one pace'. He finished fourth.

It had been as cold-blooded as an SOE silent killing and a furious Cruz-Valer, who had lost a four-figure sum, confronted John afterwards in the owners' and trainers' bar. He blamed the horse, he blamed the jockey, he blamed the trainer. There would be repercussions, he thundered. John hadn't heard the last of it. But John didn't care. William Hill and Percy Thompson showed their appreciation with a generous cash present and John, Tiny, George Bridgland and the Sparsholt stable lads all had a good drink that Saturday night.

On the Monday morning Cruz-Valer took his horse away, but Goldsmith believed he had better owners and better horses too. Horses like Querneville, the three-year-old grey filly he'd bought in France for Percy Thompson. An hour after Urgay's race she had finished a running-on second in a seven-furlong handicap at Hurst Park beaten only three quarters of a length by a smart colt called Persian Brook. The filly was improving, she loved soft ground and had yet to reach her peak. Next March, John told Thompson, she'll win the Lincoln.

23

QUERNEVILLE

It was shortly after 3.15 p.m. on the afternoon of Wednesday, 26 March 1947 and Lincoln racecourse was a peninsula with flood waters on three sides. The 200-year-old track, known locally as the Carholme, was the setting for the Lincoln Handicap, traditionally the first big event of the flat racing season and, like the Cesarewitch, one of the biggest betting races of the year. John Goldsmith, turning his coat collar up against the wind, had climbed to a vantage point high up in the 19th-century brick grandstand. In about ten minutes' time he would discover whether his first attempt at an audacious peacetime killing would succeed.

No fewer than 47 runners, a huge field by modern standards, were down at the start for the one-mile contest. It would be unimaginable for so many horses to line up in a flat race today where the safety limit is 30 over the straight mile at Ascot. A maximum of 40 take part in the Grand National at Aintree, but that's a steeplechase over four and a half miles; the pace is slower than on the flat and the runners have more time to get out of each other's way. But 70 years ago races like the Lincoln and the Cesarewitch were regarded as fair game for any stable that wanted to have a crack at them and, despite the hazardous nature of the event, thousands of pounds' worth of bets were dependent on the outcome.

Admittedly the big owners, trainers, bookmakers and punters, some British, some French, some hardened professionals, some cavalier high rollers, could hardly believe the race was on. The winter of 1946/47 had been one of the harshest in British history. Arctic snowfalls, frozen railway lines and impassable roads had led to severe food and fuel shortages with coal stocks already depleted after six years of war. On 1 March the need to conserve power had resulted in dog racing being suspended at a raft of London tracks including Walthamstow, West Ham and Wembley, and the 1947 Cheltenham Festival race meeting had been postponed until April.

Then, just as the snow began to melt in mid-March, there was widespread flooding in London, the Thames Valley and a great swathe of eastern England from Essex up to South Yorkshire, including Lincolnshire and the Wash. The Paris-based jockey Rae Johnstone, flying over from Le Bourget in a private plane, looked down with astonishment at familiar countryside pitted with lakes. At least Johnstone, like the French-trained Lincoln challengers, was coming in by air. Many English trainers wondered if their horse boxes would ever be able to get through while others had runners stranded on trains for 12 hours or more.

John Goldsmith had to battle his way across country from Oxfordshire, negotiating burst rivers and submerged roads. The Goldsmith fortunes had improved sufficiently for John and Tiny to give up renting at Sparsholt and buy a house and stables at Aston Tirrold near Blewbury. It was a small but pretty yard in idyllic country at the foot of the Downs, and now it had to pay its way. John had been aiming Querneville at the Lincoln since her good run at Hurst Park the previous autumn. And an SOE veteran who had crossed the Mediterranean by felucca and walked over the Pyrenees in January wasn't going to let a spot of weather change his plans.

John's confidence was partly based on Querneville's form in France where she had displayed abundant stamina and a preference for heavy going. By comparison many of her English-bred rivals were speedy types who had won over five and six furlongs as two-year-olds but might struggle over a mile on soft ground.

When the Blewbury gallops froze over John had taken Querneville and several other smart prospects including the French hurdler Tant Pis down to Bognor Regis, where Osberstown had been freshened up the previous year. Tiny, who rode the grey in all her work, had cantered Querneville on the beach. A lifetime around horses and riding meant that Annette was as polished an equestrian as any jockey or stable lad, and the filly answered her every call. The seashore and saltwater gallops fine-tuned her muscles and opened her lungs, and by mid-March John reckoned he had her at concert pitch.

Throughout February and March there were regular call-overs on the Lincoln and the Grand National (collectively known as the Spring Double) at the Victoria Club in London. The big bookmakers would assemble there in the billiard room after dinner on Monday nights and in a cloud of cigar smoke a whip-sharp Italian called Arthur Cassani would go through the Lincoln runners alphabetically. Credit bookmakers like William Hill, Sam Burns, David Cope and Max Parker would call out the odds they were prepared to lay each horse at and the liabilities they were prepared to incur. Mr Cassani kept a note of all the transactions struck and the following day the newspapers reported the market moves.

By the weekend of 22 March Percy Thompson had backed Querneville to win £30,000 (something like £1,030,000 in modern money), wagering £1,500 (£51,500) at 20–1. Major John Goldsmith,

DSO, had vouchsafed she was good enough and had hired an old French acquaintance, the lightweight specialist Paul 'Popol' Blanc, to ride her. Thompson, as generous as he was bold and one of nature's if not Debrett's gentlemen, had assured the jockey that he was included in the bets the bookie had placed on the filly. If Querneville won, Percy won, the John Goldsmith stable won and Popol won, sharing 'a small fortune' as Blanc excitedly told Rae Johnstone on the Chantilly gallops.

On Saturday, 22 March, Querneville's seaside galloping companion Tant Pis won the Imperial Cup at Sandown Park. The valuable two-mile handicap hurdle race was second only to the Champion Hurdle in prestige at the time and, with a big field to beat, the French-bred showed 'great resolution' in the terrible ground. 'Major Goldsmith bought him on the continent for the West End actress Miss Joan Maguire,' enthused the *Sporting Life*. Clive Graham of the *Daily Express*, a much-respected journalist and punter, was particularly impressed. With regard to 'the trainer's other French hope' Querneville he observed that 'a stable in form is often one to follow and confidence seems sky high'.

Not that Querneville was the only gambled-on runner in the 1947 Lincoln. At least a dozen other horses had been backed to win five-figure sums as turnover on the race and betting levels in general reached heights never seen in Britain before or since. Querneville's rivals included seven representatives from France whose owners and trainers were already enjoying an incredible run in the big English races. The most fancied of the raiding party was Rae Johnstone's mount, Vagabond II, a classy seven-year-old who had to carry top weight but had excellent form on soft ground. Vagabond, who was nearly blind in one eye, was trained by the Russian émigré Joseph Ginsbourg and owned by Victor Darlan, a suave Parisian high roller who, like Cruz-Valer and Lulu Chataignoux, had managed to end the war in profit. Darlan and his friends had travelled over early, staying at the Savoy Hotel, and on Monday, 24 March they backed their horse to take out a similar sum to Querneville.

There were plunges too on Harry Guggenheim's Ouragan VII, who had been wintering in the south of France, and Roi d'Atout, who was a stablemate of the Cesarewitch winner Monsieur l'Amiral, owned by the expatriate Englishman 'Hans' Barnard-Hankey and trained by Emile Charlier.

John Goldsmith respected all of the Gallic challengers but he didn't fear them. He had confidence in his filly but he also knew that there could easily be another English dark horse or two, potentially much better than the formbook might suggest and ready to go close at a big price.

The three-day Lincoln meeting was meant to begin on Monday the 24th but that morning the stewards took one look at the water-logged ground and decided to abandon. Extraordinarily, racing was allowed to go ahead on the Tuesday, but the first two furlongs of the straight mile were still under water so it was decided that the Lincoln would have to be run on the round course with a sharp left turn into the home straight after half a mile where the track was only wide enough for ten horses to gallop abreast. By Wednesday afternoon the going was treacherous and the turn had been churned up into a sea of mud. Other parts of the track too were so cut up that the ground staff had been using wooden mallets to try to smooth over the turf.

Wednesday began with a light frost and bright sunshine but by the afternoon the skies were grey and a bitter wind was blowing in from the east.

In the weighing room beforehand the mood among the senior jockeys was unusually sombre. Gordon Richards, who was to be champion 26 times in an incredible career that culminated in him becoming the first jockey to be knighted in 1953, was worried about 'the younger boys that haven't much experience'. His colleague Harry Carr, who rode for the King, pointed out that it was going to be a long season with many other opportunities. He for one would be going 'the longest way round' and anyone who wanted to follow him was welcome.

There wasn't enough room in the paddock for all the runners and, because of the flooding, they had to go the long way round to the start – just as many of the spectators trying to reach the course had had to drive or walk along the narrow hilly streets of the old city rather than take the usual road from the station, which was under water. The weather had reduced the size of the crowd but it was still the richest ever Lincoln and there were more than 50,000 people present. Smart women in fur coats, men in Homburgs and bowlers, trilbies and flat caps and, for many of them, going racing and having a flutter was the one moment of excitement in otherwise drab and humdrum lives.

The Lincoln was the third race on the card, and after the second, for which there were two false starts, Percy Thompson got down from his boards bookmaker's pitch and went down the rails where the big credit bookmakers like William Hill and Max Parker were standing. In a matter of minutes he backed Querneville again at 100–6 (approximately 16–1) to win another £10,000 (or £350,000 in modern money) and at least half of that was for the trainer and stable staff. There was further backing too for Vagabond, the Gordon Richards-ridden Poolfix and the 1946 winner, Langton Abbot.

John Goldsmith, the saddling up done and the last instructions given to Popol Blanc, huddled down into his trenchcoat and lit a French cigarette. Breathing in the old familiar smell of crushed grass and tobacco smoke, he glanced briefly in the direction of Lincoln Cathedral on the hill and then trained his wartime binoculars on the one-mile start.

Querneville was as cocked and ready as a cowboy's gun. It was now or never.

The starting tape wasn't wide enough to accommodate all the horses and the starter, Captain Chandos Pole, resplendent in bowler hat and riding boots, ordered the runners to line up in two groups, one in front of the other. Querneville, who was wearing a white noseband, was drawn 30 and Vagabond, whom John Goldsmith thought was the biggest danger, was drawn 34, which should have meant there were another 13 horses on his blind side. But Popol Blanc and Rae Johnstone had been left in no doubt as to which group they should be in and Johnstone remembered scenes like 'a rugger scrum' as they jockeyed for a front row position and 'anyone who wasn't swearing wasn't trying'.

At 3.29 p.m. one of the most dangerous flat races ever run in Britain finally got under way with a cut-throat charge towards the left-hand bend. Blanc, Johnstone, Richards and the other jockeys on the most fancied runners rode for all they were worth as a forest of hooves and legs crashed through the mud. The apprentice Frankie Durr, riding Val de Grâce, got to the turn first with Querneville in the first eight but Vagabond was trying to recover after being kicked. As they swung into the home straight the field was already strung out with more than 300 yards between the first and last, clots of mud raining down on the stragglers.

With three furlongs to go Ptolomée II, ridden by Doug Smith, took it up from Val de Grâce and another outsider called Cevos, with the Hurst Park one and two Persian Brook and Querneville right behind them. A quarter of a mile from home Persian Brook, ridden by Doug Smith's brother Eph, was in the lead but then at the furlong marker Querneville hit the front.

Up until this point Popol Blanc had done everything right and, with the end of the race in sight, John Goldsmith's and Percy Thompson's hopes were soaring. But then, in a sudden panic-stricken moment, Blanc picked up his whip and hit Querneville three times. The filly, who was giving her all, bitterly resented such attentions and veered off a straight line, losing vital ground and allowing a 100–1 outsider called Jockey Treble, sporting the all-black colours of the Rotherham bookie Syd Oxenham and ridden by the teenage Manny Mercer, to shoot up on her inside.

There was no time for the grey to get her balance back and there was no photo finish either, not in 1947. The Judge, a Jockey Club official watching through binoculars from a box on the line, called the result and the winning distances as soon as the horses had gone past. First was Jockey Treble by a neck. Second was Persian Brook, and a head away third was Querneville. There was a three-length gap back to Ptolomée II in fourth place and the closest French-trained runner was Vagabond, who finished sixth.

Percy Thompson didn't back horses each way. All of his money and all of the stable's money had been wagered on the nose and, thanks to Popol Blanc, they'd lost the lot.

One man who was there and saw it all was Sir Peter O'Sullevan who was reporting on the race for the Press Association, which filed copy for both the national and regional papers. The then 29-year-old O'Sullevan would go on to become the undisputed voice of racing on BBC television and a hallowed journalist and tipster with the *Express*. One of Peter's other distinctions was that he spoke excellent French and, as early as 1946, he made regular pre-season trips to Chantilly to scout out the best French hopes for the months ahead.

When shrewd French trainers wanted to place a bet on their horses with the English bookies, Peter's bilingual skills were at their disposal and he would also back the horses for himself and then tip them to his readers.

In March 1947, O'Sullevan's main Lincoln bet was on Vagabond II whose jockey Rae Johnstone had become a good friend. But he also knew all about Querneville's form in France and the confidence behind her and he knew what Popol Blanc stood to gain if she won. Looking back at the race in his 97th year, Sir Peter still believed that it was the weight of money that affected Popol's judgement. 'As well as seeing the winning post he saw the fortune he'd been promised floating in front of his eyes and that was his undoing.'

John Goldsmith, comporting his face in defeat as in victory, made his way down off the stand to the unsaddling enclosure where the press were waiting for him. 'I thought Blanc rode rather wildly,' said Meyrick Good of the *Sporting Life*. 'But then the French lightweights are always free with their whips.' John shrugged but said nothing as Popol, coated in mud, dragged his saddle back disconsolately to the weighing room. Percy Thompson looked his trainer in the eye and lit them both a cigarette. 'Next time,' he muttered as they walked away. 'Next time we'll get them.'

'Bookmaker's projected big coup comes unstuck' was the headline in the following day's *Daily Express*, Clive Graham's copy sitting under a dramatic photograph of the mad, scrambling race described by jockey Charlie Smirke as 'worse than the invasion of Sicily'.

Fingers may have been burned on the Carholme and shoes and suit trousers splattered with mud but, as Graham accurately predicted, the bookmaker wouldn't have to wait long to get his money back.

The day after the Lincoln the bacchanalian circus of owners, trainers, jockeys, gamblers and racing correspondents crossed the

Pennines for the three-day Grand National meeting at Aintree, which ran from Thursday, 27 March to Saturday the 29th. The comforts of Woodhall Spa gave way to the Cunard splendour of Liverpool's Adelphi Hotel with jump racing taking centre stage rather than the flat. But as well as the races over the big fences there were four flat races each day, and on the Saturday afternoon 'John Goldsmith's latest French import Bambino II', Clive Graham's bet of the day, won the Maghull Stakes by six lengths. The four-year-old, fit from hurdling in France, ran in the colours of Mrs Rosemary Marks but all the stable's owners were tipped off about its ability and it was backed down from 10–1 to 5–1 at the off. It was customary for the trainer to receive a 'present' afterwards from his grateful patrons and Mrs Marks, Percy Thompson and the rest of them all obliged.

That summer Querneville would land a similar touch in a small race at Wolverhampton,[36] but before then John Goldsmith had been given another special assignment by Percy Thompson; only this time they wouldn't target a big ante-post betting race like the Lincoln or the Grand National but a modest handicap at Windsor. The name of the horse, who will live forever in bookmaking history, was Montignac.

36 On 9 June 1947 Querneville won the six-furlong Ruckley Stakes at Wolverhampton by three lengths. She was backed in from 3–1 to 9–4 favourite.

24

THE BIG LOSER

Before a racehorse can compete in a handicap on the flat in Britain it has to have run in the UK three times so that the official handicapper can assess its form and give it a rating. Montignac, a four-year-old French-bred colt, had already won over hurdles at Auteuil in 1946. But from the moment he arrived at Aston Tirrold, John planned his 1947 campaign on the flat in England every bit as meticulously as any of his SOE missions.

The horse's three preliminary runs were each in a better class of race than a handicap and his performances designed to get him a rating or weight that would seriously underestimate his chances when the big day finally came. It's fair to say that he was not intended to win any of his prep races, and if he had shown any inclination to do so his riders were under instructions to stop him. Considerations of what was proper or legitimate didn't arise. The aim was to part the bookmakers from their money, and John was prepared to be as single-minded in pursuit of that aim as he had been when blowing up a train or a bridge.

Montignac's first run in England was in a mile-and-a-half contest at Kempton Park on Easter Saturday, 5 April. He looked well in the paddock beforehand and, with John's horses in cracking form, there was money for him in the ring. His odds contracted from 7–1 to 9–2 but, with Eph Smith in the saddle, he whipped round at the start and took no part. There was no suggestion that the incident was deliberate but, having come under what is officially known as 'starter's orders', the French import was recorded as having had his first UK run.

Montignac reappeared at Newmarket on Wednesday, 30 April, which was 2,000 Guineas day. The big race was won by Gordon Richards on Tudor Minstrel, one of the most brilliant Guineas winners of the 20th century who made all the running and romped home by eight lengths. Half an hour later Montignac lined up in the Chippenham Stakes over one and a half miles and worth £628 (nearly £22,000 today) to the winner. He was meeting some decidedly useful rivals at level weights and getting no more than 4lb from the others. He was prominent for a mile but had no chance in the last two furlongs and finished third, beaten 12 lengths.

The third and final prep run was in the Victor Wild Stakes back at Kempton on 10 May. Once again Montignac was meeting some quality opponents, most of them at level weights. The seven-runner race was won by a French horse of Marcel Boussac's called Laurentis who had Gordon Richards on board. Montignac, who was ridden by Popol Blanc, finished 16 lengths away in sixth place. His starting price was 20–1.

John Goldsmith was entirely satisfied. The 7st 5lb weight his horse was subsequently allotted in the Round Tower Handicap, due to be run at Windsor over a mile and a half on Friday, 30 May, was probably a stone too little. With only six horses to beat and the good lightweight jockey Dennis 'Mickey' Greening booked to further ease the load, Montignac looked the proverbial 'good thing'.

Percy Thompson was given the go-ahead. The bookie-gambler was planning to place a £5,000 bet on his horse (£175,000 in 2015), investing both for himself and for the stable. He hoped to get odds of around 5–2, or two and a half times his stake, which would've yielded a profit of over £437,000 in today's money. But he wouldn't be doing it at the Victoria Club weeks in advance as he had with Querneville in the Lincoln. There were no call-overs on small races like the Round Tower Handicap. The money would have to go on with the bookmakers in the ring at Windsor, but it would be difficult to place the whole amount with one operator. There would need to be a number of transactions hopefully struck before the bookies were fully aware of the size of the gamble and slashed the price.

Percy reasoned that if his colleagues knew he was behind the bets they'd cut the odds anyway so his answer was to employ a notorious punter and card player called Hughie Rowan to put the money on for him. The 78-year-old, known in the ring as 'The Old 'Un', was a silver-haired Australian con man who had settled in Europe after World War One. In the 1920s and 1930s he used to 'work the boats', meaning he travelled back and forth on the great transatlantic liners like the *Normandie* and the *Ile de France* looking for rich mugs to fleece.

On the first night out from Le Havre or Southampton, Rowan would appear in the bar after dinner looking handsome and immaculately dressed in his evening clothes. Genial conversations would begin with his fellow first-class passengers, leading on to talk of a poker game for modest stakes. Hughie would be sure to fluff whatever hands he was dealt that first night, encouraging his new friends to return for more easy pickings the next night and the next. Then on the final night before landing the Old 'Un would miraculously get lucky, cleaning out his foolish chums right down to their shirts, vests and collar studs. Some of the suckers realised they'd been filleted but some didn't and vowed to see Hughie again on the return trip. The Australian, giving a handsome tip to the purser and chief steward in return for their help, said he'd look forward to it.

Rowan used his profits from the card games to support his other great passions: entertaining pretty women half his age and betting on racehorses. He would turn up at meetings like Epsom carrying a battered old suitcase containing up to £15,000 in cash (nearly £525,000 in modern money) and spray it around liberally throughout the afternoon. The bookies who fielded his bets are long dead but the 93-year-old Benno Miller, the Bond Street commission agent who knew Percy Thompson and acted as a go-between for wealthy punters, remembers him vividly. 'The trouble with Hughie,' he says, 'is that he couldn't ever see a favourite losing. But no matter how much he lost on one race he'd always be back for the next.'

By 1947 Rowan was backing a lot more seconds and thirds than winners and the racecourse bookies were inclined to patronise him, accepting his big bets without cutting the odds or laying off. His new reputation as a Big Loser suited Percy Thompson ideally. If Hughie went down the rails at Windsor backing Montignac with fistfuls of readies the bookmakers would just think it was business as usual and accept the bets without flinching and without immediately realising he was working for Thompson.

The day of the race was a fine, dry, early summer's day, sunshine streaming through the horse chestnut trees and dappling the horses' coats as they walked around the Windsor paddock. The heart of the old grandstand with its fireplace, wooden panelling and prints of old Derby winners on the walls has changed little in the past 70 years and, despite the noise from the aeroplanes overhead, the view from the outdoor terracing is still one of pleasure boats passing on the river, rowers skulling up to Dorney and open fields beyond. On a summer Sunday in 2014 there were no more than half a dozen bookies on the rails and maybe twice that on the boards, but in the late 1940s the racecourse was always packed and the betting ring heaving with money.

The punters got off to a great start. The favourites won the first four races and the second, third and fourth of them resulted in a treble for Gordon Richards. Many racegoers followed the champion's mounts blindly and the hat-trick put the crowd in a holiday mood. One day at Chepstow in 1933 Richards had gone through the card riding all six winners and five more the next day. But he wouldn't be able to do that at Windsor as he didn't have a ride in the Round Tower Handicap, which was the fifth race on the programme and due off at 4 p.m.

Fifteen minutes beforehand John and Annette Goldsmith went down to the boxes in the pre-parade ring to saddle up Montignac and then they accompanied him into the paddock. At ten minutes to four Mickey Greening and the other riders walked out of the weighing room to meet their trainers. By this time Hughie Rowan was busy in the betting ring, but, in an attempt to throw the enemy off the scent, Percy Thompson had gone into the 'Members' Bar' with the Reading bookmaker Alf Turner and nonchalantly ordered a bottle of champagne.

When the runners cantered down to the start John and Tiny went to a pre-arranged spot in the owners and trainers section of the stand and just before the race was due to get under way Percy Thompson joined them there. Hughie Rowan was nowhere to be seen, but when Percy trained his binoculars on the bookies' boards he knew something was wrong. It was a very strong betting market at Windsor but to prevent Montignac's odds from falling too far Rowan, who was known often to back two runners in a race, was meant to be backing the second favourite Glide Away too. In the circumstances Percy had expected a £5,000 bet to cause Montignac's opening price to contract to something like 2–1 or 11–8. But minutes before the off there was no money for Glide Away whereas his horse was trading at a prohibitive 8–13, or 13–8 on, which meant you would have to wager £13 to win £8 and so on.

Windsor is a figure-of-eight track and mile-and-a-half races begin on the far side of the course, initially running parallel with the river. An outsider called Avon Prince led for the first two furlongs but then Montignac went to the front, setting a good pace as befitted a guaranteed stayer and two-mile hurdle winner in France. Mickey Greening cut across to the inside rail as he manoeuvred deftly round the bend at the top end of the course and, turning into the home straight, he had the running rail on his right. Glide Away, who was trained by the Queen Mother's friend Major Peter Cazalet and ridden by Michael Beary, got his head in front with a quarter of a mile to run but Montignac was just idling. Greening gave him one tap with the whip and the French-bred asserted himself again, running on to win 'a shade cleverly' in that expression so beloved by the *Sporting Life* by one and a half lengths. How easy was that? thought John Goldsmith.

After they'd greeted the victor in the unsaddling enclosure, where John told Clive Graham that a return to hurdling was probable for Montignac the following winter, they all retired to the bar. Hughie Rowan was already there with a girl on each arm and a glass in his hand. It should have been a great celebratory moment and champagne all round but as John, Annette and Percy looked at Rowan, who was by now surrounded by an enthralled group of journalists, punters and betting ring faces including Geoffrey

Hamlyn, they realised that the Montignac coup was blown and had been since before they'd ever set foot on Windsor racecourse.

Rowan told Percy sheepishly that he had averaged even money to his £5,000 stake, which meant that Thompson had won just £175,000 in modern money rather than the £400,000 plus he'd been expecting. John's share had fallen dramatically too. Minutes later the bookmaker Jack Stein arrived with a tally of all of Hughie's bets on Montignac which he proceeded to read out. It transpired that in total Rowan had staked no less than £40,000 on Thompson's horse (a staggering £1.4 million today), taking all prices from 5–2 down to the eventual 8–13 SP.

The press were saying that Hughie's combined winnings – not counting Thompson's profit – were more like £55,000 (£1,925,000 today). If true it was one of the biggest wins and boldest plunges of the 20th century. Unfortunately the truth was less heroic. As Percy Thompson and John Goldsmith soon discovered, Hughie had tipped off the bookmaker Max Parker – who was Jack Stein's brother and to whom Rowan owed at least £20,000 (£700,000 today) – about the extent of stable confidence in the 'job'. At least half of the £40,000 bet in the ring at Windsor was Parker's, his agents piling money on to Montignac as soon as betting began. Rowan didn't put Percy's and the stable's bets on until Maxie's business was all done by which time the bigger prices had long gone.

There were no dead bodies on the terraces, as there had been on the slopes of Mont Ventoux, but John Goldsmith knew what an ambush looked like. In the Lincoln it was Popol Blanc flailing his whip that had undermined the coup. Two months later John had again trained a horse to the minute and executed his part to perfection. But thanks to Hughie Rowan and Percy Thompson's faulty security it was the wily Max Parker who had scooped the pot.

Hughie's share of the payout didn't last long. At Royal Ascot the following month he lost a reputed £80,000 (£2.8 million in modern money) over the four days. His worst result came in Friday's Queen Alexandra Stakes run over two and three quarter miles and the longest contest in the flat racing calendar. Hughie's money went on the 8–11 favourite Reynard Volant who was ridden by Eph Smith, trained in Newmarket by Jack Jarvis and had won the two-and-a-half-mile Ascot Stakes on the opening day of the meeting. Good horses had often doubled up in the two long-distance events and Hughie couldn't see Reynard Volant losing. But among his rivals was the French-trained Cesarewitch winner Monsieur l'Amiral, ridden by Charlie Smirke and owned by those two expatriate gamblers Hans Barnard-Hankey and Captain Ian Henderson. The high rollers were going for a touch on their horse too and stakes of more than £20,000 (£700,000 in 2015) forced Monsieur l'Amiral's odds down from 6–1 to 7–2 at the off by which point most bookies were refusing to take any more bets on him.

It was an extraordinary race. Monsieur l'Amiral who, according to his trainer Emile Charlier, 'always takes miles to warm up' was almost 20 lengths adrift with a mile to run as Reynard Volant looked all over the winner. But then the indefatigable 'Smirkie' started to get a tune out of his horse and, slowly, inexorably and horrifically for Hughie Rowan, he began to close the gap. Reynard Volant still had seven lengths to spare as they swung into the home straight but 'Monsieur' gradually wore him down. Taking the lead inside the final furlong, he won by a length.

It was the penultimate race of the week. The very last was the five-furlong King's Stand Stakes and Hughie backed the favourite, Port Blanc, in that one too, and it lost. The next day Hughie went to Windsor for an evening meeting and had £5,000 to win £1,000 on

THE BIG LOSER

Glendower ridden by Gordon Richards in the final race on the card.
It won, reducing Rowan's liabilities by a paltry grand. The game, it
seemed, was no longer worth the candle.

The Australian had been living in the Russell Hotel near St
Pancras which, appropriately considering Rowan's old ocean-going
life, was partly designed by Charles Fitzroy Doll, who also designed
the first-class dining room on the *Titanic*. Bomb-damaged Fitzrovia,
as the neighbourhood was known, was a favourite 1940s haunt of
bohemians, drunks, chancers and petty crooks and Hughie had
always been assured of a good audience in the local pubs. But on the
afternoon of 27 June he returned to the hotel's conflation of pomp,
marble and stained glass and asked a porter to come up to his room
in 20 minutes as he'd have some rubbish to clear away. He then went
upstairs and hanged himself with a pyjama cord from the hook on
the back of his bedroom door. Only the hook wouldn't bear Hughie's
weight. The cord snapped and his body fell to the ground, causing
him to have a heart attack. When the porter duly arrived minutes
later he found Rowan lying dead on the floor.

By a strange irony, another old associate of John Goldsmith's,
Hans Josef Kieffer, met his death by hanging that same day. The
former SS officer and SD head of counter-espionage at the avenue
Foch in Paris had escaped detection in the first year after the war
but in 1946 he was tracked down in Germany by British war crimes
investigators. Vera Atkins was one of those who interrogated him
before his trial and he told her that Henri Déricourt had been the F
Section traitor not Gilbert Norman, though he added that Norman
'had not the integrity of Prosper', by which he meant Francis Suttill,
who had been extremely brave. When Atkins brought up the fate of
Noor Inayat Khan and the other female SOE captives Kieffer, who
was the father of three children and kept a photograph of his eldest

daughter in his cell, broke down in tears. Vera Atkins was unmoved. 'If one of us is going to cry it's going to be me,' she said. 'You will please stop this comedy.'

Kieffer was found guilty of ordering the murder of five SAS prisoners in a wood near Paris in 1944 and sentenced to death.[37] The British hangman Albert Pierrepoint executed him at Hamelin Prison on 27 June 1947, and the end came a lot quicker for him than it had done for Gilbert Norman, Jimmy Amps, Rowland Dowlen and John Young.

---

37 Twelve uniformed SAS men had landed by parachute at the beginning of July 1944. Thanks to a captured wireless set, the SD were able to intercept them. Four of them were killed in a gun battle and five were taken prisoner. They were made to change into civilian clothes and were then driven to a wood near Noailles and shot.

25

JOURNEY'S END

On 24 June 1947, a week after Royal Ascot, a famous cartoon by Osbert Lancaster appeared in the *Daily Express*. It featured a caricature spiv with a thin moustache, loud tie and a long drape suit. Standing next to him were a respectable middle-aged couple. 'Don't be stuffy,' the wife was saying to her husband. 'I'm sure the young man will give you the name of a really good tailor who doesn't bother about coupons.'

The cartoon amused John Goldsmith and reminded him of his wartime incarnation as Jean Delannoy the French black marketeer. Spivs were everywhere that year, including outside Epsom racecourse on Derby Day where they were selling everything from nylons and collapsible picnic tables to racing tips and information. Not a few of them tipped the Goldsmith-trained Aigle Royal II in the seven-furlong Epsom Plate, and quite right too. The French-bred, backed in from 8–1 to 11–2 on course, took the lead with a quarter of a mile to run and ran out a comfortable two-length winner. The next day's report in the *Sporting Life* was effusive in its praise for the winning trainer. 'Major John Goldsmith has done remarkably well with the horses he bought in France during the last twelve months or so,' enthused Meyrick Good. 'Montignac, the big Windsor winner, being one of them and now Aigle Royal.'

John's big Epsom winner helped some punters recover the losses they sustained on the Derby. Everyone's selection had been the Guineas winner, Tudor Minstrel, and a massive nationwide gamble resulted in Gordon Richards' mount going off as the 4–7 favourite. But Tudor Minstrel barely stayed a yard beyond a mile. Pulling his way to the front early on he was a spent force by Tattenham Corner and finished a well-beaten fourth. The race was won by yet another French-trained challenger, Pearl Diver, who was ridden by Urgay's jockey, George Bridgland.

The terrible winter of 1947 had given way to a summer heatwave and from late May right up to the St Leger meeting at Doncaster in September, Britain baked under blue skies and a scorching sun. Buckingham Palace announced the engagement of Princess Elizabeth to Lieutenant Philip Mountbatten. The Boulting Brothers were filming *Brighton Rock* with Richard Attenborough as Pinkie and the public were gripped by the real-life crime story of three young tearaways on trial at the Old Bailey for shooting Alex de Antiquis, a 'have-a-go-hero' and father of six, during a failed jewel robbery in central London.[38]

In the world of betting and racing there continued to be a fine line between acceptable spivvery and more sinister black marketeering and fraud. It was a time when exotic European figures suddenly popped up from the ruins bearing large amounts of cash or items like diamonds and paintings. One of the most mysterious was the

---

38   Charles 'Harry Boy' Jenkins, aged 23, and Christopher Geraghty, aged 21, were convicted of murder in July and hanged by Albert Pierrepoint, in a double ex-ecution, at Pentonville on 19 September 1947.

Hungarian gambler Baron Hatvany who had owned a priceless art collection in Budapest that had been looted by both the Russians and the Nazis. The Baron claimed to have retained some items and used their value to buy a string of French-bred horses. 'Could you believe him?' wonders John Goldsmith's friend Gerry Albertini. 'Well, life was like that then and so many people of that type turned up after the war. He had a moustache and a hunched back and was an incredibly lucky punter who won so much on the 1948 Autumn Double that he could afford to live at the Hyde Park Hotel.[39] He was also as mean as mouse shit and would arrive at a party with his own sandwiches and biscuits. Then, when he'd finished those, he'd proceed to eat everyone else out of house and home.'

The Baron liked to bet heavily on his horses and wanted John Goldsmith to train them for him. John was happy to lay one or two of them out for a coup, but after a number of unsatisfactory experiences he decided he'd had enough of the Baron's manipulative Cruz-Valer tricks and passed him on to Captain Ryan Price instead. It seemed an appropriate choice. The piratical Captain was another war hero who had swum ashore on D-Day with Lord Lovat's Commandos and fought his way across France, Holland and Germany. In a training career that encompassed victories in almost all the major races he was extremely partial to a gamble. But Hatvany eventually fell out with him too and switched stables for a second time.[40]

As the 1940s wore on John trained more and better horses for Percy Thompson and for other owners like Mrs Bobby McAlpine,

---

39   The Autumn Double – the Cesarewitch along with the Cambridgeshire, another big handicap and betting race run over nine furlongs which also takes place at Newmarket in October.

40   The best horse John Goldsmith trained for Hatvany was called Oui Oui, who was placed at the Cheltenham Festival. The Baron died in London in 1958.

of the building firm, who was a Cheshire friend of Tiny's mother – chasers and hurdlers long forgotten now but bywords in their time for quality and big-money plunges. There was the almost all-white Solo II. The giant Soda who was almost 18 hands high and, like Black Hawk in 1939, was unluckily brought down when going strongly in the Grand National. The French Champion Hurdle winner Vatelys, who was ridden at Auteuil by Alec Head, who would go on to become a champion flat racing trainer. Campeador, Royal Oak and Master Fox. But the best of them all was a brilliant French-bred steeplechaser called Le Jacobin who was the two-mile champion of his day.

At the 1948 Cheltenham Festival, John ran the four-year-old in the National Hunt Juvenile Chase over two miles. On the back of a prep race over hurdles at Windsor, the handsome bay, who ran in Percy Thompson's purple colours with a mauve star front and back, was backed down to 3–1 favourite in a field of 21. His jockey that day was Bobby Bates who, despite his Anglicised name, was born in Marseille and spoke very little English.

New to the Cotswolds he might have been but Bates navigated Cheltenham racecourse like an old hand. Gerry Albertini was there – it was his first National Hunt Festival – and he has never forgotten it. The second favourite Starwings, ridden by George Vergette, went off into a long lead 'and was still in front as they came out of the mist running down the hill'. But Le Jacobin was only just behind him and Bates had stolen the inside rail. Vergette rode a spirited finish but Le Jacobin, 'clearing the last like a gazelle', was always holding him and sprinted four lengths clear.

As John Goldsmith looked down from Cheltenham's old wooden firetrap of a grandstand and saw his best horse storming up the famous hill he must have felt as if it was moments like this that he had been fighting for. Le Jacobin would be the high point of his training career. Next time out the French-bred won at Windsor by 20 lengths and then returned to Cheltenham for another effortless triumph in April. All told he won 26 races over fences and on the flat between March 1948 and February 1951 and was one of the best-loved horses in training.

Despite these successes, Percy Thompson was an increasingly difficult man to work for, and it was his gambling that was the problem. One muddy Wednesday in December 1948 he persuaded John to run four of his best horses at modest Plumpton racecourse in East Sussex. The bookmaker needed funds and thought he could get some from a short odds 'accumulator' on four good things. The nature of the bet meant that any money won on the first horse would go on to the second and, if that won, the combined winnings would go on to the third, and so on. But while two of them – Soda and Master Fox – won, two of them fell, including Querneville who was now jumping fences, and Bobby Bates was concussed and had to be carried from the track on a stretcher.

The jockey recovered remarkably quickly and rode seven winners for John in a four-day period at the end of the month. Among them was the giant gelding Soda who landed a valuable four-mile steeple-chase by six lengths at Cheltenham on the 29th. Percy Thompson's money went on at all prices from 8–1 to 11–2, and he wasn't the only one to profit. Tiny tipped the winner in advance to Clive Graham who observed that 'trainers' wives are generally pretty shrewd judges'. The Sporting Life agreed, declaring that 'John Goldsmith has a grand stable of jumpers at Aston Tirrold and Percy Thompson owns pos-sibly the two best cross-country specialists in training in Soda and Solo who Goldsmith sees as a Gold Cup prospect'.

Solo gave a thrilling display of quick and accurate fencing to win at Cheltenham the next day and, on the same card, the Imperial Cup victor Tant Pis 'took thousands out of the ring', according to Geoffrey Hamlyn, when winning a two-mile handicap hurdle. Then on the 31st it was the turn of Montignac, back over hurdles as John had promised, who pulled off another betting coup in a selling race at Manchester. The result was a lifeline for Clive Graham who, as one of his New Year resolutions in the *Express*, vowed that henceforth he would concentrate on John Goldsmith-trained runners and 'never again bet, and lose, my car on the outcome of a horse race'.

John and Tiny celebrated the advent of 1949 in one of their favourite haunts, the Berkeley Hotel. The West End was buzzing with the news that the racehorse owner and gambler Prince Aly Khan had flown into London with the newly divorced Hollywood star Rita Hayworth, the couple taking rooms at the Ritz. The Aly, a notorious philanderer when it came to the women in his life, was much more faithful to the men who trained his horses. By contrast, John Goldsmith was having more trouble with Percy Thompson, who had become a bad payer, rarely settling a training bill on time.

The bookmaker had started sending horses to other trainers too, including Coubrador, a French-bred hurdler that was laid out by George Todd for the 1949 Cesarewitch at Newmarket. 'They hooked the horse up all year,' remembers the commission agent Benno Miller. 'He was ridden by Harry Wragg's brother Adam but he got tired before the horse and would have been better off watching from the stands.' Percy backed Coubrador to win nearly £2 million but, in one of the most exciting finishes in the 110-year history of the race, a dozen horses were still in with a chance at the two-furlong marker. Wragg came late but too late and Coubrador was beaten a head by Pat Rank's runner, Strathspey.

Thompson attempted to recover his losses when Coubrador ran in a hurdle race at Kempton over Christmas. With the amateur rider

John Hislop in the saddle the supposed world beater was backed down to 15–8 favourite but fell halfway round. Thompson, who had been watching from his pitch in Tattersalls, looked 'a very rueful man' as he walked back to the car park at the end of the afternoon.

The black market boom years were coming to an end. Master spivs like the currency racketeer Max Intrator and the car dealer Stanley Setty were either dead or in jail and the supply of gambling high rollers had dried up.[41] Percy Thompson was owed money by punters who couldn't pay and, in turn, had debts all around the ring and to the big off-course credit bookies, like Max Parker, too. In March 1951 one of his biggest clients, an Egyptian gambler and friend of King Farouk, was killed when his light plane crashed in the Rhône Valley on a return flight from London to the south of France. With no chance of recovering the huge sum the Egyptian owed him and having also taken a hit on a series of stock market investments, including an infant television company, Percy 'knocked' or defaulted on his liabilities. The big player was bankrupt. His London and Brighton offices were sold, his racehorses were sold, and at one point he wanted John Goldsmith to sell his stable yard too to bail him out. 'When Thompson went belly up John was hit very hard,' recalls Gerry Albertini. 'He'd incurred all these costs on Percy's behalf for saddlery and feed and vets' bills and farriers and transport and entries and now there was no one there to pay them.'

The size of the Goldsmith string was halved at a stroke, which was a grievous situation for any trainer to be in. He'd lost his number

41 The Berlin-born Intrator, also known as 'Palestine Max', was supposedly one of the prototypes for Graham Greene's Harry Lime in *The Third Man*, which opened in London on 2 September 1949. In October 1949 the car salesman Setty was murdered by his business partner Donald Hume who scattered Setty's dismembered body from a plane over the Essex marshes.

one rider too. Bobby Bates, who should have been champion jockey, went back to France after Thompson's downfall and in 1952 he was killed when he fractured his skull in a fall at Auteuil.

But that year, John had an even bigger tragedy to contend with. In 1949 Tiny had given birth to a second daughter, Gisele, who was born, like her sister, in Newbury, her parents having been at the races there earlier in the day. Where Gaie was a tomboy and full of spirit, Gisele was blonde, blue-eyed and extremely pretty. With his beautiful wife, his two contrasting yet well-matched daughters and his burgeoning reputation as a trainer, John's life seemed to have achieved a state of perfect harmony. But on 2 April 1952, the day after Gaie's eleventh birthday and when Gisele was not yet two and a half, their mother died suddenly of a coronary thrombosis. She was 32 years old.

John Goldsmith had lost not just the love of his life but his best friend and indispensable companion. She was the woman who had waited for him, prayed for him, ridden his horses, supported him emotionally, professionally and financially and borne his two daughters. How could he possibly go on without her? 'To begin with,' remembers Gerry Albertini, 'he went to pieces.' Drink, despair and mounting financial problems could have been the end of him. 'What kept him going was the little girls.'

Precious the company of his two daughters might have been, but that summer John was in no condition to take care of them. Salvation came in the shape of an offer from an American friend, John Tyson, who had been in the OSS during the war – the US equivalent of SOE – and who should've been a colleague of John's on the missions to the prisoner of war camps in Germany in 1945. Tyson and his wife offered to look after Gaie and Gisele until John had managed to sort himself out. The couple lived in a big house in Radnor, Pennsylvania, one of the socially smart towns on the so-called 'Main Line' which connects the Pennsylvania suburbs to Philadelphia. It was the setting for the 1940 Katharine Hepburn–Cary Grant romantic comedy *The Philadelphia Story* (based on the socialite Helen Hope Montgomery Scott), and one of the ritziest addresses on the Eastern Seaboard.

Leaving their father to grieve alone, the girls set sail on the *Queen Elizabeth* in June 1952 and didn't return until a few weeks before Christmas. They were accompanied by their nanny Ethel, or Nanny Palmer as she was known, who wore a proper uniform with a starched apron and a hat. The Tysons were a wealthy family and for six months their guests enjoyed a level of comfort far removed from the rationing and austerity that still afflicted post-war Britain. They returned in December on the *Queen Mary*, and according to Gaie the sisters had 'a riotous time on board. There was a big storm and practically everyone was ill, Nanny included. But we were both fine and we felt we had the run of the ship.'

John's daughters were reunited with their father on Didcot Station. They had brought him a pair of American cowboy boots as a present and Gaie remembers him putting them on beneath his pyjama trousers to feed the horses on Christmas morning.

A new pattern of life gradually evolved, beginning with a new nanny. Edna Booth from Derbyshire was a friend of the departing Ethel and she was just 16 years old, little more than five years older than Gaie, when she first came to work at Aston Tirrold. In the years that followed she became a good friend to the girls, even as she was dragooning them to bed or to school on time. Eventually she became an even closer friend of their father, and on 3 October 1959 John and Edna were married.

Gaie and Gisele have many happy memories of the years they all spent together in Oxfordshire with what Gaie describes as 'a tremendously hands-on father who was great fun to be with'. John had bought an Alvis and the girls would sit in the open boot and bounce up and down as they were driven around the local lanes singing Elvis Presley songs at the tops of their voices.

Gaie loved everything to do with the stable and racing and riding. Gisele learned to speak French and loved hearing about her father's passion for French wine. 'He knew them all and could describe every grape and bouquet,' she recalls. He continued to love oysters too and took his daughters out to lunch at Wheelers in Old Compton Street where the racing and betting-mad owner, Bernard Walsh, was a good friend. As they got older the girls were sometimes taken to the old SOE favourite the Gaiety Club, and to dinner at the Special Forces Club in Knightsbridge.

Following Percy Thompson's bankruptcy there were never more than about 30 horses in the stable at Aston Tirrold. The days of the big betting coups and of champions like Le Jacobin had passed. John's runners were now more likely to be seen at the smaller tracks like Warwick, where Gaie remembers 'he had a favourite mare who always won', and Brighton, where the prize money was surprisingly good well into the 1960s and something of the old pre-war flavour and banter still prevailed. With no rich patron to place stable commissions, John did his betting with the amiable Ted Sturman, who traded as Fred Binns. 'He used to be the banker in the chemmy games[42] at the Adelphi during the Grand National meeting,' says Gerry Albertini. 'People thought that he was fat but it was just a thick money belt he wore around his waist packed with ten-, twenty- and fifty-pound notes.'

---

42 Chemin de fer, a high-stakes card game extremely popular in racing and smart social circles in the post-war decades. Similar to baccarat, which James Bond plays in *Casino Royale*.

Albertini had horses with John in the 1950s including a French-bred steeplechaser called Savic II who 'unfortunately wasn't much good'. But the owner always appreciated getting a telegram from his trainer talking of 'gradual improvement' when Savic came second instead of third and, even when the results weren't going their way, the two spent many convivial hours together in each other's company. 'One day he invited me to lunch and we went out beforehand and tried to shoot a few pheasants but neither of us could hit a barn door. John was laughing. He used to say that in SOE he'd always been pretty useless with a gun and much better with a knife and a garrotte. He really was an incredible expert on French wine though and he was going to serve me a couple of very good bottles at lunch. But when we got back to the house we found that someone had left the bottles on the Aga and they'd boiled. John was furious.'

Money may have been tighter and winners less frequent but John had certain standards which never dropped. All of his suits were tailor-made by Huntsman of Savile Row, who had made Jean Delannoy's spiv's get-up in 1942. His grey hair was cut regularly by Cyril Topper in London and every Sunday he polished all his shoes. According to Gaie he would take and polish everybody else's too and 'not be at all amused by a boyfriend who didn't look after his shoes'.

As well as good wine, John still enjoyed his packets of Gauloises and Disque Bleu, the scent of the black tobacco forever reminding him of the war. When he ran out of French cigarettes he smoked John Player untipped. But in 1967 his health took a knock when he had to have a cartilage operation and lost a lot of blood. At the age of 58 John Goldsmith started to think back over the life he had led and to wonder how much time he had left.

In March 1969 the now 33-year-old Edna accompanied her husband on an emotional return journey to Paris. They took

Madame Tantzy and her devoted beau Monsieur Henri, still alive aged 88, out to dinner at the Tour d'Argent and the following day they went on a pilgrimage to the Hôtel Continentale.[43] There had been many changes and renovations since 1943 and the room John was locked up in was now a linen room. But a helpful young manageress showed them up to the third floor and when they looked out of a window, 60 feet up, John could see the ledge. It was still there, along with the glass roof of the palm court below. They went back downstairs and looked up at the ledge from the atrium floor. John wryly. Edna wonderingly, fearfully, admiringly.

Outside on the street they counted the number of steps John would have taken as he hurried from the side entrance of the hotel on the rue de Castiglione down to the crossroads and then left along to the place de la Concorde. Unlike that early Wednesday morning 26 years earlier, the great square was roaring with traffic and packed with tourists.

It was the final month of de Gaulle's presidency. He'd survived assassination attempts at the height of the Algerian crisis in 1962 but the *événements* and student riots of May 1968 had almost finished him off. Seeking the backing of the army he'd managed to mobilise enough traditional support to stay in office. But he was increasingly seen as old, conservative and out of touch, and in April 1969 he would resign and retire to his country house in the village of Colombey les Deux Églises in south-eastern France.

The General's anointed successor was his former Prime Minister Georges Pompidou, a banker who promised the French modernity, prosperity and change along with a tacit agreement to bury

---

43   In 1969 the hotel was renamed the Inter Continental Paris. In 2005 it became the Westin, and since 2010 it's been known as the Westin Vendôme.

uncomfortable memories of their wartime past. But the old SOE agent in his racing man's sheepskin-collar coat gazing at the Continentale and the Meurice, where the Germans used to hang swastika flags overlooking the rue de Rivoli, and at Maxim's and Prunier and at Longchamp racecourse and Auteuil and at the great houses on the avenue Foch, still saw the past at every turn.

After 48 hours in the capital John Goldsmith – or was it Jean Delannoy? – crossed the Seine to the Gare du Lyon and took a train south for a reunion with Camille Rayon in Antibes. The Maquis chieftain had become a rich man. As well as owning a restaurant, La Maison des Pêcheurs, he had set up a company that financed the building of the first yacht marina on the Côte d'Azur. Port Vauban would be followed by 20 more in other towns along the coast including Port Camille Rayon in Vallauris Golfe-Juan.

Le Grand Patron told John that he intended to drink a bottle of champagne every day for the rest of his life.

The two old *copains* were joined for lunch by André Bartoli and Paulo Leonetti, the mild-mannered insurance salesman and the extrovert hairdresser who had hidden and protected John back in those strange days in 1942. They all talked about their time in the Resistance and about the ones who made it and the ones who didn't survive, and they toasted their memory and the felucca landings and the arms drops and the battle with the Germans on Mont Ventoux and they all drank champagne together until long after the day had ended.

John Goldsmith drew on that reunion and other wartime memories for his autobiography, *An Accidental Agent*, published by Leo Cooper in August 1971. By then the author was seriously ill. Complications with his cartilage operation two years before had developed into leukaemia.

John had always wanted to explore the Far East and, with the help of his friend Sir Peter O'Sullevan, he was hoping to work as a stipendiary steward for the Hong Kong Jockey Club. John and Edna had gone out to Hong Kong together, and when the gravity of his condition became clear it was his third wife, the former nanny, who looked after him and supported him. He decided not to return to the UK and implored his daughters not to come out and see him in his declining state but to remember him as he was.

John Goldsmith died in Hong Kong on 1 January 1972. He was cremated and his ashes brought back to England and buried with Tiny and his father in the churchyard at Aston Tirrold. He was 62 years old.

For Gaie and Gisele their father's early death was a unique and very personal tragedy. Edna too was devastated. Tiny was the love of John's life but John was the love of Edna's life. He was mourned by the racing world, and not just by owners, trainers, jockeys and journalists. His old bookmaking adversaries also stood up to salute a man with few peers at placing a horse or preparing it to peak on a given day. Benno Miller, the old commission agent who remembers Percy Thompson and Hughie Rowan, says that 'everyone in the betting ring from the 1940s to the 1960s knew that John Goldsmith was an extremely brave, tough and upstanding gentleman'. He could have added that not every trainer of that era was similarly respected.

The newspaper obituaries quoted from the citation for John's DSO and listed his French honours too but the testimonials were not especially lengthy or numerous. Agent Valentin, who was always modest about his accomplishments, might have preferred it that way. But today his name is rarely mentioned in conjunction with other great SOE heroes and heroines like Odette Sansom, Peter Churchill and George Starr, and it's an omission that sorely deserves to be redressed.

John Gilbert Goldsmith was not a professional spy. He was an English racehorse trainer who happened to have been born and brought up in Paris and spoke fluent French. But at one of the darkest points in European history he joined that small, select group of amateurs and volunteers who found the necessary blend of courage, ingenuity and flair to play a most dangerous game, for the highest stakes, and win.

POSTSCRIPT

Family

John's eldest daughter Gaie married the trainer Fulke Johnson Houghton, scion of one of England's most famous racing families. Gaie was by Fulke's side throughout a long and distinguished career during which he saddled many big race winners including dual victors of the Irish Derby and St Leger and Ile de Bourbon, hero of the 1978 King George VI and Queen Elizabeth Stakes. In 2007 the couple handed over the reins to their daughter Eve who has maintained the family tradition and trains at Blewbury to this day.

Gisele, who remains a fluent linguist, is a businesswoman and lives in Hertfordshire. She is married with grown-up children.

John's third wife Edna is still alive and lives in southern England.

Racing

John Goldsmith's old patron Percy Thompson ended up living in relative obscurity in Brighton. The bookmaker Victor Chandler – father of the present Victor – found him there in the 1960s and gave him a job working as a settler behind the counter in his betting shop on the London Road. The once legendary gambler died on the south coast ten years later.

Querneville's jockey, Paul 'Popol' Blanc, retired from race riding in 1958 and was employed by the French racing authority, the Société d'Encouragement, at Longchamp. When Sir Peter O'Sullevan went over to Paris for the Prix de l'Arc de Triomphe he would often reminisce with Popol about the 1947 Lincoln and what might have been.

The bookmaker Max Parker, who profited from the Montignac coup, bought Ladbrokes in 1956 for a rumoured £250,000. Maxie died in 1966 and was succeeded as Ladbrokes Chairman by his nephew Cyril Stein.

SOE

Colonel Maurice Buckmaster was employed in the 1950s and 1960s as Ford's Director of Public Affairs. He wrote several magazine articles about SOE and published two volumes of memoirs. He died at his home in Forest Row in East Sussex, aged 90, in 1992.

Vera Atkins was awarded the Croix de Guerre in 1948, the Légion d'Honneur in 1995 and the CBE in 1997. She died in Hastings in 2000, aged 92, and is buried in Zennor in Cornwall.

Brigadier Colin Gubbins, unwanted by the War Office, left the army in 1946. A keen fisherman and shot, he retired to the Highlands and Islands and died in Stornoway, aged 79, in 1976.

Selwyn Jepson continued his writing career after the war, turning out more thrillers and several television scripts for the BBC. He died in 1989.

Bill Sykes, the SOE expert on demolition and silent killing, left the firm after the liberation of France and retired to a boarding house in Bexhill-on-Sea. He died there, aged 52, in May 1945.

Roger de Wesselow resumed his publishing career with Welbecson Press and died, aged 69, in 1959 of respiratory problems caused by the gas he inhaled in World War One. His grandson James is a former managing director of Racing Post Books.

Arthur Staggs, John's contemporary under Major de Wesselow's command at Wanborough Manor and the only other member of Party 27P who went to France and survived, died in Bedford in 2013. He was 100 years old.

France

Henri Déricourt, the former SOE air transport officer and suspected traitor, was arrested at Croydon Aerodrome in 1946 attempting to take gold and platinum out of the country without a licence. Flown to Paris, he went on trial before a military tribunal in 1948 accused of consorting with the enemy. The former deputy head of F Section, Nicholas Boddington, controversially testified on Déricourt's behalf that he had been authorised to make contact with the Germans. He was found not guilty.

Still flying in and out of war zones, Déricourt died in a plane crash in Laos in 1962.

General Charles de Gaulle died in November 1970 shortly before his 80th birthday and was buried at Colombey les Deux Églises. As his body was lowered into the ground the great bell at Notre Dame began to toll and was followed by all the bells in all the churches across France.

De Gaulle's old wartime rival Henri Giraud had died in 1949. He had been elected to the new French Chamber of Deputies and participated in the drawing up of the constitution of the 4th Republic. De Gaulle scrapped the constitution when he returned as President in 1958.

General René Chambe became a prolific peacetime author and acknowledged expert on aviation. He died, aged 94, in 1983.

André Girard, head of the disastrous Carte resistance network, went into self-imposed exile after the war and died in New York, aged 67, in 1968.

Jean Leonetti, whose trousers John Goldsmith borrowed in 1942, succeeded his father Paulo as Mayor of Antibes–Juan-Les-Pins. He later became a UMP member of the French parliament.

Camille Rayon stuck to his vow to drink champagne, usually a magnum poured by his Vietnamese manservant, every day for the rest of his life. On his 100th birthday in 2013 all the yachts in Port Vauban sounded their horns at midday in his honour. Le Grand Patron died in Antibes in September 2014. He was 101.

There is a memorial to the Maquis of the Vaucluse and Mont Ventoux outside the village of Sault and commemorations take place there every year.

In May 1991 a special monument was unveiled at Valençay in the department of the Indre. It marked the 50th anniversary of the first SOE F Section landing on French soil. The memorial is dedicated to the 104 F Section agents – 91 men and 13 women – who gave their lives so that fascism would be defeated and France might be free.

ACKNOWLEDGEMENTS

When I was researching my previous book *Doped* I met a number of betting and bookmaking veterans who told me about the colossal gambles that took place on British racecourses in the late 1940s and early 1950s. One of the most revered figures of that era, they said, was the trainer John Goldsmith who was renowned not only for his skill at preparing his horses to peak when the money was down but for his fearless wartime record. Goldsmith, it seemed, had been an agent in the Special Operations Executive, SOE. He had been dropped behind enemy lines three times and caught by the Gestapo in Paris in 1943. By the end of the war he had been awarded the DSO, Military Cross, Croix de Guerre and Légion d'Honneur.

Intrigued and wanting to know more I went to the National Archives in Kew where I was able to read John Goldsmith's SOE file and the files of related agents and operations. A fascinating story opened up before me. I grew up haunted by tales of the Special Operations Executive, of The White Rabbit and Violette Szabo and the courage of the many disparate men and women who 'set Europe ablaze'. Now here was an SOE agent whose 'unusual qualities of bluff and daring', as Colonel Maurice Buckmaster described them, had been forged in the worlds of racing, gambling and horse dealing which I knew well.

I read John Goldsmith's autobiography, *Accidental Agent*, which has long been out of print. I spoke to his daughters Gaie Johnson Houghton and Gisele Steel and to others who knew him and those quotations in the book without a direct footnote or attribution are all taken from the archives or from witness interviews and conversations. I also went to many of the locations in both Britain and France that played a part in John's life and gradually I was able to assemble a picture of that life not only in the Second World War but also before and after.

I am particularly indebted to Gaie and Gisele. It would have been impossible to embark on this book without their support and co-operation and I only hope I have done justice to their father and his remarkable story.

I should like to thank Alan Byrne and everyone at the *Racing Post* for backing the project, especially Julian Brown and Liz Ampairee for all their hard work and James de Wesselow – whose grandfather Roger was John Goldsmith's commanding officer at Wanborough Manor – for his enthusiasm and encouragement.

I am deeply grateful to my editor Ian Preece for his calm insight and perception and I'd also like to thank Brough Scott for his shrewd analysis, the line editor Daniel Balado, page designer John Schwartz and Jay Vincent for his wonderful jacket design.

I have been greatly helped by the reminiscences of the infinitely courteous Gerry Albertini, the astute Benno Miller and my first and foremost racing hero Sir Peter O'Sullevan who died in July, 2015. The Voice of Racing will forever be remembered by those of us for whom his superlative commentaries were the essential backdrop to our lives. But I think also of Peter's generosity of spirit and compassion for both humans and animals which co-existed so happily and stylishly with his consummate skill as a punter.

When I was in Paris I was lucky enough to enjoy the kindness and hospitality of Tom and Lisa Farrell at their home in St Cloud while the equally generous Jan Hollway let me have the run of her house in Provence and Sarah Winnington-Ingram and her family couldn't have looked after me better at Arisaig House. But more than anyone I want to thank my wife Sara for her fantastic tolerance, forebearance and support. I could never have got this far without her.

BIBLIOGRAPHY

Binney, Marcus – *Secret War Heroes.* (Hodder and Stoughton, 2005)

Buckmaster, Maurice – *They Fought Alone.* (Biteback Publishing Ltd, 2014, Odhams, 1958)

Churchill, Peter – *Of Their Own Choice.* (Hodder and Stoughton, 1952)

Foot, M.R.D – *SOE in France.* (Frank Cass Publishers, 2004)

Goldsmith, John – *Accidental Agent.* (Leo Cooper, 1971)

Hamlyn, Geoffrey – *My Sixty Years In The Ring.* (Sporting Garland Press, 1994)

Helm, Sarah – *A Life in Secrets: The True Story of Vera Atkins and the Lost Agents of SOE.* (Abacus, 2006, Little Brown, 2005)

Johnstone, Rae – *The Rae Johnstone Story: An Autobiography* with Peter O'Sullevan. (Stanley Paul, 1958)

Lambie, James – *The Story of Your Life.* (Matador, 2010)

Marks, Leo – *Between Silk and Cyanide.* (Sutton Publishing, 2007. The History Press, 2008)

Marshall, Bruce – *The White Rabbit.* (Cassell, 2000. Evans Bros Ltd, 1952)

Millar, George – *Maquis*. (The Dovecote Press Ltd, 2013. Heinemann Ltd, 1945)

O'Sullevan, Peter – *Calling The Horses*. (Stanley Paul, 1989. Hodder and Stoughton, updated edition, 1994)

O'Sullevan, Peter – *Peter O'Sullevan's Horse Racing Heroes*. (Highdown, 2004)

Pegg, Norman – *Focus On Racing*. (Robert Hale Ltd, 1963)

Perrault, Gilles – *Paris Under The Occupation*. (The Vendome Press, 1989)

Richards, Brooks – *Secret Flotillas, Vol II* (Pen and Sword Books, 2013)

Riols, Noreen – *The Secret Ministry of Ag. And Fish*. (Macmillan, 2013)

Savile, John – *Insane and Unseemly: British Racing in World War II*. (Matador, 2009)

Shortt, Philip – *Mitterand: A Study in Ambiguity*. (Vintage, 2014)

Sissons, Michael and French, Philip, Edited by – *Age of Austerity 1945–51*. (Penguin, 1963)

Suttill, Francis J – *Shadows in The Fog*. (The History Press, 2014)

Sweet, Matthew – *The West End Front*. (Faber and Faber Ltd, 2011)

Verity, Hugh – *We Landed By Moonlight: The secret RAF landings in France 1940–1944*. (Crecy Publishing Limited, 1998)

Yarnold, Patrick – *Wanborough Manor School for Secret Agents*. (Hopfield Publications, 2009)

INDEX

JG stands for John Goldsmith

Upton, Rosemary 199
Urgay 209–211
US Army:
  3rd, 36th, 45th Infantry Divisions
    181;
  3rd Army 186; 82nd,
  101st Airborne Divisions 190

Vagabond II 216–217, 218, 219, 220,
  221
Val de Gr^ace 219
Valençay, memorial to SOE agents 249
Valentine Infantry Tank 10, 135
Valkonski (caretaker/ publican) 202
Vatelys 235
Vaughan-Fowler, Peter 104
velo taxis 107
Vélodrome d'Hiver 143n
Verdun, Battle of 187n
Vergette, George 235
Verity, Hugh 98
Vichy collaborators 187–188
Victoria Club, London 215
Villa Caracasa 55
Vogt (SD man) 130

Wall, Georges 109, 122–123, 128, 129,
  134, 143, 146
Walsh, Bernard 241
Walwyn, Fulke 199
Wanborough Manor 25–26, 192;
  women agents 92, 93
Warwick (racecourse) 241
Wedermeyer, Max 178–179
Wehrmacht see German army
Welbecson Press 27, 248
Wertheimer, Pierre 58

Wesselow, James de 248
Wesselow, Roger de 26–28, 29–30, 92,
  155, 248;
  reports on recruits 31–32
Wesselow, Rosamund de 28
West, Sir Algernon 25
West Park, Finchampstead 26
Westland Lysander (aircraft) 96,
  101–102
Wheelers (restaurant, London) 241
White, Dick 104n
Wiese, Friedrich 183
Wilford, E. E. 197
Wincanton (racecourse) 201
Windmill Girls 100
Windsor (racecourse) 199, 230;
  Jalgreya 1946 200;
  Round Tower Handicap 1947
    224–225, 226–229;
  Le Jacobin 1948 235, 236
Wolverhampton (racecourse) 5, 222n
women agents 92–93
Wood Note 200
Workman 7
Wragg, Adam 237
Wragg, Harry 162, 207
Wye (racecourse) 201

Yates, Dornford 21n
Yeo-Thomas, Forest Frederick 'Tommy'
  150
Young, James 'Jimmy' 36, 38
Young, John Cuthbert 24, 32, 43,
  49–50, 93, 160, 161, 193

Zeller, André 112, 163

PHOTOGRAPHIC
ACKNOWLEDGEMENTS

Plate 1: top left, top right and bottom: the family of John Goldsmith

Plate 2: top left: Henrik Chart; top right: James de Wesselow; bottom left: the family of John Goldsmith

Plate 3: bottom: Getty Images

Plate 4: top: Getty Images

Plate 5: bottom: Getty Images

Plate 6: top and middle: Getty Images

Plate 7: top, middle and bottom: Getty Images

Plate 8: Top left and bottom: Getty Images; top right: the family of John Goldsmith

RACING POST BOOKS

What the Critics said about *Doped: The Real Life Story of the 1960s Racehorse Doping Gang* – winner of the William Hill Sports Book of the Year Award 2013

"Dope tale will have us hooked ... an explosive real life story ...
a real page turner."
Claude Duval, *The Sun*

"He has captured the Sixties milieu to a tee and served up
a richly enjoyable slice of Turf history."
Independent on Sunday

"Forgive the cliché, but this really is a book that I couldn't put down."
Anton Rippon, Sports Journalists Association

"This is a fascinating book, very well written."
Dave Ord, www.sportinglife.com

"*Doped* is a crackling, eye-opening read."
David Ashforth, *Racing Post*

"... impeccably-researched and furiously-paced ... unputdownable ...
a breathless story of greed and corruption that shocked the nation."
Sport magazine

"an absolutely thrilling read."
William Hill Sports Book Award judges

"a marvellous evocation of the period with late night stable visits by dopers,
Soho gangsters, milk bars and Ford Zephyrs."
The Sunday Times

"*Doped* superbly evokes a lost world of seedy glamour when
spivs, racketeers and glamour pusses rubbed shoulders with
aristocratic high-rollers. It would make a fantastic film."
Independent